Understanding Teaching Ex in Higher Education

As debates rage around whether it is down to subject-knowledge, communication skills, taking a research-led approach or being a technological whiz, this book provides the first in-depth examination of teaching excellence in higher education. Identifying and examining interpretations of teaching excellence, it considers what 'excellent' means and implies for practice.

Using as its central case study the practice of the UK's most 'excellent' university teachers, as awarded by the National Teaching Fellowship Scheme, this book draws upon insightful interviews with award winners and considers their teaching approaches and development plans. Reference to similar schemes in the USA, Canada, Australia and South Africa offers a comparative perspective and helps the reader locate national policies and practices within the growing worldwide 'excellence movement' in higher education.

Lecturers in any higher education establishment who are passionate about raising the standards of teaching will find much in this book to stimulate their thinking and development. It will make an exceptional companion for students on postgraduate certificate, diploma and masters courses that address teaching and learning in higher education.

Alan Skelton is Senior Lecturer in Higher Education at the School of Education, University of Sheffield. He directs the M.Ed in Teaching and Learning for University Lecturers course and is a member of the Research Centre for Higher Education and Lifelong Learning. He recently conducted an ESRC-funded evaluation of the National Teaching Fellowship Scheme for higher education teachers in England and Northern Ireland.

Key issues in higher education series

Series editors: Gill Nicholls and Ron Barnett

Understanding Teaching Excellence in Higher Education

Towards a critical approach

First published 2005 by Routledge
2 Park Square, Milton Park, Abingdon, Oxon, OX14 4RN

Simultaneously published in the USA and Canada
by Routledge
270 Madison Avenue, New York, NY 10016

Routledge is an imprint of the Taylor & Francis Group

Typeset in Times New Roman by Keyword Group
Printed and bound in Great Britain by MPG Books Ltd, Bodmin, Cornwall

British Library Cataloguing in Publication Data
A catalogue record for this book is available from the British Library

Library of Congress Cataloging in Publication Data
Skelton, Alan.
Understanding teaching excellence in higher education: towards a
    critical approach/Alan Skelton.
      p. cm. — (Key issues in higher education)
    Includes bibliographical references and index.
    ISBN 0-415-33327-X (hardback : alk. paper)
1. College teaching—Evaluation. 2. Teacher effectiveness.   I. Title.
II. Series.

LB2331.S54 2005
378.1'25—dc22   2005002946

ISBN 0-415-33327-X (hbk)
ISBN 0-415-33328-8 (pbk)

Contents

PART 4
Future horizons

Acknowledgements

I would like to thank the Economic and Social Research Council for supporting the study I undertook into the National Teaching Fellowship Scheme (award number R 000 22 3509). This research provided the stimulus for this book and informs several of the chapters. Richard Higgins made a substantial contribution to the ESRC research and I learned much from working with him. All of the National Teaching Fellows from the 2000 scheme agreed to be interviewed at a time when they were constantly being asked to talk about their work by the educational press and other media. This says a great deal about their professionalism and generosity of spirit.

I also want to thank Vaneeta D'Andrea, Hugo Dobson, Sarah Ewbank, Bruce Macfarlane and Stephen Rowland for their comments on specific chapters of this book; David Gosling for his interest in taking forward some of the practical implications of the work presented in Chapter 3; Barbara Cambridge from the American Association for Higher Education for inviting me to a collaborative meeting that informs Chapter 10; and to those teachers from the Carnegie Scholars Program who volunteered to talk to me during this meeting.

This book has only been possible with the support of the School of Education at the University of Sheffield. I would like to thank Jon Nixon, in particular, for his support and encouragement over the last two years.

Finally I would like to acknowledge two previous publications that inform Chapter 3 of this book. They are:

(2002) 'Understanding "teaching excellence" in higher education: a critical evaluation of the National Teaching Fellowship Scheme'. End of Award Report, The Economic and Social Research Council, July.
(2004) 'Understanding "teaching excellence" in higher education: a critical evaluation of the National Teaching Fellowship Scheme', *Studies in Higher Education*, 29: 451–68 (for information about this journal, please see: http://www.tandf.co.uk).

Part I
Beginnings

Chapter I

Introduction

Teaching excellence: an emergent and intensifying discourse

Teaching excellence is now part of the everyday language and practice of higher education. Policy makers declare its value to national economies, institutions market themselves through excellent teaching quality scores, and an increasing number of teachers are recognized and rewarded for their excellence at prestigious award ceremonies. At the time of writing in the UK, a new Higher Education Academy (HEA) has just been established which is to be entrusted with the goal of 'delivering' excellence in learning and teaching within the sector (DfES, 2003).

These developments could not have been contemplated two decades ago. Since that time, the argument that teaching should be treated seriously as a professional activity with equal status to research has been made repeatedly and with increasing intensity, leading to the formalization of staff development support for teaching and the introduction of a whole raft of measures designed to raise its status within higher education. These measures include teaching quality assessment and enhancement mechanisms, educational development grants funded by central government, certificated courses on learning and teaching, and awards for teaching excellence. Teaching is now firmly on the agenda and excellence in teaching is associated by many politicians with securing national advantage in the global knowledge economy.

It is surprising that although teaching excellence has taken on a greater significance in our lives, it is rarely the subject of serious research investigation. Much of the work on teaching excellence in higher education has a practical emphasis, which sets out to promote it through policy initiatives, mechanisms and structures. This book adopts a different approach in taking teaching excellence to be something worthy of *critical* investigation. This involves recognizing that teaching excellence is a contested concept and that we each need to develop an informed personal perspective on what it means for practice. The purpose of this introductory chapter is to 'set the scene' for this investigation and to identify what a critical approach involves in more detail. It considers three contextual factors that are influencing how we currently think about teaching excellence in higher education: managerialism, the market and performativity.

The chapter considers the impact of these contextual factors on our understanding of teaching excellence. It argues that they are helping it to shake off its exclusive connotations. Teaching excellence is increasingly subject to measurement and control, and all teachers are encouraged to improve their practice by meeting prescribed standards. Teaching excellence is no longer viewed, therefore, as ephemeral and beyond the reach of mere mortals. It is actively promoted by and embedded within policy initiatives and pinned down by 'expert panels' who define it for the sector. We therefore have a teaching excellence that is increasingly visible but taken for granted and under-explored. Few would challenge the idea that we need to promote teaching and learning within higher education. Few would oppose the view that teaching excellence can be used strategically to raise overall standards. But what sort of 'teaching excellence' do we want and what are the alternatives?

There is increasing concern among many educationalists about how a culture of measurement and control is influencing how we think about teaching excellence. We are encouraged to think of teaching as a simple, practical activity that can 'deliver' predetermined 'outcomes'. But perhaps what is more significant and worrying is the lack of real debate and deliberation within the sector about the meaning of teaching excellence. This book seeks to address this situation by adopting a critical approach. Such an approach recognizes that teaching excellence is a contested, value-laden concept. It takes the view that in order for it to be a valuable and meaningful concept for teachers and students in higher education, there has to be real deliberation about what it means and what it 'looks like' in practice.

It is not sufficient for teachers to comply in a passive manner with those understandings of teaching excellence given to them by politicians or experts; they have to develop for themselves a personally informed judgement and take responsibility for this. I conclude the chapter by describing the structure of the book, its intended audience and the content of specific chapters. The book seeks to promote discussion about teaching excellence in higher education. It is only through such discussion that we will develop a teaching excellence that is fit for the long term: one that is robust and confident, and one that we can trust and respect.

Higher education teaching in context: managerialism, the market and performativity

A new way of conceptualizing teaching in higher education (and excellence in teaching) has emerged in recent years. In the light of globalization, educational reform has taken place in many countries, informed by policies and discourses associated with managerialism, the market and performativity (Ball, 2003). Changes have been introduced across different phases of education, including the higher education sector, where a commitment to student expansion has become a policy norm.

Managerialism emphasizes the three 'E's of economy, efficiency and effectiveness (Morley, 1997), and these terms and standards of judgement have come to dominate discussions about teaching within the sector. Managerialism reflects a desire on the part of the state to maximize its economic return from higher education through the application of 'scientific' models of management (Pollitt, 1993). The aim is to shake up the sector by making institutions more accountable for their essential services, less financially secure and increasingly subject to the market and consumer choice.

The introduction of a market culture into higher education has created some tensions as, before educational reform, universities were predominantly run like 'publicly funded corporations' (Harrison, 1994:52). Morley notes that: 'By 1983 universities were beginning to be perceived, by the government, as offering poor value for money, being too distant from the wealth-creating sectors of industry and commerce, and being too dependent on government funding' (Morley, 1997:233). From this date onwards, public funding of universities in the UK declined, whereas the use of quasi-markets to encourage competition between institutions increased (for example, through research assessment exercises and teaching quality audits). Competition is a key feature in the market economy which seeks to drive out inefficiency and waste. Universities now need to market themselves aggressively and compete to attract new groups of students. Teaching excellence is one way of staying ahead of the competition and securing a good position in exercises which rank institutions (for example, the performance of UK institutions is now made public in league tables).

'Performativity' requires teachers 'to organise themselves as a response to targets, indicators and evaluations' (Ball, 2003:215). Teaching excellence in the performative university can be measured through high-level achievements such as receiving institutional and/or national awards for excellence and publishing research into teaching and learning. These outstanding achievements need to be tethered to everyday indicators of quality and success, as evidenced in student completion rates and evaluation scores. Excellence understood in these terms requires people to fashion their teaching according to externally set standards. They need to suspend their own judgements about teaching, comply with what is expected of them, and display appropriate behaviours, undertaking 'intensive work on the self' (Dean, 1995). This can lead to a 'values schizophrenia' (Ball, 2003:221), where people begin to ask themselves: 'Are we doing this because it is important, because we believe in it, because it is worthwhile? Or is it ultimately because it will be measured or compared? It will make us look good!' (ibid.: 220). Whereas in the traditional university, teaching excellence would have been assumed or thought of as idiosyncratic and ephemeral, today it is named, celebrated and subject to measurement and control. Within the performative university, it can turn teachers into capable but docile subjects, disciplined by the constant calls for information and endless paper trails.

New information and communication technologies (ICTs) support the flow of data in the performative university. Their current uptake and proliferation is characterized by a TINA effect (Morley, 2003:ix): an assumption that 'There Is No Alternative' to ICTs as governments attempt to cope with globalization and its implications for higher education and employment. Although ICTs help create and sustain the very globalized world order to which they appear to be the solution (Clegg *et al.*, 2003a), resistance to them appears futile, as 'The space left for practitioners in Higher Education is either to embrace the new media enthusiastically or to stand aside and watch its inevitable unfolding' (ibid.: 39). Teaching excellence in higher education is increasingly subject, therefore, to what might be termed the 'technological turn'. Resistance to the use of ICTs and new orthodoxies such as PowerPoint presentations is perceived as an inability to adapt to changing circumstances.

Can teaching excellence become a valuable and meaningful concept?

Of course it would be a mistake to assume that everything associated with recent higher education reform has been negative or problematic, since the situation is more complex than that. Teaching has clearly been the 'poor relation' of the teaching/research relationship in higher education for many years, with prestige and promotion associated with research success. There is no doubt that the performative discourse has in one sense raised the status of teaching, ensuring that some people give more time and thought to their teaching than they might have in the past, and requiring them to ask practical questions about its content, delivery and evaluation. In the process, teaching excellence has shaken off its grand, exclusive connotations. It now has a tendency to be seen as a positive 'hurrah' concept leaning towards universality rather than something cast in negative terms. Today all higher education teachers are encouraged to strive to become excellent through a process of reflection and continuous improvement. Colleagues who have received awards for teaching excellence are not set apart and revered; they are expected to contribute to the general good by passing on their expertise to others through the dissemination of good practice.

There is a growing realization, however, that reducing teaching to simply a practical matter has significant limitations since it ignores questions of value and purpose that underpin teaching in higher education and its relationship to wider society (Walker, 2001). Focusing exclusively on technical–practical matters and obsessing over operational concerns does little to excite people or to encourage them to adopt an intellectual interest in higher education teaching (Rowland, 2000). The essentially human quality of teaching and learning encounters is also side-lined as attention turns to procedures, policies and strategies for implementation. Emphasis on the three 'E's of economy, efficiency and effectiveness also deflects attention away from structural determinants of teaching excellence, namely material resources, teacher–student ratios and time for teachers to think and reflect upon their work.

In the light of this realization, the question emerges as to whether teaching excellence can be appropriated by teachers and students in higher education. Can it become a valuable and meaningful concept rather than a technical and bureaucratic concern which offers no direction and 'has no content' (Readings, 1996: 13)? Some educationalists have responded positively to this question, maintaining that teaching excellence emerges as practitioners seek to realize their educational values in practice (McLean and Blackwell, 1997). This involves reflecting on one's implicit ideas about learning and teaching in the light of educational theory and trying to implement these ideas in practice, observing how students respond. Attempts to realize values in practice can lead to a better awareness of these values and the practical and broader policy contexts in which they are expressed. An excellence understood in these terms involves a 'critical being' (Barnett, 1997), where reflective thought, self-awareness and commitment to action interrelate and guide the teacher. Teachers thereby contribute to the cultural production of excellence through their own distinctive practices. They do not simply receive dominant understandings of teaching excellence and apply them to the settings in which they work; they creatively engage with these understandings and take up, reject or modify them in the light of their own values and concerns.

This view of teaching excellence is linked to issues of professional identity. It assumes that teachers should exercise professional judgement over not only the content and process of teaching, but also its underlying values and purposes. It is important to preserve teacher autonomy from this perspective to ensure quality of educational experiences. It is subject to important controls, however, in the form of a dialogue with significant others, including colleagues, students and the wider public. Notions of academic freedom can only be justified, therefore, as part of a new and emergent professional ethic which ensures genuine educational encounters and 'freedom for others' (Nixon et al., 2001). This runs counter to the current culture of managerialism, which deprofessionalizes teachers, turning them into a 'new proletariat' who possess little or no ideological control over their work (Halsey, 1992).

It has been noted that new entrants to the profession are encouraged to think within regulatory frameworks for teaching (Zukas and Malcolm, 2002). In the light of compulsory, competence-based courses which emphasize following rules, procedures or set behaviours, they are also encouraged to view teaching primarily as a practical activity rather than one which involves serious thought (as does their research). Indeed, teaching excellence in higher education is increasingly being separated from disciplinary and pedagogical research. Expertise in disciplinary research is viewed neither as a necessary nor sufficient basis for excellent teaching and support for 'teaching-only' institutions is gathering pace in many countries, premised on the assumption that the best support for students may sometimes come from people who are not research active. Teachers who are recognized as excellent in award schemes may have little knowledge of educational theory or pedagogical research. As Yorke (2000: 113) notes, 'many teachers deemed "excellent" may have only a sketchy knowledge of the literature of pedagogical research, which is a matter of concern in that they may provide models of teaching activity which are ignorant of, or run counter to, the evidence from research'.

The question of whether excellent teachers need more exposure to educational theory and pedagogical research is an issue currently exercising the minds of many in the sector. Can teachers learn how to become excellent through appropriate education and training, or is excellence a set of innate qualities and skills? Educational developers are beginning to think about what design of professional development course will support teaching excellence, drawing upon recognized traditions and practices (Gosling, 1996). Should they be generic, interdisciplinary or subject-focused? How (if at all) do they need to differ from entry level courses? What evidence is there to suggest that professional development can 'add value' to the quality of teaching in higher education?

Teaching excellence, higher education expansion and the learning process

Our current preoccupation with teaching excellence and how best to support it may reflect, paradoxically, a concern from some quarters that it is under threat. As many countries move towards 'mass' systems of higher education without significant increases in funding, there are fears that teaching quality is in decline. These anxieties may be premised on a view of teaching excellence which is associated with the traditional university and a cloistered elite of scholars. According to this view, the recent rapid expansion of student numbers and the attempt to accommodate it through the quality movement has led to a 'dumbing down' of higher education, as traditional standards cannot be maintained.

An alternative view is that a mass higher education system offers opportunities to fundamentally reassess what is meant by teaching excellence. Responding to increasing diversity within the student body allows teachers to think differently and more creatively about their approach and not to rely so heavily on methods based on transfer theories of learning (Fox, 1983). The challenge of 'mixed-ability' teaching, previously the preserve of school-based education, may soon present itself more widely in higher education, requiring teachers to reflect upon how they might differentiate between students. The need for vocational courses which are relevant to 'non-traditional' students may encourage higher educators to question their epistemological assumptions: teaching excellence in a mass system may involve 'putting knowledge to work' (Symes and McIntyre, 2000) and adopting elements of work-based learning in courses across the curriculum (Boud and Solomon, 2001).

Whilst a new and unified idea of teaching excellence could be constructed in the light of massification, it is also possible that a range of forms might emerge, linked to different types of institution within a diverse system of provision. Here any fundamental idea of the university would be rejected, with teaching excellence linked to the histories, identity and 'missions' of particular institutions and the specialist interests of their staff. In this respect, it is instructive to consider the situation of 'teaching-' and 'research-intensive' institutions (see Gibbs, 2000). Teaching-intensive institutions, for example, may wish to lay claim to a teaching excellence based on commitment to teaching, resources and links with the community. A research-intensive institution, on the other hand, may claim a teaching excellence which is informed by the latest research findings and scholarship. Alternatively, 'customer delight' (McNay, 2003: 26) could become the driving force behind teaching excellence, as institutions pay more attention to what attracts students and their consumption habits. It has been suggested that universities could become 'cathedrals of consumption', which draw upon insights from other settings (such as shopping malls), while offering teaching experiences that are 'genuine forms of spectacle and enchantment' (Ritzer, 2001).

Future projections like these bring into question the emphasis on teaching rather than learning excellence. There is wide recognition that higher education teaching traditionally has placed too much attention on the act of teaching and given insufficient regard to what students learn in the educational encounter. Typical concerns with the teacher's ability to speak clearly and transmit information are based on simplistic models of communication, which fail to take into consideration the students' frame of reference and 'starting points'. Much of the contemporary literature on pedagogical practice in higher education has moved towards an emphasis on the student and learning, claiming that teaching is only as good as the quality of learning that it promotes. According to this view, the performance of teaching is not an end in itself; it is aimed towards the end of supporting students' learning. Given this change of emphasis, a new professional body launched in June 1999 in the UK was named the Institute for Learning and Teaching for Higher Education (ILTHE, now incorporated into the HEA), a name which purposefully re-ordered the usual semantic flow. *Learning* excellence places value on support for learning and acknowledges the student's role in their own development. The question emerges then as to whether the discourse of *teaching* excellence represents a 'restorationist' project: a return to traditional views of teaching and an emphasis on the teacher.

The focus on learning in recent pedagogical writing also encompasses the 'teacher-as-learner'. Teaching excellence, from this perspective, is associated with a continuous process of learning, so that excellence becomes not an end-point, but a dynamic process of ongoing professional development. The concept of the 'reflective practitioner' (Schon, 1983, 1987) informs this process of development in higher education. It has become almost 'taken for granted' in the literature and embedded in planned systems of professional accreditation (Zukas and Malcolm, 1999: 2). Reflective practice involves a process of continual learning based on careful observation and experimentation. Although it has been mainly interpreted as a form of self-reflection leading to insights about one's own teaching, teacher learning through critical reflection may also involve examination of the social, economic and political contexts of higher education practice (see Kemmis, 1987; Rowland, 2000).

To summarize the discussion so far, teaching excellence has become part of the everyday language and practice of higher education. It has managed to shake off its exclusive connotations and is currently dominated by a performative, 'techno-bureaucratic' discourse (Readings, 1996). It remains to be seen whether teaching excellence can become a meaningful concept to teachers and students within the sector. To date, there has been surprisingly little in-depth discussion about what it means. Educational writing and policy documents often appear to assume that we all know what excellent teaching is, and terms like 'excellent', 'good' and 'competent' are often used interchangeably. This book looks in detail at teaching excellence and explores how the concept might become a positive force for development and change.

A critical approach to the study of teaching excellence

It is a contention of this book that we have reached a time when it is crucial for the higher education community to develop a critically informed understanding of teaching excellence: whilst teachers in higher education should be concerned about the quality of their teaching and want to improve, identifying the direction of that improvement is a serious intellectual endeavour. Given the growing interest in and importance attached to teaching excellence, it is imperative that all those involved in higher education reflect deeply on what it means and the different ways it can be expressed in practice. We can no longer choose to base our teaching simply on tradition, the latest trend or what regimes of inspection tell us to do: how, what and why we teach are difficult and challenging questions that cannot be answered easily.

A critical approach recognizes that teaching excellence is a contested concept which is historically and situationally contingent. This means that there are different understandings of what teaching excellence means and how to practise it. Differences in interpretation may occur across time and space, as understandings of excellence are shaped by the historical and cultural context within which teachers are located. But students, teachers, politicians and employers may all have different understandings of teaching excellence at any given moment in time within a particular system of higher education. Listening to these different 'voices' helps to deepen our understanding of teaching excellence and to inform our practices as teachers.

A critical approach seeks to identify the values and assumptions that underpin any understanding of teaching excellence. Taken-for-granted understandings of excellence, dominant discourses and notions of 'good practice' are not taken at face value; they are interrogated to reveal the principles upon which they are based. Understandings of teaching excellence are inevitably informed by broader ideologies of education (Williams, R., 1961) and models of the higher educator (Zukas and Malcolm, 1999). Although policies which seek to promote teaching excellence may claim to be neutral and value-free, they intentionally or unintentionally connect with particular values and interests: a critical approach to teaching excellence seeks to make these explicit and therefore subject to public scrutiny (Barnett, 1997).

A critical approach to the study of teaching excellence invokes a particular intellectual stance towards knowledge, the self and others. Recognizing the 'critical stance' as a distinctive characteristic of a *higher* education, Curzon-Hobson (2003) states: 'The critical stance is characterized by a willingness to challenge, recreate and imagine in a manner that is searching, persistent and resolute'. It involves 'an enquiring and reflexive disposition ... [which] is underpinned by a recognition of one's freedom to choose, the responsibility that comes with this projection, a rejection of uncritical acceptance of value and meaning, and a celebration of self-will and the will of others' (ibid.: 202). The critical stance is contrasted with absolutism (an enduring truth or essence) and radical perspectivism (anything goes), since both 'negate the confrontation with one's inability to choose choice itself and the personal responsibility imbued with the exercise of self-will' (ibid.: 204).

The critical stance therefore involves bringing conflicting perspectives to bear on thought, action and self-reflection (Barnett, 1997). It involves developing a personal standpoint in the light of such perspectives, taking responsibility for this and recognizing that one's own understanding is subject to change. The critical stance can only be achieved in dialogue with others who offer different ways of seeing the world. Although temporary comfort can be found in living according to the expectations of others, following such a path is ultimately alienating, since in doing so one becomes dislocated from one's self. Similarly the critical stance recognizes that all of us inhabit a world that precedes us, one that is already constituted by rules, values, beliefs and practices. Understanding what freedom is available to us within such a context, making decisions in the light of this and taking responsibility for our actions is characteristic of the critical approach.

The challenge in higher learning about teaching excellence, therefore, 'is to encourage students and teachers to recognise and exercise their freedom to change what is possible *and* take responsibility for these acts that constitute, structure and limit their lives and those lives around them' (Curzon-Hobson, 2003: 210: original italics). This book seeks to support higher education teachers in reflecting upon and developing an informed, personal perspective on teaching excellence. It rejects the idea that 'ordinary' teachers should simply accept and operationalize understandings of teaching excellence passed down to them by experts or politicians. Any 'deep learning' about teaching excellence involves considering different perceptions and interpretations to facilitate real dialogue. This book aims to support such a process.

The October 1999 edition of the journal *Teaching in Higher Education* was devoted to the subject of 'critical thinking', exploring its meaning and practice from a wide range of disciplinary perspectives. From the discussion, it is possible to identify a number of characteristics that might contribute to a 'critical approach' to higher education study:

- Developing an informed, *personal* perspective through active engagement. Recognizing that ultimately one has to develop a personal perspective in the light of available knowledge, experience and our own values and commitments. Criticality is *not* about being told how to see the world and accepting 'received wisdom' (Parker, 1999: 474).
- Avoiding 'convergence', premature judgement and 'closure'. Recognizing that 'our bodies of knowledge are systems of conjectures, which are rational only to the extent that they are always open to debate' (Scoggins and Winter, 1999: 487).
- Recognizing that current understandings, realities and practices could be different and *better*. This involves considering alternatives and also freeing ourselves from 'ideological delusion' (Barnett, 1997: 97). It means understanding the ideological interests that underpin existing

discourses and practices. It means working towards a world that is less subject to the abuse of power and ideological manipulation. For this reason, the critical analysis of teaching excellence is informed by a range of critical theories. These theories have in common a commitment to the principles of democracy, social justice, liberation, equity and emancipation (Clegg *et al.*, 2003a; Walker, 2001).

- 'Criticality' involves a critical disposition towards knowledge, the self and action. Higher education has historically been committed to the development of a critical engagement with knowledge, but has placed less emphasis on how to act in accordance with such knowledge and the implications this has for the self. This book aims to support people in thinking critically about teaching excellence. But it also hopes that this thinking will inform teaching practices. For this to happen, the book carries implications for 'the self'. Crème (1999) refers to the Chinese student who stood in front of a tank in Tiananmen Square. This vivid picture was used in the book *Higher Education: a critical business*, written by Ronald Barnett (Barnett, 1997), to demonstrate 'an ultimate act of intellectual, personal and political affirmation' (Crème, 1999: 461). Barnett's notion of 'critical being' integrates the intellect, the self and action. Clearly teachers who refuse to accept received wisdom, who develop an informed personal perspective, who take responsibility for this and are prepared to act in accordance with their understanding and values, place themselves at some risk. The 'negotiation of/with the self' involves a dialogue about the extent to which one can realize personal values and commitments in situations that are already constituted and constrained.

- The importance of *comparative* materials, perspectives and practices. This helps to contextualize, 'locate' and 'situate' our existing understanding (see Parker, 1999). Comparative perspectives offer an opportunity to see the world anew, to consider alternatives, to shake up taken-for-granted ideas. The insights offered by marginalized and subordinated groups in society can be particularly instructive since they are well placed to 'deconstruct' dominant discourses and practices.

Our existing understanding about teaching and learning in higher education has been influenced by particular perspectives. There is a need to consider comparisons in order to address current gaps and imbalances in our knowledge and understanding. For example, the current literature on teaching and learning in higher education is dominated by psychological ideas and theories. It emphasizes the transaction between individual teachers and learners and ignores the wider social, political and economic context within which higher education is located (Malcolm and Zukas, 2001: 34–6). A critical approach to the study of teaching excellence recognizes that different disciplinary perspectives can be brought to bear on questions of teaching and learning in higher education. It takes the view that it is important not to be confined to dominant psychological interpretations of excellence; there may be other equally valuable ways of making sense of the phenomenon.

Much current discourse is also dominated by practical questions which emphasize how to recognize, reward and promote teaching excellence. A critical approach to teaching excellence sets practical questions like these within a broader context. It maintains that decisions about practical matters cannot be divorced from structural questions about the purpose of higher education and its relationship with wider society.

Identifying dominant, marginalized and subordinated perspectives is a central concern of a critical approach to teaching excellence. It seeks to understand why particular understandings have been accorded a particular status and what implications this might have for those who work in the sector. Some marginalized and subordinated understandings of teaching excellence may reflect the social positions of those who voice them. A critical approach anticipates that giving expression to these voices can be a basis for social and educational change.

A critical approach also asks serious questions about higher education policy related to teaching excellence and how it is interpreted by teachers and students. Current policies which aim to recognize, reward and promote teaching excellence in higher education need to be examined in the light of their assumptions. 'Rational-purposive' policies, favoured by politicians and institutional managers, are overly rational and coherent, and fail to recognize that teachers and students at grass-roots level mediate recommended practices (Trowler, 2002). It is important, therefore, to recognize that policies on teaching excellence are always subject to creative interpretation on the ground. What policies as texts reveal about teaching excellence in higher education has to be set against the reality of how policies are received and interpreted. Eliciting the views of 'ordinary' teachers and students about teaching excellence can provide insights into the impact of policy initiatives.

Background to the book

I direct and teach on a masters course for university lecturers at the University of Sheffield, in the UK. My research interests focus on teaching and learning in higher education. From my perspective, practical questions about teaching and learning are always connected to larger structural questions about the changing nature of society and the place of higher education within it. It seemed to me that a masters course for university lecturers might claim, with some legitimacy, to be concerned with supporting teaching excellence. But what precisely might this involve and how does it connect with the broader purposes of higher education?

I was fortunate to obtain an Economic and Social Research Council (ESRC) grant to explore teaching excellence, through a study of the National Teaching Fellowship Scheme (NTFS) for teachers in England and Northern Ireland. The NTFS seeks to recognize and reward teaching excellence in higher education by identifying twenty teachers per year, conferring on them the title 'Fellow' for life and awarding each person £50,000 to spend on the development of their teaching.

The book draws upon this study, which was undertaken between 2001 and 2002 (see Skelton, 2004). It was organized in three phases. In phase one, a literature review of work relevant to teaching excellence in higher education was conducted. This involved looking at previous studies of teaching excellence, literature on teaching and learning in higher education and related work undertaken in other sectors, for example, schools and adult education. The review encompassed both 'practical' writing on how to promote teaching excellence and 'theoretical' discussions about its nature and underlying values and purposes. Documentary analysis of the aims, procedures and criteria of the NTFS was undertaken and its contribution to teaching quality enhancement explored. A comparative analysis of award schemes was carried out, looking at similarities and differences between the NTFS, other UK schemes and those in Australia, the USA, South Africa and Canada. Non-educational and educational press reporting of the NTFS was examined, looking, in particular, at the extent to which their coverage had allowed readers to engage critically with questions related to 'teaching excellence'. Finally, four focus groups with teachers and students from two local universities (one teaching-intensive, one research-intensive) elicited their perceptions of teaching excellence. These phase one processes helped to generate semi-structured 'interview guides' (Patton, 1990) that formed the basis of work in phase two.

In phase two, interviews with all twenty of the first cohort of NTFS teaching fellows were conducted. These interviews explored the Fellows' perceptions of 'teaching excellence', the process by which they were selected within their institutions, what they aimed to do with the award of £50,000 and how the award affected their professional lives. Interviews with six members of the National Advisory Panel (NAP) of the NTFS were also undertaken. The NAP is the expert panel responsible, with the help of the ILTHE, for devising the criteria for teaching excellence in the NTFS. The interviews involved an equal balance of men and women, participants from different types of institution ('teaching/research-intensive') and a student representative. The aim was to understand the process that had occurred within the NAP to generate the criteria for excellence, what deliberations had occurred and how different interpretations had been resolved. Interviews were also conducted with representatives from a wide range of institutions that had not participated in the NTFS to ascertain their reasons for non-involvement. It was anticipated that 'non-participating' institutions might be well placed to think critically about the assumptions underpinning the NTFS and its understanding of teaching excellence. Representatives of the ILTHE and HEFCE were also interviewed during this phase to gain their perspectives on the NTFS.

In phase three, a content analysis of the data generated from these interviews was conducted, identifying common themes, contradictions and alternative cases. There was a movement back and forth between theoretical ideas generated in phase-one and phase-two data to keep the analysis dynamic (see Lather, 1986). The study focused on the first year of the NTFS (2000) to try to understand what assumptions about teaching excellence were feeding into the development of the scheme and its procedures and criteria. During the writing of this book, however, it became clear that the initial structure of the scheme remained intact during the first three years of HEFCE funding (2000–2003).

Book structure and audience

Teaching excellence has different dimensions and can be studied from different perspectives (Elton, 1998). Where teaching excellence resides is a contentious issue: should we focus on the individual teacher, collaborative teaching teams, students who have taken responsibility for their learning, resource-based institutions, community relations, national systems or global movements?

This book examines developments at a range of levels and draws upon the ESRC study as an important foundation. It considers award schemes for individual teachers, institutional strategies and identities, disciplinary understandings of teaching excellence, cultural conceptions of excellent teaching, the perceptions of 'ordinary' teachers and students, and the quality of professional development courses. It explores the perspectives of different groups of people. The emphasis is on looking at a range of contemporary expressions of teaching excellence and subjecting these to critical scrutiny.

The book has been written for a diverse audience. Participants on courses about higher education teaching, academic practice and research into higher education will find that it opens up questions about the nature of teaching excellence and whether it is a useful concept. It offers an opportunity for professional reading for individual teachers who want to improve their understanding of teaching, and acts as a sourcebook for researchers and scholars of higher education. For institutional managers and administrators in teaching and learning units, it offers a critical guide to current developments relating to teaching excellence. Teachers who have received awards for teaching excellence and those responsible for developing such schemes in institutions will find much of the material in the book informative and relevant to their interests and experience.

The book consists of four main parts. Part 1 comprises the first two chapters and is called 'Beginnings'. It offers an introduction to the book, establishes key themes and provides a critical framework for exploring understandings of teaching excellence in higher education. Part 2 comprises Chapters 3–5 and is called 'Familiar faces'. It focuses on the three dimensions that have dominated our thinking about teaching excellence to date: awards for individual teachers who are deemed to be excellent (*individual* dimension), teaching excellence at the institutional level (*institutional* dimension) and disciplinary understandings of teaching excellence (subject *discipline* dimension). Part 2 considers some of the discussions that have taken place about teaching excellence at these different levels and locates them within a contemporary context. Part 3 comprises Chapters 6–9 and is called 'Alternative explorations'. It opens up new areas for enquiry, such as: how teaching excellence is viewed from the perspective of 'ordinariness'; the way in which the 'internationalization' of higher education is raising awareness of the cultural specificity of teaching excellence; the role the press plays in mediating understandings of excellence within the wider community; and the relationship between professional development and teaching excellence. Finally, Part 4 comprises Chapters 10–12 and is called 'Future horizons'. It considers how teaching excellence in higher education might develop in the future, examining current initiatives and research activity. It also pulls together strands from preceding sections of the book and offers some tentative conclusions.

Contents of chapters

Part I: Beginnings

In Chapter 2 I outline a critical framework for understanding teaching excellence in higher education. This framework is offered as something useful in its own right – a device to support a critical engagement with teaching excellence and a means to support meta-level deliberations about what it means and how it can be practised – and also as a reference point to inform discussions in subsequent chapters. Four different ways of understanding teaching excellence are outlined, each with their own surface features and deeper connections with educational ideologies and discourses. In order for people to obtain some critical purchase on teaching excellence, it is important to get a sense of the different ways in which it can be expressed and practised. Policies and practices that seek to promote teaching excellence are never value-free. A critical appraisal of different interpretations of teaching excellence helps to make their underlying assumptions explicit and available for critical interrogation.

Part 2: Familiar faces

Chapter 3 focuses on award schemes for teaching excellence and, in particular, the NTFS for teachers in England and Northern Ireland. It examines how teaching excellence was understood in the scheme, how it planned to promote teaching and learning more broadly within the sector, and the impact of the scheme on the professional lives of the award winners. The chapter draws upon interviews with all twenty of the first cohort of NTFS Fellows, documentary analysis and a comparative study of award schemes from other countries, notably Australia, the USA, South Africa and Canada.

How teaching excellence is understood and expressed within different institutional contexts is the subject of Chapter 4. This chapter looks at a range of issues, including: the case for looking at teaching excellence at institutional level; the emergence of formalized institutional teaching and learning strategies; the relationship between institutional identity and teaching excellence; the creation of Centres of Excellence in Teaching and Learning; and institutional responses to teaching award schemes.

Chapter 5 considers some of the arguments that support the growing assumption that teaching excellence can only be understood and supported within a disciplinary framework. These arguments are set in context with reference to the emergence of interdisciplinary study in the 1970s and the creation of theme-based subjects. Recent work on new understandings of disciplinarity which has addressed some of the criticisms of the established academic curriculum is then examined. This work suggests that disciplines need to be reflective and that teaching excellence needs to be both located within the deep structures of disciplines yet prepared to question these structures and consider alternatives. In the final section of the Chapter 1 consider how this might be achieved through a process of critique.

Part 3: Alternative explorations

'Ordinary' teacher and student perceptions of teaching excellence are the subject of Chapter 6. It suggests that people 'on the ground' have an important creative role to play in deconstructing assumptions underpinning higher education policy and 'official' discourses of teaching excellence. The chapter draws upon focus-group discussions with teachers and students from two universities in Sheffield, UK. Images and metaphors of excellence are explored to further understanding.

Chapter 7 examines how teachers might respond to cultural variations in conceptions of teaching, drawing upon a range of theoretical models. It argues that given that higher education institutions are becoming more international and culturally diverse, any adequate understanding of teaching excellence has to be informed by this diversity. This involves recognizing the cultural specificity of teaching excellence and learning from cultural differences.

The media play an important role in shaping people's understanding of teaching excellence. Far from simply taking ideas about teaching excellence produced in one context and reporting them faithfully for audiences, the press mediates these ideas through a process of selection and emphasis. Chapter 8 offers an analysis of regional and educational press coverage of the NTFS, looking at how the scheme was reported and what tools were offered to readers to develop an informed, critical understanding of teaching excellence. Press mediation is considered to be a significant process in and through which user communities learn about and develop their understanding of teaching excellence.

Chapter 9 focuses on the relationship between teaching excellence and professional development. It considers how teaching excellence might be supported through professional development courses. It examines current and emerging provision for teachers in higher education, the assumptions underpinning different types of courses, the question of whether excellent teachers need to have been exposed to formal training, and arguments about what would characterize an approach to professional development that would foster excellence.

Part 4: Future horizons

In April 2004, I attended a meeting in San Diego, California, organized by the American Association of Higher Education (AAHE). The purpose of the meeting was to bring together award-winning teachers/scholars from the UK, Canada and the USA and to foster collaborations between people with an interest in teaching excellence. Chapter 10 discusses this meeting and uses it as a basis to reflect on future developments. It draws upon interviews with US scholars undertaken during the visit to suggest ways in which a more integrated understanding of teaching excellence (which incorporates notions of 'scholarship') might be achieved.

The penultimate chapter (Chapter 11) examines research into teaching excellence in higher education. Four themes which are considered are: who will undertake this research? How will it be conducted? What should be the focus of research into teaching excellence in higher education? And what role might evidence play? Background information on the current state of pedagogical research in higher education and recent calls for an 'evidence-based' approach to teaching and learning is provided. I look at the different ways in which people have researched teaching excellence to date before outlining a number of alternative visions for future practice.

The final chapter brings together strands from different parts of the book and offers some tentative observations and conclusions. It identifies the dominant ways in which teaching excellence in contemporary higher education is being constructed. The implications of this situation for the higher education sector are discussed and alternative suggestions for policy and practice outlined. I argue that a critical approach to the study of teaching excellence can make an important contribution as part of a mature pedagogical research community.

Chapter 2

A critical framework

Introduction

As noted in Chapter 1, teaching excellence has now become part of our everyday language and aspiration for practice in higher education. But what we mean by the term often seems unclear as terms like 'excellent', 'good', 'outstanding', 'competent' and 'best' (practice) are often used interchangeably by practitioners and educational policy makers (DfES, 2003). It is also apparent that when people refer to teaching excellence they often mean quite different things. This can be confusing and not conducive to dialogue. It seems timely, therefore, to try to achieve a greater level of conceptual clarity. If teaching excellence is to be a positive force in higher education, we need to gain some critical purchase on it and how it might be understood.

In order to do this, some serious questions need to be asked about teaching excellence. First of all, we need to identify what we mean by 'higher education' so that any expression of teaching excellence is directed towards this end. As Barnett (1992: 15) notes, it is impossible to discuss concepts like quality and excellence 'unless we have a reasonably clear conception of what might be included under the umbrella concept of "higher education"'. Any consideration of teaching excellence must therefore address the broader concept of higher education to which it contributes. Some 'dominant' and 'alternative' concepts of higher education are outlined by Barnett (ibid.: 18–21). The dominant conceptualizations are systems-based. Higher education is viewed as a total system, 'in which students enter as inputs, are processed, and emerge as outputs' (ibid.: 20). Alternative concepts 'take seriously the educational processes to which students are exposed, or which are intimately concerned with the students' development' (ibid.: 20). These different conceptualizations are listed below:

Dominant – higher education as:

- The production of qualified manpower
- Training for a research career

- The efficient management of teaching provision
- A matter of extending life chances.

Alternative – higher education as:

- The development of the individual student's autonomy
- The formation of general intellectual abilities
- The enhancement of the individual student's personal character
- The development of competence to participate in a critical commentary on the host society.

Different conceptualizations of higher education will have a significant bearing on what we understand by teaching excellence. For example, an excellence devoted to the production of a skilled workforce will have a different quality to that which seeks to develop student autonomy. In the former there would be a concentration on skill formation to meet the requirements of particular professions. In the latter, the emphasis would be on allowing students to make decisions about the nature and purpose of study, and on developing their ability to exercise independent judgement. In order to arrive at a deeper understanding of excellence, therefore, it is important that meta-level questions about the meaning and purpose of higher education are addressed. Although it may be tempting to focus on operational concerns about how to promote teaching excellence, avoidance of meta-considerations leads ultimately to a teaching excellence which lacks direction and purpose.

A second important question asks whether teaching excellence is an exclusive or inclusive concept. Is it the preserve of the 'chosen few', an elite group of 'superteachers' who, by nature of their skills and qualities, are destined to teach and set an example for others? Drawing upon Barnett (1992), it is possible to associate this view of excellence with a highly selective system of higher education:

> Excellence has classical origins, attaching both to persons and to objects where they fitted fully the ends for which they were destined . . . So far as persons were concerned, it implied a hierarchical society, where one's station in life (as warrior or senator) was given, and where the virtues appropriate to one's role could be specified relatively narrowly. This, then, was a conception of excellence which just some individuals were assumed to be capable of meeting.

(Ibid.: 59)

This view is quite different to how teaching excellence is currently being understood in higher education in many countries. There is now a pervading 'culture of excellence', which requires all teachers to sign up to a process of continuous improvement. A recent advert for a washing machine which proclaims 'excellence comes as standard' captures the prevailing mood. Excellence is now a 'hurrah' concept which has shaken off its exclusive connotations. But in doing so, has it lost some of its meaning and formative power? If everybody can be excellent, is something lost in the process? Or in different terms, 'Is the culture of excellence resulting in mediocrity?' (Morley, 2003: ix).

A third question that might be asked is *where* does teaching excellence reside? Is it to be located, for example, in the individual teacher, in teams of teachers responsible for courses, in the quality of students' work, within the subject discipline, at the institutional level, or perhaps more broadly in the higher education system itself (and its structure) which gives rise to the material conditions that influence the work of teachers? Use of the term *teacher* excellence might imply that excellence is an individualistic concern, dependent on the special qualities of the individual teacher. This view of excellence underpins many of those adver-tisements seeking to recruit people to the teaching profession which invite us to remember that 'special teacher' from the past. *Teaching* excellence, on the other hand, might direct us to the broader context of teaching and learning, the provision of resources, and team working in teaching and support for learning. The NTFS has attracted some criticism in the educational press for not paying sufficient attention to this broader context (Currie, 2000a). Even though the NTFS is part of a broader teaching quality enhancement programme, its particular responsibility for identifying excellence has led people to question its individualistic emphasis and the message this sends to teachers and students in higher education.

A fourth question that emerges is whether teaching excellence can take on different meanings. There certainly seem to be arguments to support this view since, as mentioned earlier, teaching excellence is inevitably linked to broader understandings of what is meant by higher education. Teaching excellence also appears to be both situationally and historically contingent. For example, in some cultures, teaching excellence may be associated primarily with the transmission of authoritative knowledge, with students regarded as apprentices in the service of their tutors. In others, teaching excellence may be linked to students developing their own ideas and viewpoints, with teachers acting as 'facilitators' of other people's learning. In any given culture, understandings of teaching excellence may also change over time and, with the aid of history, be seen to be 'temporally specific'. For example, some have already begun to observe a growing mistrust in teaching that is technologically enhanced and economically relevant, as doubts surface about the benefits of new technologies and the benign impact of globalization (Clegg *et al.*, 2003).

In any particular situation or context, teaching practices which are deemed to be excellent are often the outcome of a struggle over meaning, in which some interpretations become accepted as more valuable than others. For example, the state, higher education teachers, institutional managers, professional associations, students, employers, parents, local communities and the wider public may all have views on what constitutes teaching excellence, and differences in perspective may indeed exist within these groupings. How a particular understanding of teaching excellence comes to be recognized as more valuable or appropriate in a specific setting is therefore of great interest and has implications for the sector. Dominant, orthodox and preferred understandings can inhibit discussion and preclude a consideration of marginalized and subordinated 'voices' on teaching excellence. Dominant views may be presented as natural and 'common sense', disguising what underlying interests these views serve. This book maintains that the consideration of alternative views can enhance people's understanding of teaching excellence, helping them to develop an informed and critical personal standpoint.

In the remaining part of this chapter I outline four 'ideal-type' understandings of teaching excellence in higher education. These are:

- Traditional
- Performative
- Psychologized
- Critical.

The aim of the discussion that follows is to gain some purchase on teaching excellence by comparing and contrasting different ways it can be understood. Ideal types, by their nature, have some accepted limitations, for as Williams, J. (1997) states, 'They provide an academically neat blue-print for a messy reality' (ibid.: 28). Each ideal type, for example, appears as a unified whole when in actuality there are vigorous debates and points of difference within them. Ideal types can only represent, therefore, a 'distillation of the real world' (Salter and Tapper, 1994: 183). Their purpose is to inform a process of critical reflection about teaching excellence, to aid 'deep learning', moving beyond surface and taken-for-granted assumptions.

The four ideal-type positions offer a critical framework for analysis. This framework is offered as something useful in its own right – as a device to support a serious engagement with teaching excellence (an 'enquiring reflexive disposition' – Curzon-Hobson, 2003: 202) which necessarily involves meta-level deliberations about what it means in practice. It also will be used in the context of this book as a reference point for discussions in subsequent chapters. The framework is informed by previous work on ideologies of education which underpin teaching excellence (Williams, R., 1961), different discourse positions which inform higher education policies and practices such as access arrangements (Williams, J., 1997), and discussions of different models of higher education (Salter and Tapper, 1994) and the higher educator (Zukas and Malcolm, 1999). In drawing upon this work, two assumptions are made. First, meta-level understandings about the nature of higher education and its relationship to wider society inevitably underpin discussions about teaching excellence. Second, 'conversations' between different sectors of education (for example, school-based education, adult education, higher education and so on) can be a useful vehicle for analysis (Malcolm and Zukas, 2001). The four positions demonstrate that understandings of teaching excellence can differ fundamentally in terms of underlying assumptions and purposes. They also offer different answers to questions posed earlier in this chapter relating to the broader purposes of higher education to which a teaching excellence seeks to contribute, where teaching excellence is meant to reside and how inclusive/exclusive the quality is thought to be.

The four ideal types have a temporal character. The first ('traditional') evokes an early period in history when there was some consensus about 'the idea of a university' and also, by association, teaching excellence. It is tempting to think that traditional understandings of teaching excellence have been thoroughly marginalized in the light of postmodernity, as institutional diversity (for example, 'research-' and 'teaching-intensive' institutions) has gathered pace. But it is striking that some traditional understandings of excellence continue to exert an influence on the way people think and practise. For example, it has been observed that the top tier of universities continue to be inhabited by the children of the professional middle class, despite attempts to widen access (Smith and Webster, 1997: 12). The idea that teaching excellence requires suitable 'raw material' in order to flourish may still hold sway, therefore, in some quarters, and this clearly differs from a view of excellence linked to mass higher education and the ability of teachers to develop suitable pedagogical responses to student diversity.

The second ideal type ('performative') reflects contemporary understandings of teaching excellence which have been shaped by changing relations between higher education and the state. Again it would be tempting to assume that the thinking and practice of current practitioners and, in particular, new entrants to the profession is consistent with performative understandings of excellence which emphasize measurement and control. It has been argued, for example, that many academics find it difficult to see beyond the language and practice of performativity when it comes to their teaching, since they have 'grown up' with it in the 1990s and know few if any other ways of constructing teaching differently (Zukas and Malcolm, 2002). My own recent experience of working with both experienced and relatively new higher education teachers on professional development courses suggests, however, that an increasing number of people are keen to question the performative discourse and are aware of its shortcomings. Interestingly, those who have received good scores in quality assurance processes can be particularly vigorous in their critique, something that has been reported in previous studies (Morley, 2003: 40–41).

The third ideal type ('psychologized') also has a contemporary quality, since it captures those meanings of teaching excellence that have arisen amidst calls for the professionalization of teaching in higher education during the 1990s (ibid.: 27). Recent research has shown that psychologized understandings of teaching and learning dominate the pedagogical literature in the UK, which is informed by work undertaken in other countries (Malcolm and Zukas, 1999; 2001).

The final ideal type ('critical') has a 'future orientation'. It has had little impact on higher education practice to date. This may be due to its political interests and commitments: critical understandings of teaching excellence associate it with the goals of freedom, justice and student empowerment. Teaching according to this perspective is therefore inescapably political and at odds with the traditional emphasis on the disinterested pursuit and dissemination of knowledge. There are signs, however, that interest in critical perspectives on teaching and learning in higher education is on the increase. One reason for this is that as higher education institutions experience increasing ontological and epistemological uncertainty (see Barnett, 2000), the conventional view of universities as apolitical institutions suddenly seems problematic.

Traditional understandings of teaching excellence in higher education

Universities evolved in Western Europe in the twelfth century and were regarded as teaching rather than research institutions. They adopted a conservative teaching process which sought to inculcate an inherited body of knowledge, drawing upon European Christian traditions of scholarship (Cobban, 1999). The Graeco-Roman notion of the Seven Liberal Arts underpinned the curriculum (the 'trivium' of grammar, rhetoric and dialectic, and the 'quadrivium' of music, arithmetic, geometry and astronomy), which aimed to produce 'educated gentlemen' who were learned, humane, just and capable of taking up a leading position in society. Student scholars were offered a general education which exposed them to 'the best that has been thought and known in the world' (Arnold, 1983: 31). Such an education was associated with the development of personal wisdom and judgement, students attaining a clear and objective comprehension of all things (Newman, 1976).

The contemporary arts/science divide was absent in medieval universities. For example, the undergraduate BA Arts course at Oxford involved a combination of trivium and quadrivium subjects. Scholars who read degrees in the faculties of law, theology and medicine would broaden their knowledge through further degrees in different disciplines or be required to take the Arts course as a preparation for study (as in the case of theology). Dialectic (or Aristotelian logic and philosophy) was recognized as being important for all students in offering a rigorous training of the mind. Logical analysis fostered intellectual precision which was considered to be key in the search for universal truths. The application of rational argument to intellectual propositions and the whole training in arts was thought to be just as valuable and useful as 'vocational' subjects such as law and medicine. It was recognized as an important basis for all professional work – equally relevant for service in government, the church, law, in schools or universities, or for royal or papal diplomatic business. A general education of this kind, therefore, was understood to have direct community value.

The main methods of teaching and learning in the ancient universities were the lecture and the disputation. Ordinary lectures lasted about one hour and were given roughly three times per week in the main faculties at Bologna, Paris and Cambridge (Cobban, 1988). Regent Masters at Oxford and Cambridge (non-salaried masters or doctors who were required to teach for one to two years following their degree) gave ordinary lectures whose purpose was to provide: a detailed exposition of stipulated texts; resolution of problems raised by such texts; a lively narrative which opened up avenues for enquiry and a critical analysis of existing commentaries. Ordinary lectures were supplemented by extraordinary lectures, which considered books that were not part of the formal course. These lectures had a stimulatory function, were given by masters with less experience and were less rigorously constructed. Disputations represented an opportunity to explore complex issues that could not be handled adequately in formal lectures. They involved the debate of propositions relating to matters of current concern in the field, allowing people to develop their dialectical skills. Disputations would have no fixed agenda and anyone could raise issues for debate. They provided a welcome release from an educational diet that was predicated on a reverence for authority. Despite this release, teaching and learning in the medieval universities was essentially conservative. Methods allowed authoritative rulings to be modified but not countered by arguments based on different principles. Questioning was encouraged yet conducted primarily as a form of training within an established intellectual framework. Teaching excellence during this period was therefore associated with mastery of a discipline, the general sharpening of critical faculties, logical analysis and exposition and careful digestion of approved knowledge (see Cobban, 1988: chapter 5).

This 'traditional' understanding of teaching excellence remained basically intact until the beginning of the nineteenth century. Some additional and particular features of the English university took root from the mid-sixteenth century onwards, as teaching and learning at Oxford and Cambridge became decentralized and centred on the secular colleges. Lectures and other teaching activities increasingly took place in the colleges, with tutors becoming responsible for the students' overall experience – educational, moral and financial. In these changes we see the foundations of a tutorial system of teaching and support (involving one-to-one exchanges) being established, one in which academic and pastoral concerns became increasingly blurred. During this period, more and more accommodation began to be controlled by the universities, with the residential experience becoming associated with discipline and character formation.

But apart from these distinctive features of English universities, there existed a broad and relatively stable understanding of the 'idea of the university' in Western Europe at the turn of the nineteenth century. The university was associated with an educational experience that fostered the development of higher-order states of cognition, an enquiring rational mind and intellectual independence (Newman, 1976). Undergraduates studied for three years at the same university on a full-time basis. Excellence in teaching was associated with encouraging students to search for truth, to think logically and critically, and to rise above the limitations of common-sense thinking. Knowledge was pursued for its own sake yet had recognized community value in preparing people for the professions. The university was associated with cultural continuity as it ensured that existing bodies of knowledge and accumulated wisdom were passed on from one generation to the next (Filmer, 1997: 48–9).

This idea of the university and traditional understandings of teaching excellence gradually began to be challenged during the 1800s in the light of industrialization. The number of universities increased, with new institutions offering new subjects for study such as modern languages, science and economics. Most European universities began to combine general education with a more direct vocational preparation for the professions and work in bureaucracies. Oxford and Cambridge initially resisted such moves, but by the mid-1850s a serious debate had begun to take place in England about what constituted an appropriate higher education for a social elite. Arnold was the most influential in these debates, ensuring that liberal education and a preference for all-rounders over specialists prevailed. The period 1860–1930 was a critical period in the modernization of English society as links were made between the developing universities and the professions. By 1900 a number of new 'red-brick' or 'civic' universities had been created in England, offering a wide range of subjects which emphasized higher technical training. But the continuing cultural dominance of Oxford and Cambridge influenced the character of the civic universities, leading to imitation and a 'generalist shift' in the new institutions' curricula. Over time, the civic universities increasingly offered a similar education to the ancient universities but to a local clientele. A university education came to be seen as irrelevant to the entrepreneurial class, who failed to impose their values on the higher education system (Anderson, R. D., 1992).

After the Second World War, science and technological subjects were increasingly introduced into the higher education curriculum in England. Universities became research as well as teaching institutions, taking on an increased number of postgraduate students. By 1960 Oxford had become one of the nation's leading research centres, signifying a fundamental change in the purpose of the ancient universities (Tapper and Salter, 1992). But liberal education and traditional understandings of teaching excellence continued to exert a significant influence within the sector. For example, liberal education was endorsed by the Robbins Report (1963), civic universities developed halls of residence and tutorial systems and 'green-field' universities, with their campus environments for the new generation of school leavers with grants for maintenance and fees, were a striking testament to the success of the pastoral ideal.

Performative understandings of teaching excellence

Performative understandings of teaching excellence have emerged as nation states react to globalization pressures. Many developed countries around the world have embarked on a process of reform which seeks to make their educational systems more productive, drawing upon human capital theory. Teaching excellence within the performative university is associated with three main characteristics. The first is its ability to contribute directly to national economic performance through teaching which is relevant to commerce and industry. This involves rethinking university education to encompass work-based learning (Boud and Solomon, 2001), the 'vocationalization' of the curriculum, 'employability', 'entrepreneurship' and the increasing importance of 'Mode 2 knowledge', which is relevant to governments, industry and society (Symes and McIntyre, 2000). These are all expressions of teaching excellence within the performative university, signifying a shift in its epistemological assumptions. This shift is also informed by an increasing commitment, on the part of policy makers, to an approach to teaching based on 'instrumental progressivism'. This approach

> stresses a student-centred style of education that is individualized and flexible, and is designed to enhance the individual's opportunities for employment. Unlike previous forms of progressivism that were inner-directed, their revamped forms are outer-directed, and are tethered to the goals of performativity rather than reflexivity.

> (Ibid.: 2)

Instrumental progressivism recognizes changes in the mode of industrial production from mass production to 'flexible specialization' or 'post-Fordism'. This new mode is dependent on continuous innovation, research and development, creating specialized products and services to match demand from an increasingly heterogeneous market. Teaching excellence within the performative university is therefore concerned with the creation of a new type of learner and flexible worker. It seeks to offer programmes of study which are not premised on the traditional standard of full-time study. Rather the emphasis is on choice, modularization, credit transfer, work-based learning, accessibility, transferable skills, competency formation and continuous improvement through profiling, records of achievement and reflective practice.

The second characteristic feature of teaching excellence in the performative university is its ability to attract students on to courses which compete in the global higher education marketplace. In this respect, higher education becomes part of the knowledge economy where countries compete for a share in this market and the income and prestige that is associated with it. As we shall see in Chapter 7 on the internationalization of higher education, the UK is well placed to exploit this new market given that English is the leading global language of business and communications. New methodologies such as distance and e-learning are utilized to open up access to courses beyond national boundaries. Producing courses which have international appeal can lead to increased awareness of different cultural contexts within which teaching and learning occurs. But such production can also lead to a homogenization of culture, as dominant producers of educational materials colonize other countries through their own cultural assumptions and values.

The third main feature of excellence within the performative university concerns the way in which teaching is regulated by the state to maximize individual, institutional and system performance. A range of measures is introduced to ensure that the state achieves a good return on its investment in higher education. These measures involve requests for information on performance which are then made available for public scrutiny, for example in the form of comparative tables. They include: course entry figures, completion rates, drop-out rates, assessment scores, evaluation ratings, and higher-order achievements such as publications in teaching and learning, educational development grants, and awards for teaching (at institutional and national levels). Through these measurements of performance, the state seeks to maintain quality and secure value for money in the face of student expansion and reduced funding. All teachers are encouraged to become excellent against these measures through a process of continuous improvement and self-regulation. This involves extensive 'work on the self' as individuals are rewarded for publicizing particular aspects of performance. People experience an 'existence of calculation' (Ball, 2003: 217), which can be positive for some, but alienating for others. Teachers learn to separate their own views about teaching from those required by different audiences.

Psychologized understandings of teaching excellence

The term the 'psychologization of teaching and learning' was first introduced by Malcolm and Zukas (1999; 2001). They used it to explain the dominant emphasis in UK literature on teaching and learning in higher education – a literature which includes work written and carried out in other countries. Teaching (and excellence in teaching) from this perspective is underpinned by psychological constructions of the teacher and learner, particularly those that draw upon humanistic, cognitive and to a lesser extent behavioural psychology. Teaching excellence is associated with the establishment of universal procedures for teaching and learning, their successful implementation in practice and the achievement of specified outcomes:

> Psychological discourse constructs the educational process in such a way that it is apparently possible to predict and control what will be learnt and how. What better than the 'tools' of psychology to help us create knowledge about how best to do this? In particular, psychology's scientific paradigm is most appealing – through the 'scientific' study of human experience, one may discover general laws which govern human behaviour. One may therefore carry out objective, scientific studies on the techniques of teaching and processes of learning in order to build a 'technology of behaviour' (Skinner, 1973: 11), enabling behaviour to be understood, categorized and predicted, and practice to be improved.
>
> (Malcolm and Zukas, 2001: 35)

Psychologized understandings of teaching excellence focus primarily on the transaction between individual teacher and student. From this perspective, teaching excellence is relational: it does not reside in either the teacher or the student; rather it can be found in the interpersonal relationship that develops between them. The teacher can foster grounds for excellence by being approachable and through seeking to understand the individual needs of students. These needs are understood primarily through reference to the personality and learning style of students, which are deemed to be relatively stable categories. Once individual differences are recognized, teachers can then select appropriate methods and learning experiences from their 'toolbox' of available processes, techniques and activities. If the teachers' diagnostic abilities are adequate and appropriate experiences are offered, then it is possible that the majority of students will adopt a 'deep' approach to their learning and achieve predicted outcomes. Potential blocks to an excellent working relationship include the perceptions teachers and students have of each other, their previous experiences of educational relationships and their conceptions of teaching and learning. But if these blocks are overcome considerable formative potential is associated with the teacher–student encounter. If the teacher respects the student, identifies their individual needs, and selects learning experiences which are appropriate and sufficiently rich and enabling, the student will grow personally and achieve their full potential.

A psychologized form of teaching excellence recognizes that what is taught is often very different from what is learned. Methods that focus on the content of teaching and its transfer, such as the didactic lecture, are considered to have limited value since they fail to take into consideration the different ways in which individual learners make sense of and 'process' the material. 'Student-centred' approaches and 'constructivist' ideas and theories have become popular in the light of the critique of didactic teaching. They recognize that students actively construct meaning in the light of their existing knowledge and experiences. Constructivist theories maintain that teachers need to offer learning experiences that recognize and extend the student's existing frame of reference and understanding. Teaching excellence from this perspective, therefore, is concerned with 'starting from where the students are at' and encouraging learners to work within the 'zone of proximal development' identified by Vygotsky (Vygotsky, 1978). Teaching methods that enable students to articulate their current understandings, test them out and extend them in the company of others (for example, through co-operative group work; see Cowie and Rudduck, 1988) are therefore associated with this form of excellence. Teachers need an awareness of communication skills, how to conduct interpersonal relationships and the ability to reflect upon their own teaching. Students are also encouraged to take responsibility for their own learning by reflecting on the quality of their work, what they want to achieve and how best to go about this.

Critical understandings of teaching excellence

Critical understandings of teaching excellence are informed by a range of critical theories (for example, critical theory itself, neo-Marxism, feminism, anti-racism, Freireism). There are differences between these theories, but they all share an interest in and commitment to emancipation. Teaching from this perspective is therefore regarded as an inescapably political act rather than something that is neutral or value-free. Human beings are thought to have an interest not only in controlling or making sense of the world, but also in changing the world for the better (Habermas, 1978).

According to the critical perspective, knowledge, the curriculum, and teaching and learning practices within universities are shaped by existing political and social interests that serve to maintain the 'status quo'. Key questions for the critical pedagogue seeking to understand their experience of teaching within universities focus on issues to do with epistemological authority and control, for example: (i) What counts as knowledge? (ii) How is what counts as knowledge organized? (iii) How is what counts as knowledge transmitted? (iv) How is access to what counts as knowledge determined? (v) What are the processes of control? (vi) What ideological appeals justify the system? (see Anderson, G., 1989).

Teaching excellence from the critical perspective seeks to provide learners with access to knowledge that engages prevailing social structures and interests. This might involve locating such knowledge within wider socio-historical, political and economic movements, questioning established canons within disciplinary fields (Gates, 1992), recognizing the contributions of silenced or marginalized people and perspectives within the curriculum (Skelton, 2002) and creating new 'ideologically explicit' subjects such as Black and Women's Studies to challenge the existing social order (see Chapter 5).

The teacher's main aim, from the critical perspective, is to support a process of student emancipation which seeks to give them greater knowledge and control over their lives. The role of the teacher is to act as a critical or transformative intellectual (see Giroux, 1988), who disturbs the student's current epistemological understandings and interpretations of reality by offering new insights and theories. This involves creating teaching and learning situations which question 'common-sense' ways of thinking and behaving, leading to new forms of consciousness and ideas for effecting social and political change. Emancipation therefore involves constructing less oppressive ways of understanding the world and acting within it.

According to the critical perspective, higher education is viewed as a social site which maintains privilege through inequalities in access and participation. Teaching excellence involves not only increasing access to courses to groups of people who have been historically under-represented, but also enhancing participation through the creation of inclusive learning environments (Skelton, 2002). Such environments aim to enable people to participate in higher learning irrespective of their gender, race, social class, disability or sexual orientation. This involves challenging assumptions built into disciplinary cultures, curricula and pedagogical practices (Cronin *et al.*, 1999).

Empowerment through participation is also central to critical understandings of teaching excellence. In order for students to act confidently with critical intent in their future lives, participatory forms of engagement in teaching and learning situations are required. This may involve greater reciprocity between teacher and taught than is commonly the case. For example, students might be encouraged to contribute to the design of learning experiences and to take part in making judgements about the quality of arguments and assessed work. They may help to establish democratic principles for sharing ideas, contributing to the creation of 'ideal speech situations' (see Habermas, 1974), 'in which people, free from constraints and power relations, rationally discuss and reach agreements' (Abbas and McLean, 2003: 71). Being involved in this way helps to generate the confidence that is required for future critical action. This action may take various forms, for example: challenging oppressive epistemologies and social structures; taking part in a 'critical commentary' on the host society (see Barnett, 1992: 18–21); and engaging in a 'democratisation of knowledge in everyday life' through critical discussions with friends, colleagues and family about matters such as politics, science and relationships (see Giddens, 1994: 115).

Teaching excellence from the critical perspective focuses on the broader purposes of higher education and the underlying educational values that inform teachers' work. According to this view, teaching cannot simply be reduced to technical or practical matters; it inevitably involves moral questions about what it means to be educated. Any guiding principles for teaching cannot be derived, therefore, from what is perceived to be normal or appropriate: one has to consider whether established practice has value. Teachers are expected to engage with higher education policy and locate their practice within the broader social, economic and political context of higher education. Alternative solutions to 'teaching problems' may be found that fall outside the dominant ideology – for example, 'teaching excellence' may well be linked ultimately to the material conditions of higher education rather than the ability or commitment of individual teachers. From such a perspective, adequate funding, staff time to reflect on teaching, pay and conditions, teacher–student ratios and student fees all have a significant bearing on the quality of teaching in higher education.

Although there has been relatively little work on teaching excellence from a critical perspective to date, and few public accounts of critical pedagogy in higher education (there are some notable exceptions; see Luke and Gore, 1992), this situation seems to be changing, with a number of recent articles recognizing its value (for example, see Clegg et al., 2003: 50–51). One reason for this is that in current social conditions of increasing ontological and epistemological uncertainty (see Barnett, 2000), the orthodox view of universities – as apolitical institutions committed to disinterested, rational enquiry – suddenly seems problematic. In searching for an alternative to this view, critical understandings of teaching excellence offer to harness university teaching to the greater social goods of emancipation, empowerment, social justice and the struggle against inequality and oppression.

These four ideal-type expressions, which are summarized in Table 2.1, bring into question any notion of a monolithic view of teaching excellence. Once identified, they make it impossible to hold on to the idea that any one understanding of teaching excellence is natural or inevitable. They allow us

Table 2.1 Four meta-understandings of teaching excellence in higher education

	Traditional	Performative	Psychologized	Critical
Who for?	Social elite	Meritocracy	Individuals	Informed citizenry
Where located?	Disciplinary knowledge	Rules and regulations	Teacher–student relationship	Material conditions
Epistemology?	Pursuit of truth	Knowledge that works	Subjective interpretation	Social critique
Indicative method?	Lecture	Work-based learning	Group work	Participatory dialogue
Teacher's role?	Subject expert	Enforcer of standards	Psycho-diagnostician	Critical intellectual
Purpose?	Cultural reproduction	System efficiency	Effective learning	Emancipation

to think more deeply about how teaching excellence is currently being understood in policy and practice.

Any preliminary reflections on the relationship between these four ideal types would have to include some reference to what appears to be the current dominant understanding of teaching excellence in many developed countries. Performative interpretations of teaching excellence appear to be in the ascendant, favoured by politicians, educational policy makers and institutional managers. Their appeal is that they allow teaching to be harnessed to the needs of the economy and measured to ensure system efficiency. Proponents of the performative discourse identify it as an inevitable response to globalization, which is driving educational reform across the world.

Psychologized understandings of teaching excellence currently dominate the literature on teaching and learning in higher education and have exerted a considerable influence on practice. It is likely, therefore, that perspectives on what constitutes teaching excellence for many practitioners will be informed significantly by cognitive, humanistic and to a lesser extent behavioural psychology. Although it is clear from this chapter that performative and psychologized understandings of excellence differ in important respects, they share a belief in the possibility of identifying universal approaches to teaching that can meet the needs of individuals. The driving force, from a psychologized perspective, is to ensure that the teacher–student encounter is productive, leading to individual growth and development. The value of universal approaches, from the perspective of performative discourse, is that they enable teaching and learning to be predicted and controlled, thereby aiding system efficiency. Together, these two discourses form a powerful alliance which significantly influences the way teaching excellence is understood in contemporary higher education.

Traditional understandings of teaching excellence appear to be in decline and under attack. Higher education in many countries has shifted from an elite to a mass system, and calls for increased access and widening participation are changing what is considered to be appropriate methods of teaching and learning. For example, didactic teaching, lecture-based methods and notions of performance are currently out of favour since they are perceived to pay insufficient attention to the learning process. Teaching which is considered to be extravagant and insufficiently tethered to the mechanics of learning and its standardization is increasingly under threat. Of course attacking traditional understandings, particularly given the powerful interests they serve, can lead to a defensive reaction and covert restoration impulses. As mentioned earlier in this chapter, some elite institutions continue to retain their traditional clientele despite calls for greater access and the introduction of related performance indicators. Critical perspectives, on the other hand, are currently marginalized from key debates and policy initiatives relating to teaching excellence for being too self-interested and political, their proponents criticized for standing in the way of progress.

In Chapter 3, I turn my attention to the first of three 'familiar faces' of teaching excellence in contemporary higher education. I will look at the introduction of award schemes for teaching excellence which have become a common feature of the higher education landscape in recent years. The chapter will look in detail at the NTFS for teachers in England and Northern Ireland. The NTFS is based on similar schemes in Australia, the USA and Canada, and forms part of growing 'awards industry' and 'world-wide excellence movement' (McDonald, 1990; Fritzberg, 2000). The four ideal types of teaching excellence which have been outlined in this chapter will help us to understand how excellence is being constructed in and through award schemes. Despite their proliferation in recent years, they have been subjected to little critical analysis in the higher education litera-ture. It is important to know what understandings of teaching excellence are promoted by award schemes. Given the increasingly high priority that is afforded to such schemes and the impact they have on teaching and learning development, it is crucial that we gain a deeper understanding of the assumptions that underpin them and the potential significance of these assumptions for the sector.

Part 2
Familiar faces

Chapter 3

Awards for teachers

Introduction

Awards for teaching excellence have proliferated in recent years, often accompanied by the 'glitz and glamour' of prestigious ceremonies and enthusiastic media coverage. Although the first award was introduced as long ago as 1957 at the University of California in the USA (McNaught and Anwyl, 1993), it is only in the last decade or so that they have become commonplace in many countries, especially the UK, South Africa, Canada, the USA and Australia. Many institutions now have their own award schemes and some countries have national-level programmes. For example, the NTFS was introduced in 2000 for teachers in England and Northern Ireland, and this scheme has begun to shape the character and purpose of institutional awards (HEFCE, 2002). It has been estimated that two million dollars are spent each year around the globe on awards that cover the whole spectrum of human activity and achievement. In the USA, the country which offers the most awards (approximately 29,000 per year), there is even an Annual Awards Banquet which offers a prize for the best overall award. Awards for teaching are therefore part of a much larger and growing 'world-wide excellence movement' (McDonald, 1990; Fritzberg, 2000) and 'awards industry' (*Arena*, 2001).

Given their profileration and increasing significance in higher education, it is important to explore what significance award schemes have for our understanding of teaching and learning within the sector. While awards have an inherent 'feel-good' factor, it is important to engage with them critically, to identify their implicit assumptions and values. As noted in Chapter 1, there is an emerging discourse of teaching excellence in higher education and awards are a key aspect of this discourse. In order to under-stand how teaching excellence is being constructed in higher education, therefore, we need to examine award schemes and the specific forms they take.

The purpose of this chapter is to discuss some of the main reasons for awards, their key characteristics and intended impact. A review of previous research informs the discussion. A case study is then presented of the NTFS which offers an in-depth analysis of what kind of teaching excellence is being developed in a specific, national-level award scheme. The discussion that follows draws upon ideas presented in this chapter and the four ideal types of teaching excellence outlined in Chapter 2.

The rationale for awards, their characteristics and impact

There are many reasons why award schemes for teaching excellence have been introduced into higher education (McNaught and Anwyl, 1993; Warren and Plumb, 1999). These include:

- to recognize and reward excellent teachers;
- to raise the status of teaching and learning in higher education;
- to enhance the public image of universities;
- to redress the balance between teaching and research;
- to disseminate good practice and support educational change;
- to improve teaching quality;
- to help identify what constitutes 'teaching excellence';
- to encourage innovation and development;
- to create 'role models' for other teachers to follow.

Award schemes have developed alongside calls to professionalize teaching in higher education and to raise its status in relation to research. There are differences between specific schemes, however, and Warren and Plumb (1999: 246–9) provide a useful framework for understanding these differences and making comparisons between them. In their survey of teacher award schemes in higher education, based on eleven UK and seven overseas institutions, they identified four different types of award:

- *Traditional award schemes* – these give prizes in recognition of past performance. According to Warren and Plumb (ibid.: 247), this is 'the most common model adopted worldwide'.
- *Teaching fellowship schemes* – these confer the title 'Teaching Fellow' for a period of time and encourage award winners to meet together to share ideas and undertake collective developmental activities.
- *Educational development grant schemes* – these support specific innovations in teaching and learning.
- *Promotion/bonus schemes* – these involve the creation of promoted posts which emphasize teaching (for example Readerships in Teaching) and/ or salary increments or bonuses for teaching-related innovation and/or achievement.

Some award schemes closely resemble one of these types, while others seek to integrate two or more of them. For example, the NTFS attempts to combine traditional and fellowship schemes in recognizing past performance and encouraging future development. Successful applicants undertake individual and collective development activities. Awards for teaching excellence also vary in terms of many of their surface characteristics. For example, the number of awards, their monetary value, whether they are for individuals or groups of teachers, the selection and assessment processes they adopt, their criteria and whether they are subject-specific or operate according to prescribed themes (for example, the teacher who demonstrates 'excellent use of technology') – all these features may differ to some extent within a specific award scheme. National-level schemes tend to be better resourced than their institutional counterparts. Awards of greater monetary value tend to emphasize both reward and development, rather than the traditional gift of a prize. A comparison of four national-level award schemes undertaken in 2000 by the author revealed similarities and differences as shown in Table 3.1.

Table 3.1 indicates differences in the nature, locus and emphasis of awards. The Canadian 3M scheme, for example, offers an all-expenses-paid three-day 'retreat' in luxurious surroundings, whereas the NTFS has one of the highest monetary awards. The 3M scheme enables Teacher Fellows to meet together for a short period to exchange ideas, but the NTFS carries a higher expectation of development work, each Fellow being required to conduct a specific project or pursue development activities. The Australian Awards for University Teaching and the US Professors of the Year Program organize their awards into particular categories. Most of the awards in the four schemes are given to individuals, although the Australian scheme does have an institutional category which recognizes that teaching excellence may be dependent upon its broader context.

Research into teaching awards

Even with the introduction of national-level programmes, there has been limited research to date into award schemes for teaching excellence and their impact. Two early studies carried out in the USA on institutional-level schemes showed no clear link between excellence awards and teaching quality, with no differences being found between award-winning and non-award-winning university staff (Tollefson and Tracy, 1983; Jacobsen, 1989). A study of 33 higher education institutions carried out in 1991 in Australia found that just under half had some form of award scheme and the majority of institutions supported their introduction. Where implemented, they were perceived to have an impact in terms of recognizing excellent teachers and promoting high-quality teaching. Nine institutions, however,

Table 3.1 Comparison of award schemes

Name of scheme	Nature of awards	Locus	Emphasis
Australian Awards for University Teaching	$40–100k; 16 awards in 4 categories (individual, themed; institutional; overall)	Subject-based individual awards	Reward and development
Canadian 3M Teaching Fellowships	Expense-paid 3-day retreat	Generic: no subject-based categories	Mainly reward
NTFS (England & NI)	£50k; 20 individual awards	Generic: no subject-based categories/quotas	Reward and development
US Professors of the Year Program	$5k; 4 awards, 1 in each of 4 categories	Generic: no subject-based categories/quotas	Mainly reward

chose not to introduce an award scheme because they believed them to be 'cosmetic', inequitable and impractical (McNaught and Anwyl, 1993).

Some studies have compared excellence in teaching awards with other strategies that seek to promote teaching and learning in higher education. For example, a later study carried out in Australia found that although institutional teaching awards were commonplace, they were not rated highly by respondents as a way of improving teaching quality, and were regarded by the authors of the study as potentially alienating (Ramsden and Martin, 1996). A further study found that the perceived advantage of traditional award schemes was their relative low cost (as 'one-off' payments) and their ability to raise the status of teaching and learning within institutions. Reported limitations included their tokenistic quality, their competitive and divisive nature, and their ability to label recipients as 'non-researchers' (Warren and Plumb, 1999: 247).

In comparison, responses to promotion/bonus types of teaching award have been much more favourable. In the study conducted by Ramsden and Martin, promoting good teachers was seen to be the best way of improving teaching quality in higher education. In the study by Warren and Plumb, the advantages of promotion-based types of teaching award were reported as being their ability to increase academic status, the continuous nature of the reward (that is, not a tokenistic, one-off payment) and their use of the existing promotions system. The main limitation of this type of award was perceived to be its cost.

One approach to the study of teaching excellence that has become popular over the last decade explores the educational philosophies, concepts, teaching practices and personal characteristics of award-winning teachers (see, for example: Dunkin and Precians, 1992; Dunkin, 1995; Johnston, 1996; Baiocca and DeWalters, 1998; Kreber, 2000; Hativa et al., 2001). Researchers have sought to reveal the 'essence' of teaching excellence which is thought to reside within the award winners themselves. The teachers become the subject of study and teaching excellence is identified so that it can be promoted more generally within the sector. Award winners are often presented as 'role models' for others to follow. The nature of the awards themselves and the systems of selection that recognized the teachers as special in the first place are given little or no consideration in these studies.

Other research conducted on teaching excellence award schemes has tended to focus on operational and implementation concerns (see Chapter 11). These studies have been premised on the assumption that award schemes are a 'good thing' and the important research questions to ask about them involve the extent to which they have been successful in their own terms. Some of these studies have been politically driven in that they evaluate schemes introduced by agencies of central government and seek to reassure the public that they represent sound thinking and good value for money (see, for example, references to a formative evaluation of the NTFS in HEFCE, 2002). What they fail to do is to identify a theoretical framework within which their findings can be understood and interpreted. They also do not make their methodological assumptions explicit, although this tendency is found more generally in the higher education literature (Antoniou and Stierer, 2002).

In the remaining part of this chapter I present an in-depth case study of the NTFS. The NTFS was launched by HEFCE in April 2000 to recognize and reward excellent individual teachers. Linked to subject and institutional-level developments through the Teaching Quality Enhancement Fund, the NTFS is part of an integrated strategy to raise the profile of teaching and learning in higher education within England and Northern Ireland. The ILTHE was invited to manage the scheme, which involved a range of responsibilities including: the establishment of a National Advisory Panel (NAP); the preparation of background information to enable the panel to identify criteria for excellence; and the development of a process to select winners. Higher education institutions were invited to identify a candidate to proceed to the national-level competition. Ninety-five nominations were received and the ILTHE and the NAP met on two occasions to assess applications. Following these meetings, the first group of 20 award winners was identified in July 2000. At the time of writing, the NTFS has been running for over five years and from 2004 it has been extended to recognize and reward 50 teachers annually.

The purpose of the case study is to explore in detail what a teaching award 'says' about teaching excellence: for example, what messages are conveyed explicitly and implicitly about its meaning and purpose(s). Whilst the NTFS has specific features, it is based on similar schemes in Australia, Canada and the USA. It has potential significance, therefore, for understanding how teaching awards inform the way teaching excellence is constructed within these settings.

Case study: a critical evaluation of the NTFS

This case study of the NTFS is informed by an ESRC research study conducted between 2001 and 2002 (see Chapter 1, pp. 15–16). The ESRC study undertook a critical evaluation of the NTFS. Whilst the HEFCE itself reviewed the scheme after its first year of operation, some questions that fell beyond the immediate scope of this review needed to be addressed to enhance the scheme's credibility. As Barnett (1997: 18) has noted, any serious evaluation incorporates an element of critique, which provokes a debate from a 'wider perspective than that in which the internal debates are usually conducted'.

The study was informed by an understanding of teaching excellence as a *contested concept* which is *historically and situationally contingent*. In other words, there are different definitions of what it means to be an 'excellent' teacher, and these are located within a shifting social, economic and political context. As noted in Chapter 1, for example, many universities in the developed world have been subject to the introduction of 'new managerialist' practices (Clarke and Newman, 1997), as the state has sought to increase its economic return from higher education (Salter and Tapper, 1994). Such practices have influenced the way people think about teaching, as a new 'language of business' has taken precedence over educational terms and principles (Barton, 1994; Barnett, 1994). The concern for economic advantage in the global, knowledge-based economy has also encouraged a commitment to the expansion of student numbers in higher education (NCIHE, 1997). Whilst this commitment to expansion has not been accompanied by an increase in the unit of resource (leading some to point out that the quality of teaching is inevitably related to its material conditions; see Morley, 1997), the 'massification' of higher education has simultaneously driven an interest in pedagogical responses to student diversity (Skelton, 2002; Higgins *et al.*, 2002). Understandings of teaching excellence, therefore, are always intimately connected to the wider social, economic and political context and are underpinned by broader discourses or ideologies of education (Williams, R., 1961) and models of the higher educator (Zukas and Malcolm, 1999). The degree to which particular understandings of teaching excellence are dominant in a particular time and place reveals something about their relative status.

The study also drew upon an analysis of *development mechanisms and strategies* used to support teaching and learning in higher education. Three main approaches to developing teaching and learning can be detected: individual, guided and directed (Hannan and Silver, 2000: 6–9). In the UK, for example, up until the late 1970s an 'individual enthusiast' approach dominated, where interested lecturers experimented with new teaching methods. This gradually changed from the 1980s onwards as higher education became more accountable and institutional structures for staff and educational development were strengthened, supporting a period of 'guided innovation'. Programmes such as Enterprise in Higher Education (EHE), the Teaching and Learning Technology Programme (TLTP) and the Fund for the Development of Teaching and Learning (FDTL) also began to be introduced by national government and its agencies during this period. 'Directed' development initiatives of this kind were policy-driven and related to defined, often vocational aspects such as work-based learning and key skills (DfEE, 1998). Teachers involved in these initiatives had some scope to define them in terms of their own priorities and concerns, adopting a pragmatic form of 'action research' for reflecting upon and improving practice (McNair, 1998). As part of the Teaching Quality Enhancement Fund (TQEF) introduced by HEFCE in 1999 (which also includes development strands at subject and institutional levels), the NTFS represents a continuation of this directed policy.

The growing literature on the *professional identity* of teachers in higher education helped to contextualize the study and offered a means to explore the potential impact of the NTFS on the award winners and their colleagues in the sector. For example, the introduction of awards for teaching excellence is consistent with the view that teaching and learning need to be restored at the heart of university life (Nixon *et al.*, 1998) with the 'scholarship of teaching' becoming just as important as 'blue-skies' research or the 'scholarship of discovery' (Boyer, 1990; 1994). Teaching awards may also open up new professional identities as an emerging cadre of academics become teaching and learning experts within their own discipline (Healey, 2000). Alternatively, awards for teaching could become a 'poisoned chalice' for many academics, since the take-up of an emphasized 'teaching identity' may be costly in the research culture of universities (Leon, 2002a). They may further polarize teaching and research, accelerating the emergence of 'teaching-only' contract staff and institutions with differentiated and stratified 'research' and 'teaching' missions (see Nixon *et al.*, 2001: 232). Awards such as the NTFS may therefore further erode what is taken by many to be the fundamental 'idea of the university' (Barnett, 1990), since it is argued that university education will only be revitalized once teaching and research are brought into a closer and more productive relationship (Rowland, 1996).

These theoretical ideas informed the study which focused on the following three inter-related question areas: (1) How is 'teaching excellence' understood within the NTFS? (2) What are the key characteristics of the NTFS as a development mechanism and strategy? (3) What impact has the NTFS had on the professional lives and identities of the award winners? The methodology used to explore these questions involved three phases and was described in detail in Chapter 1 (pp. 15–16).

How 'teaching excellence' is understood within the context of the NTFS

Research undertaken during phase one suggested that teaching excellence within the context of the scheme is informed strongly by a model of 'reflective practice'. This model draws principally on the work of Schon (1983; 1987) and involves teachers reflecting upon their own teaching and disseminating 'good practice' to colleagues within the sector. Reflecting upon one's own practice involves identifying a mismatch between 'espoused theories' (how one should teach) and 'theories in use' (how one actually does teach) and proposing a practical solution to overcome this mismatch (McLean and Blackwell, 1997). The dissemination of good practice to colleagues represents a further layer of 'reflection on action': Teaching Fellows refine their ideas by sharing them with other people. The model of reflection underpinning teaching excellence in the NTFS draws mainly upon psychological theories of learning. Such a model emphasizes the transaction between individual teachers and learners and ignores the wider social, political and economic context within which higher education is located (Malcolm and Zukas, 2001: 34–6). This model may favour those people who draw upon psychological theories of teaching and learning. Teachers who bring their own and/or different disciplinary perspectives to bear on questions of teaching and learning in higher education may find that their understandings of teaching excellence are not so readily recognized by the NTFS. Previous research has established that 'reflective practice' is often presented in the higher education literature as taken-for-granted 'good practice' its conceptual dominance within the sector demonstrated by the way it has been incorporated, without explanation, into the ILTHE accreditation framework (Zukas and Malcolm, 1999: 2).

During interviews with members of the NAP in phase two, it was possible to explore the process by which the criteria for 'teaching excellence' were established and used to judge applications. As noted by McNaught and Anwyl (1993: 35), it is important to establish 'how such criteria are actually used by the selection panels, or how particular items are valued'. It became evident that the amount and quality of deliberation within the NAP was limited. This was partly due to the time made available for discussion: there were four meetings of the panel in total during 2000, only one of which focused on identifying criteria for teaching excellence. An emphasis on 'speed and efficiency' appeared to characterize the meetings. The NAP was large, with equal numbers of men and women drawn from a range of institutions. But there were significant exclusions (one respondent characterized the panel as 'white and grey'), limited student representation (one student on the panel in each year of the scheme: in 2000, the representative did not attend most of the meetings), few people with substantial experience of educational research and a high concentration of senior managers and educational developers (over half of the 24 panel members). The NAP worked within structural parameters for the NTFS preset by the HEFCE. Members of the panel expressed concern about two of these parameters: first, the emphasis on 'individual' teaching excellence in the awards and second, the decision to recognize and reward only a small group of 20 award winners rather than the larger group nominated by institutions.

Criteria for teaching excellence were generated deductively by NAP acting as an 'expert panel' rather than inductively from a consideration of real cases. Some of the complexity involved in understanding excellence only became apparent when people tried to apply the criteria. In presenting a provisional set of criteria to the NAP, the ILTHE drew on extensive research they had conducted into award schemes and some of the more focused research on how to recognize and reward teaching excellence (for example, Elton and Partington, 1993). But they did not address any of the 'meta-level' debates about education that underpin understandings of teaching excellence, for example: work on ideological traditions in education (Williams, R., 1961); different discourses of higher education (Williams, J., 1997: 27–45); and different models of the higher educator (Malcolm and Zukas, 1999). These debates were not made available to the NAP and they did not feature significantly in NAP discussions. Consequently there was little self-conscious, rational debate about alternative interpretations of excellence within the NAP.

The ILTHE presented provisional criteria for teaching excellence that were consistent with those that people need to meet in applying to join the ILTHE. The criteria at this stage consisted of a long list of behaviours, attributes and attitudes. The NAP developed their own criteria and made a distinction between teaching excellence and competence: they argued that excellent teachers need to demonstrate an 'extended professionalism' (Hoyle, 1980) beyond the classroom and contribute to the dissemination of good practice. The four criteria below were finally agreed upon and used to judge applications:

- the ways in which the application demonstrates the nominee's ability to influence students positively, to inspire them and to enable them to achieve specific learning outcomes as defined by the institution and/or the subject area;
- the ways in which the application demonstrates the nominee's ability to influence and inspire colleagues in their teaching, learning and assessment practice, by example and/or through the dissemination of good practice;
- the nominee's track record or potential, as demonstrated through the application, to influence positively the wider national community of teachers and learners in higher education in relation to teaching, learning and assessment practice;
- the nominee's ability, as evident in the application, to demonstrate a reflective approach to teaching and/or the support of learning.

ILTHE provisional criteria were appended to NAP criteria as a compromise – the ILTHE maintained that this was done to illustrate the range of evidence that might be considered, but some panel members felt the two sets of criteria were contradictory (one 'mechanistic and atomistic', the other 'organic and holistic'). NAP members had three main reservations about the selection process put in place by the ILTHE. These were (a) the initial reliance on institutional selection of excellent teachers, (b) the absence of any observation of teaching and (c) the limited and narrow range of evidence that was asked for in NTFS applications. Panel members disagreed about whether there had been inter-judge reliability in the assessment of NTFS applications. Some maintained that there had been insufficient deliberation around the meaning of the criteria and how to interpret and apply them. For example, one person said:

> When you came down to the judgement, what people were taking as evidence, which bits of the proposals struck them, what things they were using that particularly swayed them one way or another was obviously so different...and yet we didn't have time to discuss the fact that that was the case. So...it was like marking essays and you discover that somebody is giving it 80 percent and someone else is giving it 40 percent...and it's not because they are 'hard' or 'soft' markers although that's there as well, but because they actually disagree about the nature of the criteria and that was what the problem was...it was the lack of discussion about the meaning of the criteria.

In the first year of the scheme, differences in the assessment of applications and the interpretation of criteria were resolved through a 'defence-then-voting' system. This was perceived to be highly unsatisfactory for most panel members who were interviewed, since it privileged those willing and able to robustly defend their own assessments at short notice. In the second year of the scheme, more was done to encourage panel members to share and discuss their assessments, but this met with mixed success.

Phase-two interviews with fellowship holders elicited their understandings of teaching excellence in higher education. Recognizing the changing nature of the student body, the importance of teacher–learner interactions and the need to enhance students' employment prospects, they identified seven key aspects (order based on reported frequency): (1) reflecting upon and meeting the individual needs of students; (2) 'starting from where the students are at' in their thinking and encouraging them to adopt an 'active' approach to learning; (3) recognizing the importance of communication: knowing and valuing students and being available for them; (4) valuing and making use of new technologies in teaching; (5) adopting problem-solving methodologies; (6) recognizing the importance of transferable skills; and (7) offering learners flexibility and choice.

There were four different types of relationship between what Teaching Fellows said about teaching excellence in their NTFS application and what they said in interview. These were (order based on reported frequency): (a) correspondence; (b) 'playing the game' (one award winner used the term 'reflection' or a derivative 28 times in their application); (c) reframing the NTFS (using it to support their own current interests); and (d) 'strategic compliance' (Lacey, 1977: 72–3), where the individual complied with NTFS assumptions and requirements but retained private reservations about them (see Skelton, 1990). Previous work suggests that conformist teachers are more likely to win awards, with radicals, dissidents, 'villains' and those who adopt a critical perspective having little chance of success

(Brookfield, 1995). The responses of the national Teaching Fellows indicate that a more complex situation may exist, with some teachers being 'economical' about their real educational values and motivations.

The NTFS as a development mechanism and strategy

No explicit model or strategy for change appears to inform the NTFS or the work of the 20 fellowship holders. No NTFS documentation adequately conceptualizes the relationship between individual award winners and their wider constituencies. Although the TQEF as a whole is underpinned by a learning and teaching strategy (HEFCE, 1998), the aims of this strategy have not been pulled through as successfully into the NTFS as they have with the subject and institutional strands (for example, 'good-practice' guidance for producing institutional learning and teaching strategies includes a discussion of 'organizational change' – see HEFCE, 2001a). Within the documentation on the NTFS, the fellowship holders are viewed implicitly as reflective practitioners who will promote 'good practice' by disseminating the results of their project work to the wider higher educational community. But as teachers who have been identified and rewarded for their 'teaching excellence', it is also assumed that they have legitimate authority, as an 'expert group' (Gosling, 1996), to pass on their 'everyday' teaching expertise to others. The relationship that is implied between expert and other here is a passive one: the fellowship holder disseminates findings, sets an example, identifies good practice and passes this on to colleagues. An assumption is made that project findings and good practice can be transferred from one practice to another in a relatively straightforward manner. This implicit model of dissemination and change is based on 'transfer' theories of learning (Fox, 1983) and is evident in many of the HEFCE publications related to the TQEF (for example, subject centres are sometimes referred to as 'one-stop shops' and 'delivery' and 'transfer' feature frequently in the language of guidance material and 'good-practice' guides, see HEFCE, 2001a). Transfer theories of learning fail to recognize the complexity involved in educational change and the difficulty of 'embedding good practice'. It has been demonstrated that 'ordinary' teachers will not accept and apply curriculum changes unless they share the educational beliefs and values that underpin them (Fullan, 1982: 30).

The nature of the Teaching Fellows' development projects will influence the degree and level of impact they are likely to have on other teachers and students in the sector. The research demonstrated that most of the projects resemble a form of 'technical' or 'practical' action research (Carr and Kemmis, 1986; Zuber-Skerritt, 1992) – emphasizing solutions to specified teaching/learning problems, the development of teaching materials, textbooks and computer applications, and improvements in delivery methods (see HEFCE, 1998: 7). One of the potential benefits of technical/practical action research projects is that they can produce outcomes that are highly relevant to practitioners' immediate concerns and interests. They can foster collaboration between teachers (and students), and lessons learned at the local level can offer potential insights for other teachers, thereby contributing to an evolving 'grass-roots', 'evidence-based practice' (Pirrie, 2001). This type of action research, however, also has a number of recognized limitations. First, it can be under-theorized and insufficiently related to previous work in the same field, leading to problems of 'reinventing the wheel' (Bell, 1982), 'theory-building' and 'cumulation' (Yorke, 2000). Second, it tends to provide details about research methods but little about 'methodology', including any reflexivity about its own positioning relative to other research traditions and paradigms (Antoniou and Stierer, 2002). Third, it focuses on the immediate practical context of teaching and learning and ignores the wider social, economic and political context in which practices are located. Finally, generalizing from such projects can be problematic given the highly context-dependent nature of teaching and learning. These limitations may influence the degree to which the NTFS projects affect the higher education sector.

Plans for the Teaching Fellows to work collectively to promote effective teaching and learning in higher education (ILTHE, 2000: 2) have to date met with limited success. There were four main reasons why a 'shared identity' beyond camaraderie had not developed among the fellowship holders: (a) their perception of themselves as subject specialists; (b) their gravitation towards other individuals in the group of 20 who shared similar interests and/or project concerns; (c) the perception that some fellowship holders were more experienced in educational development work than others; and (d) the overall focus on achieving one's own individual project. The perceptions of the fellowship holders towards their group are typical of any interdisciplinary group, split, for example, by subject and experience. If one of the aims of the NTFS is for the fellowship holders to work together to promote effective learning and teaching in higher education, then these perceptions may need to be challenged and the potential value of the group, as a collective, may need to be explored in more detail. Some people expressed disappointment that no shared values and purposes had been established within the group of fellowship holders. They felt that this made it difficult for the group to have any significant influence on higher education policy and practice. The following comments by three people give some indication of the unrealized collaborative potential of the scheme:

> What surprised me about the scheme is, in a sense, what's not happened...they haven't actually created...a sense of a team that could use a little influence in a very constructive way.

> If there is one disappointment it's that politically... the potential for Teaching Fellows to form an informed 'voice'... I think we seem to have missed the boat slightly on that one.

> I think the national Teaching Fellows should be mobilized and should be doing things... I always wished that there had been the chance to simply apply for the award and then the people who won it, to actually do more work together, collaboratively.

The difficulty in developing a collective identity among Teaching Fellows may be related to the increasing fragmentation and 'proletarianisation' (Halsey, 1992) of the academic workforce in the UK, which has led to calls for a 'new academic professionalism' founded on shared commitments and values (Nixon *et al.*, 2001). It may also reflect an underlying tension in the NTFS between individual reward and collective development. The socio-political origins of the scheme, for example the need for it to emulate those in other countries, to attract publicity and to be treated seriously in the predominantly research culture of UK higher education, help to explain why such large sums of money (£50,000) were given to each of the award winners for development purposes. But the importance of the awards being seen to have 'added value' to the sector was evident in the initial plans for collective activity. In practice, however, this activity has not become a formal requirement; for example, non-attendance at shared meetings of the Fellows would not result in moneys being withheld. Similarly there has been a 'light-touch' management of development work which may explain why, at the point of interview, 12 to 18 months after the awards were announced, some of the award winners were only beginning to think about starting their projects.

The impact of the NTFS on the professional identity of the award winners

The award winners described the various ways in which the NTFS had enhanced their professional lives and status. For example, three people had been promoted to professorial level following NTFS recognition and in each case the award was perceived to have played an important part in this promotion. Although educational press coverage of the NTFS has featured criticism of the scheme for its failure to address the formal promotion system (Currie, 2000b), a national award for teaching excellence may represent an 'objective' measure of teaching performance that promotion panels can recognize. Two of the three promotions were in teaching-intensive institutions and the third in a teaching department within a research-intensive institution. It may be the case, therefore, that teaching-intensive institutions and departments are more able to recognize the NTFS as a legitimate basis for promotion to professorial level.

Virtually all the NTFS award winners reported that their contribution to teaching and learning had been recognized by the NTFS and subsequently acknowledged by colleagues, students, the subject community and the institution. Some people said they felt more confident in themselves and in their teaching, becoming a 'voice' for educational matters within their department. Others expressed the view that their interest in teaching had been validated, giving purpose and value to their work:

> If there are issues about teaching and learning I'm always asked about them; they expect me to be someone who's got a view and has thought about it.

> In career terms it has been vitally important because it has given me the opportunity to state that what I'm interested in [teaching] is valuable, and that those people for whom being an academic is fundamentally about research . . . those people have to recognize that what I'm doing is significant.

A number of ambivalent and less positive aspects about the award were also mentioned by some respondents. Several award winners in research-intensive institutions felt that receiving an award for teaching was problematic and that as project work took them away from their substantive research interests, the NTFS represented a 'poisoned chalice'. This was a point also made in the focus groups with higher education teachers (see Chapter 6). Other NTFS holders maintained that the award had prompted negative or ironic comments from colleagues and sometimes led to a feeling of being separate or isolated.

Most of the award winners had previous experience of educational development work (for example, involvement in the TLTP and FDTL programmes) and form part, therefore, of a growing number of staff who are involved in these activities within universities and colleges of higher education (Leon, 2002b). As a sub-set of the whole, the award winners might be thought of as 'educational developers within the disciplines' (see Healey, 2000; Healey and Jenkins, 2003) – a new cadre of staff who are located within a discipline and are undertaking educational development work specific to that discipline. This new identity appears to offer some benefits. Academics within subject disciplines who are interested in pedagogical issues can validate this interest through the new identity. It also offers a way of bringing together 'teaching' and 'research' interests through the scholarship of teaching and learning. But there also appear to be potential drawbacks. First of all, to embrace this new identity fully one would need to abandon substantive research interests in the discipline. Some of the award winners were unwilling to do this. Second, even if one were able to abandon these interests, the consequences of doing so, particularly in research-intensive institutions, might be severe and possibly costly in career terms.

Discussion

The case study shows that teaching excellence is a contested concept which becomes inscribed with meaning following a complex social process. In the creation, development and implementation of the NTFS, there has been a struggle over the meaning of teaching excellence, involving different groups of people, including government ministers, the HEFCE, the ILTHE, the NAP and the award winners themselves.

For example, the impetus for the scheme came from the Dearing Report (NCIHE, 1997), with its emphasis on raising the profile of teaching and learning within the sector. Initially government ministers were committed to the idea of producing videos of 'star performers' to identify teaching excellence. These videos would then be used to improve the work of other teachers within the sector. At this point, teaching excellence was associated with a small group of 'superteachers' and focused on individual performance.

After consultations within the sector, the star videos idea gradually lost favour and attention shifted towards a national award scheme. This was partly due to rank-and-file opposition to the star videos concept and partly due to the fact that national award schemes appeared to have been introduced successfully in a number of other countries. Key personnel and the Teaching and Learning Committee within HEFCE established basic parameters for the NTFS, notably that the award would be for 20 individuals who would each receive £50,000. To justify this amount of money, award winners would be expected to participate in individual and collective development activities. Guidance from HEFCE suggested a practical focus for such development (HEFCE, 1998: 7). At this point, therefore, teaching excellence continued to be thought of as an exclusive quality and associated with relatively small numbers of teachers (20 per year). However, the emphasis on individual performance became less pronounced with the expectation that the scheme would be a 'fellowship'.

The ILTHE, as managers of the NTFS, inherited the parameters set by HEFCE. Their research into award schemes was extensive but it did not address 'meta'-level discussions about the meaning and purpose of teaching excellence, and these were not made available to the NAP. As a consequence, the meaning of teaching excellence from this point on was considered to be relatively unproblematic, with attention shifting to procedures for assessing applications. This served to reinforce the notion that teaching excellence is an essentially 'practical' concern. One of the ways in which the

ILTHE sought to contribute to the development of the scheme was through the provisional list of criteria for teaching excellence they put forward for consideration at the first meeting. This list was consistent with the ILTHE's membership criteria that people need to satisfy in order to demonstrate their basic competence to teach. The ILTHE therefore offered a means to universalize teaching excellence, blurring the boundary between basic competence and excellence, implying that the difference between these two qualities was a matter of degree rather than of kind. The breaking down of teaching excellence into a long list of behaviours and attributes (described by one NAP member as 'mechanistic and atomistic') is a highly performative act, one that assumes that teaching can be reduced to its component parts and made amenable to measurement and control.

In rejecting the ILTHE's provisional criteria, the NAP were also implicitly rejecting their universalistic understanding of teaching excellence. In foregrounding reflection and dissemination in their own criteria, the NAP put the concept of the 'reflective practitioner' at the heart of teaching excellence in the NTFS. Many of the NAP panel who were interviewed were vociferous in their criticism of traditional understandings of excellence which focus on the performance of teaching. Excellent teachers were perceived to be those people who reflect upon their practice and attempt to develop a deeper understanding of the students' experience of learning.

The award winners also mediated understandings of teaching excellence through the way they interpreted the NTFS and in the development work they planned. At interview, when asked to talk about teaching excellence, most drew upon performative and psychologized understandings (see Chapter 2, pp. 29–32). For example, they stressed the importance of adapting teaching to meet the needs of an increasingly diverse student body differentiated by personality, learning style and motivation. They were committed to notions of instrumental progressivism and supporting the development of the flexible learner/worker. In their development projects and activities they focused mainly on changing delivery patterns to accommodate student expansion, using new technologies to support these changes.

The majority of award winners were supportive of current higher education policy or at least prepared to work within its assumptions and values. Only a few people questioned the NTFS, the work of the ILTHE and/or higher education policy and few located their own work within a broader social, economic and political context. Of those who did express some criticism, one person wanted to return to a more traditional view of teaching excellence based on the disinterested pursuit of knowledge. Several people thought that the NTFS Fellows, as excellent teachers, should be in a position to influence higher education policy through their 'collective voice'. In practice such a voice was not established, since the Fellows focused more on their individual development projects and making connections with disciplinary colleagues outside the NTFS network. Most of the collective activities that the NTFS Fellows were meant to undertake together, therefore, were left unrealized.

Conclusion

Much of the existing work on teaching excellence award schemes has focused on reasons for their introduction, differences between awards and their impact on practice. Few if any have considered what sort of teaching excellence is promoted by particular award schemes and this is what I have attempted to do in this chapter.

Early research studies found no clear link between excellence awards and the improvement of teaching quality. Studies which have compared different mechanisms for promoting teaching and learning in higher education indicate some resistance to award schemes due to their potentially competitive and divisive nature. Despite these reservations, award schemes have proliferated in recent years. Schemes linked to existing promotion systems are more attractive to teachers whereas traditional schemes, emphasizing one-off prizes, are most common, possibly due to cost considerations. Evaluation studies of award schemes have tended to focus on operational concerns, often taking the meaning of teaching excellence for granted.

This chapter has included an in-depth case study of the NTFS for teachers in England and Northern Ireland. The NTFS is beginning to exert a considerable influence on institutional award schemes and is therefore helping to shape how teaching excellence is understood within the sector. The case study shows the complex social process through which different groups of people sought to give meaning to teaching excellence in the NTFS. Through their interactions and struggles over meaning, a particular understanding of teaching excellence has emerged with the following characteristics:

- *Individualized* – the NTFS makes awards to individuals. It therefore recognizes individual teachers rather than excellent teaching (which may result from the contribution of a group or team of teachers). Initial plans to create a 'fellowship' of excellent teachers who would engage in collective activities have met with limited success. Little sense of a collective identity had developed among the award winners who were interviewed. Initial claims that individual NTFS projects and development work would lead to sector benefits need to be reassessed given the simple one-way passive relationship that is assumed between 'expert' award winners and 'ordinary' teachers.
- *Underpinned by 'reflective practice'* – teaching excellence in the NTFS is primarily about reflecting on one's own teaching, devising solutions to practical problems (see below) and disseminating these solutions to

institutional and sector colleagues. Sharing practice developments with colleagues represents a further layer of 'reflection on action'.

- *Psychologized* – the reflections that NTFS award winners are undertaking focus primarily on the transaction between individual teachers and students, drawing on theories derived from psychological theory ('personality'; 'learning style'; 'motivation' and so on).
- *Practical* – the solutions to teaching problems that NTFS development projects generate are inherently practical, involving changes to delivery methods and the creation of new materials. The overall 'signature' NTFS project is using new technologies to make teaching and learning more accessible and attractive to 'non-traditional' students.
- *Performative* – the NTFS perpetuates the view that teaching and excellence in teaching can be measured and controlled. It contributes to system efficiency by maximizing the return from individual units (teachers) and acts as a performative lever in seeking to drive up general teaching standards within the sector. Much of the development work carried out within the NTFS is consistent with notions of 'instrumental progressivism' – a 'student-centred' style of education that is designed to enhance the individual's opportunities for employment. The NTFS has already begun to influence institutional teaching awards and 'local' understandings of teaching excellence.
- *Located within current higher education policy* – the practices, perspectives and development projects of the award winners are located within current higher education policy arrangements and commitments (for example: the vocationalization of the curriculum; notions of instrumental progressivism; the widening participation agenda and the incorporation of new technologies).

In drawing upon the four 'ideal types' outlined in Chapter 2, it is possible to identify what *kind* of teaching excellence is therefore being recognized and promoted by the NTFS. Through its assumptions, structures, procedures and criteria, and in the perspectives, practices and development projects undertaken by the award winners themselves, a performative and psychologized form of teaching excellence is in the making. Key aspects of a performative teaching excellence are measurement, control and system efficiency. There is an emphasis on its ability to contribute directly to national economic performance through teaching which is relevant to commerce and industry, and its commitment to instrumental progressivism which enhances the individual's opportunities for employment. A psychologized teaching excellence focuses on the transaction between individual teachers and learners, reflective practice informed by psychological theories and identifying practical solutions to teaching problems.

There is little evidence that 'traditional' and 'critical' understandings of teaching excellence are given expression in and through the NTFS. A clear shift away from traditional understandings of teaching excellence can be detected in the scheme's emphasis on reflective practice rather than lecturing performance. The move from an elite to a mass system of higher education is also supported by the scheme, as award winners find innovative ways of making teaching more accessible for 'non-traditional' students. Many of the assumptions behind the NTFS conflict with critical understandings of teaching excellence. For example, awards for a small group of 'super-teachers' conveys the message that the effort of individual teachers is more important than the material conditions of higher education. Clearly an emphasis on placing responsibility for teaching excellence on to individual teachers is attractive to politicians. Money invested in award schemes is relatively minor compared with the cost of significantly reducing staff–student ratios, maintaining or reintroducing student grants and improving pay and conditions for all higher education teachers. A scheme which promotes a teaching excellence that is primarily practical (practical solutions to teaching problems) is also one that is inherently apolitical. Working within a given policy context and focusing on delivery methods, technological innovations and new materials diverts attention away from fundamental questions about the purpose of teaching in higher education. Reducing teaching to the practical ultimately renders it politically malleable and turns teachers into technicians.

In Chapter 4, I consider how teaching excellence is understood and expressed within different institutional contexts. The chapter looks at a range of issues including: institutional responses to teaching award schemes; the emergence of formalized institutional teaching and learning strategies; and the relationship between institutional identity and teaching excellence, including reference to 'teaching only' institutions.

Chapter 4

Institutions and teaching excellence

Introduction

The discussion in Chapter 3 focused on awards for teaching excellence. Although some awards recognize that teaching excellence is a team effort and intimately connected to institutional policy and available resources, the majority reward individual teachers. In this chapter I concentrate on institutional teaching excellence. It has been argued that to analyse teaching excellence with some precision, one needs to consider not only the contributions of individuals but also the institutional contexts within which they work (Elton, 1998). A range of issues is examined, including: the case for looking at teaching excellence at institutional level; the emergence of formalized institutional teaching and learning strategies; the relationship between institutional identity and teaching excellence; the introduction of specialist centres; and institutional responses to teaching award schemes.

Why focus on teaching excellence at the institutional level?

'Everyone remembers a good teacher' is a phrase that is frequently used in teacher recruitment campaigns. In my work with university lecturers on professional development courses, participants often have vivid memories of particular teachers from the past (both good and bad) that have remained with them over the years. It can be useful to revisit these memories to allow teachers in higher education to identify their implicit ideas about what constitutes teaching excellence. But it is also important to remember that the 'individualization' of teaching has significant limitations since, however exceptional an individual appears to be, their work is always influenced to some extent by institutional factors.

An institution's support for teaching excellence may be facilitative rather than direct, offering the necessary working conditions, ethos, incentives and support for excellence to prosper. A survey of Australian universities in 1994 investigated the extent to which institutions had developed criteria for recognizing good teaching, what mechanisms were used to promote teaching and learning and whether teaching was taken into account in promotion and appointment procedures (Ramsden and Martin, 1996). These measures form part of a wide range of principles and procedures that have been identified in the literature through which institutions might offer support for teaching excellence:

- The provision of resources (including time for teachers to reflect)
- Low teacher–student ratios
- Quality of teaching and learning spaces
- A high standard of general infrastructure, equipment and so on
- Management processes and policies that support teaching and learning
- Awards for teaching
- Funding for teaching and learning development work
- An institutional culture that values and promotes teaching and learning
- Policies and practices that support the exchange of ideas
- The availability of professional development courses
- The recognition of teaching in career progression and promotion procedures.

All these measures are potentially important for supporting teaching excellence. Institutions that value teaching and understand themselves as 'learning organizations' will seek to learn about key aspects of their practice (such as teaching and learning) and promote the exchange of ideas among staff. Institutional learning about teaching may involve investigating current policies and practices, finding solutions to recognized problems and analysing the impact of innovations. An organization committed to learning about teaching will also endeavour to develop new institutional practices in the light of this learning.

It has been suggested that opportunities for professional development and the recognition of teaching in promotion procedures are crucial for creating an institutional culture that promotes teaching excellence (Elton, 1998: 5). It is clear that courses on teaching and learning in higher education have proliferated in recent years in many countries (the relationship between professional development and teaching excellence will be considered in detail in Chapter 9). But staff take-up of these opportunities and an individual's commitment to teaching and learning are influenced by the extent to which teaching is recognized in promotion procedures, a point often made in staff surveys (Ramsden and Martin, 1996: 304). Some institutions are creating teaching-related promoted posts and there is evidence to suggest that teaching-intensive institutions, in particular, are prepared to promote people to professorial level in the light of recognized teaching achievements such as teaching excellence awards (see Chapter 3, pp. 54–5). Higher education funding councils such as the HEFCE are also beginning to link teaching enhancement funding to institutional learning and teaching strategies. This is encouraging institutions to look more seriously at the mechanisms they have in place to support a culture of teaching excellence.

Institutional learning and teaching strategies

Many institutions of higher education now have a formal learning and teaching policy or strategy. In England and Northern Ireland the production of formal learning and teaching strategies gathered pace after 1998. The HEFCE linked funding to the production of learning and teaching strategies through its Teaching Quality Enhancement Fund, which directed development at the three interrelated levels: the individual, subject discipline and institution. A total of £49.5 million was allocated to the institutional strand over the three years between 1999–2000 and 2001–2002. The invitation to apply for funds identified five national priorities: staff development, innovation, exploitation of communications and information technologies (C&IT), widening access and learning resources (HEFCE, 2001a: 3).

By June 2000, every English institution had a learning and teaching strategy. Planned activities within these strategies for the most part follow HEFCE-identified priorities. For example, the most common mechanisms cited for supporting teaching and learning were: staff development and continuing professional development for experienced staff (91 per cent of institutions); support for ILTHE membership for staff (81 per cent); exploitation of C&IT (81 per cent) and promotion and rewards for excellence in teaching (65 per cent) (see HEFCE, 2001b). With regard to promotion and rewards, a report commissioned by HEFCE noted: 'In many cases changes to promotion mechanisms are an intention rather than a clear plan, and much work needs to be done to develop the details of workable mechanisms for different contexts, especially contexts where research is more highly valued' (ibid.: 14).

A good-practice guide published by HEFCE in 2001 concluded that learning and teaching strategies were becoming more coherent and linked to a planned process of change, with many institutions creating new management structures and procedures to ensure plans were being implemented. The strategy documents were also becoming more comprehensive and sophisticated, recognizing contextual and cultural shifts that needed to occur before change could take place. The guide commented, however, that there was additional scope for 'joined-up thinking' in which learning and teaching issues were related more closely to institutional policy on widening participation and research (HEFCE, 2001a: 4–5). The guide also noted that strategic support for learning and teaching needed to be linked more closely to the identity of an institution and its broader aims and purposes, commenting: 'Goals are more likely to be effective if they reflect the institutional mission' (ibid.: 6).

The relationship between institutional identity and teaching excellence

Through the production of formalized learning and teaching policies and strategies, institutions are working towards developing 'cultures of teaching excellence'. There is a growing expectation that all higher education institutions will seek to promote a culture of teaching excellence as a 'core' activity. At the level of policy, the quality of teaching and learning is now regarded as crucial to both national economic competitiveness and the attractiveness of higher education institutions in the global marketplace.

Running alongside this expectation that all higher education institutions will strive towards teaching excellence is a reform agenda that recognizes and promotes institutional diversity. In the light of this agenda, there is a recognition that institutions with different histories and missions will understand and practise teaching excellence in different ways. For example, a recent HEFCE report concluded:

> Some higher education institutions are examining the relationship between learning and teaching and research strategies. In particular, making the benefits of research strengths more explicit to under- graduate teaching, and maximising those benefits, might be a key feature for those institutions claiming that teaching excellence is based on excellence in research. (HEFCE 2001a: 9)

There are of course different ways in which institutions may seek to configure the teaching–research relationship in support of teaching excellence. 'Research-led' teaching has become the most popular way of expressing this relationship, but its meaning is not always clear. Carol McGuinness from Queen's University in Belfast, Northern Ireland, offers the following interpretation of teaching that is research-led:

- Teaching about specific research topics which are being studied by an academic at a point in time (in a module or part of a module);
- Teaching which emphasizes the current developments/research direc- tions in own area of research (cutting edge);
- Teaching more generally in own area of scholarship;
- Teaching with emphasis on research methods/processes or ways of accumulating knowledge in a particular discipline;
- Teaching as 'inquiry-based' learning vs. more didactic approaches to teaching;
- Students as researchers;

- Designing degree programmes which capitalize on current research expertise in a school or across schools;
- Linking research in the context of degree programmes for professional development (e.g. teachers, doctors, lawyers, managers), evidence-based practice;
- Learning environments which support a research-led focus, e.g. good access to primary sources in library, good information technology support, well-funded laboratories.

(See http://web.gg.qub.ac.uk/people/staff/whalley/misc/teaching/resled.html)

The University of Sydney in Australia adopts an even broader definition, suggesting the following dimensions to assess the extent to which research-led teaching is taking place:

1. *Research staff* – teaching is undertaken by world-class researchers who are actively researching and publishing.
2. *Evidence-based teaching* – teaching and learning is designed in the light of pedagogical literature and evidence of students' experiences.
3. *Research-based curriculum* – the curriculum reflects research processes and activities (e.g. team working, giving presentations and papers).
4. *A culture of inquiry* – there are debates and discussions within the subject discipline about pedagogical matters.
5. *A community of scholars* – students are inducted into the culture and community of researchers within the discipline.
6. *Research-aligned teaching* – teaching is organized by the particular research strengths and interests of staff.
7. *Teaching-led research* – teaching stimulates disciplinary research as ideas, theories and concepts are engaged with critically by students.

(See http://www.itl.usyd.edu.au/RLT/issues/dimensions.htm#one)

The final dimension is interesting to note since it places 'teaching' before 'research'. Many 'new' universities in the UK (former polytechnics and colleges of higher education granted 'university' status following The Further and Higher Education Act of 1992) are seeking to develop a teaching excellence that is founded on 'teaching-led research' rather than 'research-led teaching'. This involves not only point 7 above, but also research into teaching practices within the institution and developing teaching and learning practice and policy in the light of this research.

The argument that excellent teaching follows naturally from high-quality disciplinary research has generated a considerable amount of discussion within the sector. In a recent White Paper on the future of higher education, the UK government appear to distance themselves from this argument, stating:

> our belief [is] that institutions should play to diverse strengths, and that excellent teaching is, in itself, a core mission for a university. It is clear that good scholarship, in the sense of remaining aware of the latest research and thinking within a subject, is essential for good teaching, but not that it is necessary to be active in cutting-edge research to be an excellent teacher.

(DfES, 2003: 54)

The paper outlines proposals that waive the necessity of having research degree awarding powers to become a university and cites evidence which disputes any relationship between disciplinary research and the quality of teaching. This latter point is supported with the comment:

> not every teacher needs to be engaged in 'research' as a narrowly defined activity but might be expected to engage in scholarship to inform their work as teachers. These findings are backed up by the experience of our current colleges of higher education. These higher education colleges have standards of teaching that, in many cases, match or even surpass those of full universities.

(Ibid.: 54–5)

California State University (CSU) is referred to in the White Paper as an example of institutional teaching excellence understood in these terms. CSU is identified as a 'teaching-centred comprehensive university' which specializes in professional training across its 23 campuses. In the light of this example, it is possible to interpret the White Paper as a 'redistributive' strategic plan, designed to recognize the contribution that teaching-intensive institutions make to teaching excellence within the sector. In the focus groups that were conducted in my research into the NTFS (see Chapter 6), several participants felt strongly that teaching-intensive institutions should be recognized for the excellence of their teaching. Their argument was that as the research assessment exercise rewarded the research performance of research-intensive institutions, there ought to be a counter-balance to this, whereby institutions noted for their teaching received some equivalent recognition and financial reward for the quality of their work.

Where teaching excellence resides within higher education is therefore currently being contested. The idea that there may be 'equal but different' understandings of teaching excellence is gathering pace, yet this argument ignores the realities and implications of an increasingly stratified system of higher education. Differences in the financial resources, student and staff populations and consequent status of institutions make the notion of 'equal but different' problematic. For example, it has been noted that 'The stratification of the higher education sector has led to a greater degree of institutional specialization and to sharper divisions of labour within the academic workplace' (Nixon *et al.*, 2001: 232). Such stratification is leading to a situation where 'the gulf is widening between a small number of affluent and highly selective institutions where competition for admission is fierce and mostly privileges the wealthy – and hard pressed public and private institutions' (Gamson, 1998: 109).

The discourse of 'research-led' teaching excellence that is emerging in research-intensive institutions is therefore problematic due to its connotations with elitism and privilege. It also appears to assume that excellence flows naturally from cutting-edge research, which may not necessarily be the case. On the other hand, a teaching excellence understood as 'subject scholarship' is also limiting since it allows teaching to be separated from both disciplinary and pedagogical research – a separation that may lead to teaching being viewed essentially as a practical activity devoid of any real intellectual substance. If an excellence as scholarship also becomes associated with teaching-intensive institutions within a stratified system of higher education, then even though this may be just and redistributive, it may mean that teaching excellence is afforded little status and weight.

Institutional centres of teaching excellence

In January 2004, HEFCE-funded higher education institutions were invited to bid for funding to establish Centres of Excellence in Teaching and Learning (CETL). The purpose of CETLs is to recognize excellent teaching and to provide further investment to maximize their potential impact across the sector. A sum of £315 million is available to fund CETLs over a five-year period from 2004 to 2005 and a two-stage competitive bidding process is being used to select institutions. HEFCE expect to fund about seventy CETLs and are limiting the number of bids per institution to ensure that a wide range of institutions is represented (HEFCE, 2004).

At the time of writing, details of the institutional bids that are proceeding to stage two of the process have just been released. The range of expressions of teaching excellence is fascinating and highly diverse. For example, the University of Leicester is seeking support for the SPLINT Centre which specializes in 'Spatial Literacy in Teaching', the University of Nottingham is developing a 'Visual Learning Lab' and the Royal Northern College of Music is creating a CETL for 'Dynamic career building for tomorrow's musician' (see http://www.hefce.ac.uk/learning/tinits/cetl/s2bids.asp).

The CETL programme is therefore consistent with a policy of supporting and promoting institutional diversity. There is a wide range of expressions of teaching excellence linked to institutional characteristics and purposes. CETL appears to be more a 'postmodern' celebration of difference than an initiative which seeks to be redistributive. Different expressions of excellence, whether located in research- or teaching-intensive settings, are being recognized, rewarded and held up as 'equal but different'. The overall aim of the CETL programme appears to be performative: to drive up overall standards within the sector by stimulating activity and promoting diversity. Within the CETL programme there is no clear and unifying 'idea' of what teaching excellence is meant to be (see 'traditional' understandings of teaching excellence in Chapter 2). Rather, the emphasis is on the different ways it can be expressed and how these can be harnessed to performative goals.

Over the next five years it will be important to assess the impact of the CETL programme on institutional identities and understandings of teaching excellence within the sector. A number of questions could usefully be addressed: (a) will CETLs be used by institutions to affirm or reposition their existing identities (for example research- and teaching-intensive institutions)? (b) Beneath the surface appearances of CETLs, what understandings of teaching excellence are being promoted through the programme? (c) Will CETLs be used by institutions to forge a more specialized teaching identity? (d) Can CETLs disturb the current dualism that distinguishes research- from teaching-intensive institutions? (e) How successful will the CETL programme be in offering teaching-intensive institutions a foothold in an ever more competitive and stratified higher education system? And finally, (f) will 'super-institutions' emerge, recognized for the quality of both their teaching and research?

Institutional responses to award schemes for teaching excellence

Many higher education institutions now have formal teaching and learning strategies which identify measures for supporting teaching excellence. Some institutions are taking part in schemes like CETL in a bid to become specialist centres, developing a teaching excellence of a particular kind. We know relatively little about what influences institutional take-up of initiatives to promote teaching excellence and why they become successful. What helps and hinders their participation and ultimately contributes to their success? In this section I consider this question by drawing upon the ESRC research I conducted into the NTFS. Part of this research involved looking at institutional participation and non-participation in the NTFS. There were three main reasons for this interest. First, given that the NTFS aims to promote teaching excellence across the sector, it was important to establish the extent of institutional involvement. Second, I wanted to know whether participation in the NTFS was influenced by institutional 'identity' or 'mission' (for example, involvement of teaching- and research-intensive institutions). Finally, it was important to establish why some institutions chose not to participate in the scheme. The view was taken that establishing grounds for non-participation would give some insight into the perspectives of institutions 'outside' the scheme and help identify its underlying assumptions and values.

Participation levels for the first two years of the scheme were analysed. Institutions were categorized into the following types: (1) 'old' universities (institutions designated universities before the 1992 Further and Higher Education Act, including the ancient universities of Oxford and Cambridge); (2) 'new' universities (see p. 65); (3) University of London colleges; (4) higher education (HE) colleges; and (5) further education (FE) colleges (with higher education provision). In year one of the NTFS, 95 out of 132 (70 per cent) of all eligible institutions across these five types put forward a nominee to the national stage of selection, which demonstrates that there was keen sector interest in the scheme. Concentrating on universities, the majority took part (89 per cent), with broadly similar proportions of old and new institutions represented (89 per cent and 86 per cent respectively). Given that figures for year two of the NTFS follow a very similar pattern, it is not possible to conclude that the NTFS is a 'redistributive' mechanism which is giving teaching excellence back to teaching-intensive institutions. Equal proportions of teaching- and research-intensive institutions are taking part in the scheme.

A lesser proportion of University of London colleges participated in the NTFS (65 per cent), and only 40 per cent of HE colleges put forward a nominee. Interpreting these figures in the light of further interview data (see below), it is possible to suggest that the size of an institution, for example, having a smaller pool of staff from which to draw upon and less staff resource to support the application process, may affect its ability to participate in the NTFS. This may also explain why only three FE colleges (with higher education provision) participated in year one.

Interviews were conducted with representatives from four non-participating institutions to consider their perspectives on the NTFS. These varied in terms of size and category and whether they had not participated in one or both years:

1. A university of London college, which participated in year one (with an unsuccessful nominee) but not in year two: interviewee was an academic staff developer (henceforth referred to as Institution A)
2. A higher education college in the South of England, which did not participate in either year: interviewee was the Vice-Principal, responsible for academic staff development (referred to as Institution B)
3. An old university in the South of England, which did not participate in either year: interviewee was an administrative leader within a learning, teaching and quality support unit (Institution C)

4. A university college in the South of England, which participated in year one (with an unsuccessful nominee) but not in year two: interviewee was the Principal (Institution D).

During these interviews, seven main reasons for institutional non-participation in the NTFS were identified: principled objections to the scheme; insufficient time and resources; lack of interest from staff; lack of interest from management; difficulty interpreting the requirements of the scheme; reluctance to put the institution's reputation 'on the line'; and resistance to the ILTHE.

Principled objections to the scheme

- Competitive award schemes are elitist and divisive. They are driven by the 'cult of celebrity'. The institution had no plans to participate in future years (Institution A).
- The NTFS is considered to be tokenistic and superficial. It involves 'picking at the surface . . . [and] paying lip service' to the problems of trying to raise the profile of learning and teaching in higher education. Rewarding excellence diverts attention away from raising overall standards (Institutions A and C).
- As a scheme which rewards teaching, the NTFS reinforces the separation between teaching and research in higher education (Institution B).
- The NTFS is patronizing and underpinned by a deficit model. The views of user communities are more significant than awards in testifying to the quality of an institution's teaching and learning provision (Institution B).

Insufficient time and resources

- There was insufficient time to select a nominee in the first year. It was not possible to set up an internal, transparent selection process in the time available (Institution A).
- Insufficient time was available for the institution to help develop their nominee's application and this was compounded by the amount of documentation involved (Institution C).
- The application process coincided with the Easter break when many staff were away from the university (Institution C).
- There were other more urgent institutional priorities, together with limited resources for dealing with them: 'we had a QAA review and three new foundation degrees, I had to say what are the priorities for a small institution . . . It would be nice to have had the time and the space and I guess the larger institutions have always got more person power. I think scale is helpful because you've got a bigger pool of people and

more dedicated staff to support people applying for an award'
(Institution D).

Lack of interest from staff

- There was a staff perception that the chances of winning an award were
limited (because of the two-stage selection process: institutional then
national), and so the effort to put together an application did not seem
to be justified (Institutions A, B and C).
- Staff perceived that the competition at the national stage would be too
strong. This was a view particularly held by staff with little experience of
education research and/or development (Institution A).
- The experience of failure: one institution had an unsuccessful nominee
in year one, for whom the experience had been one of 'failure'. This
discouraged other applicants (Institution A).
- Staff were more concerned about developing their standing as
researchers within their discipline (especially in the early days of their
careers), rather than showing an interest in educational development
(Institution B).
- Staff without an idea for a development project were put off by the
extra effort that the project part of the application demands: 'I can see
why you've got to "sing for your supper" ... [but] unless I had a "pet
project" I wanted funding for I might not bother. I suspect this will put
people off' (Institution C; also similar comments Institution B).

Lack of interest from management

- Teaching initiatives were not regarded as a priority given the strong
research profile of the institution. An interest in teaching plays 'second
fiddle to the research agenda' and participation was not a strategic
priority (Institutions A, B and C).
- Participation will have little impact on the institution's standing
(Institution B).
- There was initial reluctance to get involved with something 'new'
(Institution C).
- Staff were encouraged not to apply for a relatively significant amount of
funding for a research/development project since they were perceived to
lack experience in bidding for, setting up and managing large projects
(Institution B).

Difficulty interpreting the requirements of the scheme

- Concerns were expressed about the quality of the NTFS documentation
made available to institutions. This rendered the requirements of the

scheme difficult to discern (Institution B, similar concerns expressed at Institution C).

- Confusion about the basis on which to select a nominee: 'The thing I'm puzzled about is why do they have to do the project? What is the fellowship being awarded for?' (Institution C).

- The NTFS was interpreted as primarily a bid for research funding by some institutions: 'I think if you cannot actually think of something which is either novel and then needs to be disseminated, or a problem which needs to be researched and solved, then I'm not quite sure how you justify £50,000'. The 'claim that it is a reward for good teaching seems to me to be slightly extraordinary' (Institution C).

Reluctance to put the institution's reputation 'on the line'

- There was a reluctance to submit a 'weak' application and 'put the [name of institution] stamp on it'. There was a lack of confidence in potential nominees, so a tendency to suppress applications for fear of damaging the standing of the institution with the ILTHE (Institutions B and C).

Resistance to the ILTHE

- Distrust of the ILTHE may discourage members of staff from applying, particularly if they are already uncertain given the effort required to put an application together (Institution C).

An assumption is often made that institutions that do not respond positively to educational change are suffering from inertia and/or mismanagement. This example of the NTFS demonstrates that a wide range of factors contributed to institutional non-participation, not all of which could be subsumed under the category of 'reluctance to change'. Institutions rarely respond passively to directed educational change, mediating the 'brute sanity' (Fullan, 1982) of policy makers. Some institutions chose not to participate in the NTFS due to principled objections, and difficulties were experienced due to economies of scale, short-term deadlines, competing priorities and confusion about the nature of the award and its paperwork. If institutional support for teaching excellence in higher education is to be nurtured and used to best effect, then reasons for non-participation in change initiatives need to be carefully considered by policy makers as a basis for future strategy.

Summary

However excellent an individual teacher appears to be, their work is always located in a broader institutional context. Institutions can create a culture of teaching excellence by providing the necessary resources, infrastructure, development opportunities and climate in which individual and teams of teachers can prosper. Two mechanisms appear to be linked strongly to the development of a culture of excellence. The first is the availability of professional development courses for lecturers. The second is the formal recognition of teaching in promotions procedures and the creation of teaching-related promoted posts.

The identification of mechanisms such as these, which support teaching excellence, is now a common feature of the learning and teaching strategy documents produced by higher education institutions. The recent emergence of such strategies and policies, sometimes linked to central government funding, is creating a situation of 'directed educational change' as institutions plan developments in the light of national priorities. Given that teaching is seen as a core activity, all higher education institutions are being encouraged to strive towards a culture of excellence. But some institutions are also seeking to develop an identity primarily on the basis of their teaching, and this has given rise to fierce debates about what such an identity might involve. Two main arguments have been put forward. The first maintains that excellence understood as 'research-led' teaching flows naturally from cutting-edge disciplinary research. The second suggests that excellent teaching is scholarly, which means keeping up to date with (rather than producing) the latest developments in one's subject field. Both arguments have weaknesses and intensify an unhelpful split between teaching and research. CETLs seem to be a 'third-way' postmodern solution, celebrating difference and producing expressions of teaching excellence of infinite variety. Any sense of a uniform 'idea' of teaching excellence now seems to be out of the question!

As part of their teaching and learning strategies, many institutions are developing awards for teaching excellence. In the UK, these awards tend to be based on the NTFS, which requires institutions to select their own candidates to go forward to a national-level competition. Following an analysis of institutional participation in the NTFS, a number of reasons were identified for non-participation in the scheme. Although it is often assumed that non-participation can be explained by reference to inertia and blockages to change, some institutions had principled objections to the NTFS and experienced practical difficulties relating to the timing of the scheme and its paperwork. In order to foster support for teaching excellence, therefore, policy makers need to develop an understanding of institutional perspectives on specific initiatives as well as their experience of change. It is also clear that 'directed' educational change is always subject to some institutional mediation.

Concluding comments

A performative understanding of teaching excellence (see Chapter 2) underpins recent policy to make funding available to institutions that produce teaching and learning strategies. The production of such strategies and institutional cultures that support teaching excellence is associated with system efficiency and the attempt to raise overall teaching standards. There is no doubt that the shift towards a mass higher education system has led to a focus on institutional teaching excellence. The realization that non-traditional students would need additional learning support has turned attention towards institutional infrastructure and resources. Although traditional understandings of teaching excellence have always emphasized the importance of the institution, this importance has centred on the processes of socialization and character formation. Today institutional teaching excellence is measured more by operational systems, procedures, policies and the drive to standardize practice across different departments. Recognizing the contribution that teaching-intensive institutions make to teaching excellence suggests a step towards ensuring a more equitable system of higher education: something that is consistent with the critical perspective outlined in Chapter 2. The continuation of separate funding streams for research and teaching, however, and the differential status afforded to research-intensive institutions, ultimately means that a two-tier, stratified system remains, with institutions that are associated primarily with teaching (even if this is excellence in teaching) being seen as the 'poor relation'.

Chapter 5

The contribution of subject disciplines

Introduction

In this chapter I critically examine the relationship between teaching excellence and subject disciplines. I begin by looking at some of the arguments that support the growing assumption that teaching excellence can only be understood and supported within a disciplinary framework. I then go back in time to consider the emergence of interdisciplinary study in the 1970s, what this implied for teaching excellence and what happened to some of the new theme-based subjects that were introduced during this period. In the light of this discussion, I consider recent work on new understandings of disciplinarity which seeks to address some of the criticisms that have been made of the established academic curriculum. This work suggests that disciplines need to be reflective and that teaching excellence needs to be both located within the deep structures of disciplines yet prepared to question these structures and consider alternatives. In the final section I consider how this might be achieved through a process of critique. The chapter seeks to address some crucial questions about the relationship between teaching excellence and subject disciplines. For example, is the subject necessary for any understanding and practice of teaching excellence? What arguments support such a view? Are there any alternatives to a subject-based understanding of teaching excellence? And what are the constraints that make such alternatives difficult to realize in practice?

The restoration of the subject

In recent years there has been a re-emphasis on the importance of the subject discipline in many countries. With the move towards 'mass' systems of higher education without a matching increase in the unit of resource, there has also been a shift back towards lecture-based teaching and 'knowledge delivery'. Although the emergence of interdisciplinary work in the 1970s threatened to destabilize the established curriculum and open up new understandings of teaching excellence, it never managed to break free from the margins and is currently in decline (Bird, 2001).

In the UK, the LTSN subject network, subject benchmarking, the QAA's Subject Review, the research assessment exercise (with its strongly bounded subject-based panels) and the FDTL and TLTP development programmes, which offered funding to support subject-based educational development projects, have all contributed to restoring an emphasis on traditional subject disciplines. Professional development courses for university lecturers are also increasingly moving away from generic programmes to subject-based initiatives (Gosling, 1996; Healey, 2000). In the light of these changes, there is a growing assumption that teaching excellence can only be understood and supported within a disciplinary framework. In this chapter, I examine this assumption, identifying arguments for and against a subject-discipline-based understanding of excellence. The next section reviews some of the arguments that support such a view. It is important to examine these arguments since the central defining role of the subject discipline is often presented as 'common sense'.

Teaching excellence within the subject discipline

According to Becher (1989), subject disciplines provide the epistemological structure and social organization through which individual academics come to make sense of their work in higher education. He states: 'the attitudes, activities and cognitive styles of groups of academics representing a particular discipline are closely bound up with the characteristics and structures of the knowledge domains with which such groups are professionally concerned' (Becher, 1989: 20). Although he acknowledges that disciplines are subject to historical variation involving the emergence of new fields within the discipline, the death of old ones, border disputes and the 'occasionally dramatic metamorphosis of those in middle life', he maintains that there is a recognizable continuity to disciplines, their 'differentiation over time ... seldom such as to obliterate all significant resemblance' (ibid.: 21).

From such a perspective, subject disciplines precede the individual academic and provide a 'ready-made' community, tradition, value system, mode of enquiry, conceptual structure and set of established behaviours and practices within which academics make sense of their work. This 'deep structure' of the discipline is usually tacit and only learned through a period of immersion within the discipline. Teaching excellence from this perspective is inevitably linked to this deep structure, with the established aims, concepts and methods of the discipline informing what it means to teach and learn in appropriate ways. One of the criticisms that is often made of higher education teaching is that, until recently, with the introduction of formalized professional development, people have learned from experience or based their own teaching on the typical practices they have witnessed within their discipline. According to the view proposed here, this informal learning represents an important familiarization with the knowledge structure and cultural conventions of the discipline, which may be implicit but nevertheless invaluable in understanding how to operate successfully within disciplinary cultures.

The work of Hirst (1974) supports the view that the epistemological structure of academic disciplines determines how they should be taught and, by extension (for our purposes here), how teaching excellence ought to be understood. Hirst argues that there are logically distinct forms of knowledge which give rise to cohesive academic disciplines such as mathematics, physics and history. These disciplines have a grammar of key terms and concepts and a logical order with respect to how the concepts relate to each other and are organized. Teaching (and excellence in teaching) from this perspective has to involve communicating the epistemological structure to learners. There are different ways to communicate this structure through teaching, however, since as Hirst points out with reference to teaching science, 'Logical order is the end product in scientific understanding. It is a pattern which in teaching is pieced together as one puts together the pattern of a jig-saw ... There is a great variety of ways in which the jig-saw can be made up ... The logical order emerges as you go along' (Hirst, 1974: 122). Although Hirst recognizes (ibid.: 124) that in some disciplines ('moral and historical matters') there may not be a clear hierarchical ordering of concepts, he concludes that, generally speaking, teaching has to concern itself much more rigorously with the detailed analysis of the logical features inherent in different forms of knowledge for it to be rationally defensible. Taking issue with Dewey, whom he regards as being mistaken for elevating scientific method above subject knowledge, he argues that subjects have a grammar and logical conceptual structure which must be communicated through teaching. Otherwise teaching becomes almost incomprehensible: 'it will not be the teaching of a subject at all' (ibid.: 129).

Healey (2000), writing about the scholarship of teaching and learning, argues that such scholarship needs to be developed within the context of academic disciplines. He states that 'scholarship of teaching shares ... characteristics of excellent and scholarly teaching, but, in addition, involves communicating and disseminating about the teaching and learning practices of one's subject' (Healey, 2000: 172). Writing with particular reference to the discipline of geography, he supports a disciplinary-based scholarship of teaching with two supporting arguments: first, that the primary allegiance of most academic staff is to their subject or profession; and second, that there is a strong perception among academic staff of significant differences between disciplines. He argues that this perception is reinforced by research evidence which identifies disciplinary differences in activities, subject matter, learning styles, attitudes to teaching and research, patterns of communication and learning goals. Healey concludes that the scholarship of teaching in higher education should be related to the content of particular disciplines. He cites the Carnegie Academy for the Scholarship of Teaching and Learning in the USA as an example of an educational development initiative organized along these subject discipline lines (see Chapter 10 for further details).

The emergence of interdisciplinary study

During the late 1960s and 1970s, following attacks on the established curriculum of universities, subject-based teaching in higher education began increasingly to be questioned. In the light of student protest movements, interdisciplinary work began to grow, and joint honours degrees were created (Barnett, 1990). New theme-based subjects such as Black and Women's Studies emerged, staffed by lecturers from different disciplines. This challenged the assumed boundedness of academic study and the authority of discrete subject areas. 'Traditional' teaching was also criticized for focusing too heavily on the transfer of subject-based knowledge. The emergence of a 'student-centred' learning movement emphasized the importance of socially relevant curricula and interactive teaching methods. Facilitation of the students' learning became a key focus for educators and the 'didactic authoritarian pedagogue', who relied on lecture-based teaching, gradually began to lose favour (Northedge, 2003b: 169–170).

Barnett (1990) argues that from a liberal perspective, interdisciplinary study has great potential since traditional subject disciplines place unnecessary restrictions on the pursuit of knowledge. He states: 'They [academic disciplines] are bounded packages of knowledge and experience, each with its own internal character. They stand for narrowness and limitations on the development of the mind... Disciplines are anathema to any real, open and liberating educational experience' (Barnett, 1990: 175). Teaching excellence from such a liberal perspective would not be located within subject disciplines. It would seek to encourage students to look beyond discrete subject areas and pursue their enquiries across disciplinary boundaries. Barnett (ibid.: 176) notes that some experimentation with interdisciplinarity took place in the 1970s across the Western world, involving teachers from different disciplines working together. He concludes, however, that the conventional disciplines have re-established themselves in recent years, with interdisciplinary initiatives either becoming marginalized or stripped of their radical potential. He argues that multidisciplinary courses continue to exist but they tend to be 'a collection of units... with few horizontal connections made across the disciplines' (ibid.).

This distinction between multi-, inter- and transdisciplinarity is significant for the discussion in this chapter and a useful set of definitions is offered in the work of Gibbons *et al.* (1994). They suggest that the first 'is characterised by the autonomy of the various disciplines and does not lead to changes in the existing disciplinary and theoretical structures'. Interdisciplinarity, next, 'is characterised by the explicit formulation of a uniform, discipline-transcending terminology or a common methodology'. Finally, transdisciplinarity 'is essentially a temporary configuration and thus highly mutable. It takes its particular shape and generates the content of its theoretical and methodological core in response to problem-formulations that occur in highly-specific and local contexts of application' (ibid.: 28–30).

Bird (2001) explains that support for interdisciplinarity in the USA in the 1970s emerged in the context of student protests about the Vietnam War and other liberatory movements (for example, the Civil Rights movement and Feminism). Four key principles underpinned calls for a transformation of the higher education curriculum and an overthrow of traditional academic disciplines. These were relevance, experience, liberation and totality (ibid.: 466). The first principle involved challenging the perceived irrelevance of the academic curriculum to focus on important contemporary themes such as war and civil rights. 'New' knowledge would also draw upon personal experience rather than hide behind an 'ivory-tower', detached academic view of the world. Liberation involved looking at ways in which knowledge in higher education might support a more equal and just world rather than be the servant of the 'industrial–military complex'. Universities were viewed as bastions of conservatism and subject disciplines a means of preventing people from understanding the 'totality' of what was happening in their lives.

Bird examines the case of one of the new interdisciplinary subjects which emerged in the 1970s, Women's Studies, which, along with Cultural Studies and Black Studies, represented a challenge to the established higher education curriculum. The case study offers a fascinating account of how established disciplines are able to incorporate new knowledge without ceding too much territory, thereby ensuring that disciplinary boundaries are 'redrawn rather than demolished' (ibid.: 463). Various structural constraints made it difficult for Women's Studies to break out from the margins, and recent interviews with women in both the UK and the USA suggest that many degree courses had either closed or were under threat. Delaying devices used by committees responsible for course approval, refusal to honour agreements about appointments and their continuation, difficulties in being located within administrative centres and the research assessment exercise were all cited as impediments to continuation. The 'pull of the disciplines' meant that many women had moved back into faculty or departmental bases and away from inter-disciplinary work.

Bernstein (1971) writes about the emergence of integrated curricula at the beginning of the 1970s. He argues that at this point, integrated curricula are more of a theoretical possibility than an empirical fact, but he concludes his article by trying to explain an observable movement towards the institutionalization of integrated codes. In his analysis, he identifies two main types of curriculum. The first he calls a 'collection'-type curriculum, where 'contents stand in closed relation to each other, that is ... the contents are clearly bounded and insulated from each other' (ibid.: 49). The second he calls an 'integrated' type of curriculum, 'where the contents stand in an open relation to each other' (ibid.) and are subordinate to some relational idea or theme. Clearly there are links here between integrated curricula and interdisciplinary work, and the idea of the latter being driven by a relational theme requires the more radical horizontal connections between teachers that Barnett (1990: 176) refers to. Bernstein maintains that collection-type curricula (such as those found in secondary schools and universities which are organized along subject-based lines) are highly effective in maintaining the existing social order and power relationships. School subjects and academic disciplines create a strong sense of membership: they attribute identities, so that people know who they are and where they 'fit' in the hierarchical structure created by collection codes (some subjects/disciplines have higher status than others, which is reflected in the amount of time allocated to them, who teaches them and so on). Subjects tend to have strong 'framing' (Bernstein, 1971: 49–51), which 'refers to the strength of the boundary between what may be transmitted and what may not be transmitted', and this framing in turn has implications for the degree of control teachers and students have over the curriculum and the relations that exist between them. Whilst Bernstein recognizes the potentially transformative power of integrated curricula to create more democratic educational systems, he also accepts that such curricula have their own limitations, create uncertainty and require changes in the distribution of power and principles of control. He states: 'It is no wonder that deep resistances are called out by the issue of change in educational codes' (ibid.: 63). In seeking to account for the movement towards integrated curricula, Bernstein gives two main explanations. The first is technological: in order to respond to changes in the industrial process, people in the twenty-first century need to have general and transferable skills that can be applied to a range of operations. These changes reduce the significance of disciplinary knowledge and specific skills. His second argument is that the move away from collection codes reflects a deeper moral crisis: a growing ontological and epistemological uncertainty that we will return to later.

Subject or discipline? Towards a 'new disciplinarity'

With the restoration of the subject discipline has come a new body of work which has sought to develop new understandings of disciplinarity and its place in higher education. This work has attempted to both build on some of the existing claims made for disciplines and also to respond to some of the challenges implied by interdisciplinary study and its critique of the established academic curriculum.

Parker (2002), for example, makes an important distinction between 'subject' and 'discipline'. She states:

> 'Subject' is reassuringly concrete – a subject can be defined, has a knowledge base which can be easily constructed into a programme of knowledge acquisition and, perhaps most importantly, of quantitative assessment ... a discipline is a more complex structure: to be engaged in a discipline is to shape, and be shaped by, the subject, to be part of a scholarly community, to engage with fellow students – to become 'disciplined'.
>
> (Ibid.: 374)

She argues that much of the recent emphasis on subject disciplines in teaching and learning in the UK actually focuses on *subjects* rather than disciplines: 'What we have is Subject Review, Subject Centres, not Discipline Review, or Learning and Teaching Discipline Centres' (ibid.). For Parker this is a crucial distinction, since the focus on a narrowly conceived subject has led to skill-based, training-derived models of university education being adopted in both the UK and the USA. According to this view, subjects can be broken down into a set of competencies or skills and then tested. The role of the teacher is simplified to focus on the efficient delivery of the course and the achievement of the specified competencies or skills. Parker argues that this model of education is being applied to all sectors (from school to university education) and is a response to the perception that educational standards are in decline. She suggests that the new training model is associated with a move towards performativity, leading to a situation where knowledge is commodified and valued not for its own sake but for its functionality (see Chapter 2, pp. 29–31).

Moore and Young (2001) also recognize that a performative 'technical instrumentalism' has begun to influence what happens in all sectors of education, including universities. They state:

> all subjects taught at university from Fine Art to Pure Mathematics have to incorporate key skills and show their students how to

apply their knowledge...Subject specialists are increasingly expected to make explicit not only how their subject links with other subjects, but also how it facilitates team work, communications or number skills.

(Ibid.: 448)

The current conception of 'subject', for Moore and Young, therefore, represents an uneasy and confused compromise between two competing educational ideologies that drive current educational policy. They call the first of these 'neo-conservative traditionalism', which wants to restore traditional academic disciplines as the 'gold standard' of higher education given their ability to promote a 'proper respect for authority and... traditional values' (ibid.: 447). They refer to the second ideology as 'technical instrumentalism', which focuses on the links between higher education and the economy and the need to be competitive in the global, knowledge-based economy of the future. They argue that recent postmodern critiques of knowledge have failed to offer a convincing alternative to the positions advocated by these two dominant contemporary ideologies. In the light of this, they suggest that from a 'social realist' perspective, a curriculum of the future needs to draw upon the knowledge and practice of existing disciplinary networks while being responsive to actual social and economic changes (for example, the proliferation of knowledge and the global economy). In other words, if the current 'restoration of the subject' in higher education leads to either (a) an emphasis on traditional academic disciplines which are impervious to the wider social and economic context or (b) an emphasis on subjects understood as connected, skills-based entities within a modular curriculum and taught by 'facilitators', both of these renderings of the 'subject' are problematic. Moore and Young therefore share Parker's concern about a narrowing of disciplines into subjects. They also suggest the need for academic disciplines to locate themselves more adequately within changing social and economic circumstances.

In the light of her criticisms of the subject, Parker proposes a 'newly-invigorated model of disciplinary education' (Parker, 2002: 374). Within this model, a case is made for a distinctive approach to disciplinary teaching. Such an approach would recognize and build on the following assumptions:

- Teaching is both an expression of and a participation in the discipline.
- It seeks to communicate a discipline's essential pedagogic structure: the disciplinary processes and modes of communication.
- The teacher reflects on and communicates that which is unique to and indicative of the discipline.

- Learning is a specific process of induction into the processes of the discipline.

Teaching excellence from such a perspective would move beyond this distinctive approach not only to induct students into the deep structure of disciplines but also to encourage reflection on these structures. A teaching excellence located within reflective disciplines would involve asking questions such as those listed below:

- What types of relationship between teacher and student are considered to be appropriate to the discipline?
- What is the relationship of research to teaching?
- Where does the curriculum start and end?
- What is assessed?
- How strongly does the discipline mould its practitioners? (that is, how much space is there for creative expression?)

Whilst Parker's work makes the important distinction between subject and discipline and identifies reflection as a process through which some of the limitations of disciplines can be overcome (unquestioned assumptions, practices and boundaries which may limit student learning), her argument would be strengthened by a deeper engagement with questions of power. Many accounts of academic disciplines fail to address how power operates within disciplines. For example, socio-cultural theories of learning (for example, Wenger, 1998), which emphasize participation in 'communities of practice' or 'knowledge communities', create an impression of academic disciplines as benign entities where novices are supported by established members and border disputes about curriculum and pedagogical processes are resolved harmoniously by rational consensus. Within such theories, teachers enable participation in knowledge communities through three main roles: clarifying meanings; offering learning experiences that encourage deep engagement with knowledge; and coaching students to participate in knowledge communities through prevailing practices (in academic disciplines through reading, writing and speaking the disciplinary discourse: see Northedge, 2003b).

What this neglects is the way in which positional power operates within disciplines (that is, the behaviour of key 'stakeholders' within disciplines: those who hold positions of power who control access to journals, research grants, positions on national bodies and so on) and also how power understood as normative practice and discourse operates to influence decisions about what counts as 'appropriate' disciplinary knowledge and methodology (although this may be more amenable to change through reflective scrutiny). Bird (2001: 467) views the 'tribes and territories' disciplinary metaphor critically, stating that 'Disciplines/disciples fiercely defend their spaces, patrol boundaries, and regard those who either intrude or disrupt with suspicion'.

Teaching excellence, reflexive disciplines and critique

A new form of disciplinarity which emphasizes not only induction but also reflection on existing practice may address some of the potential limitations of a teaching excellence located within the disciplines. Reflexive disciplines make public their deep structures and encourage reflection on them. They are dynamic rather than fixed, and require an active engagement on the part of teachers and students. In the context of philosophy teaching it has been argued that the 'ground rules' of the discipline should be made explicit and subject to scrutiny. This involves: 'encouraging them [students] to develop a meta-awareness about both the discipline itself and the educational process in which they are engaged' (Burwood, 1999: 449). There needs to be a critical dialogue about the discipline: 'What is desired is a way to allow students to find their place within a disciplinary culture from a position of empowerment, rather than subordination and thus perhaps lead to a democratization of disciplinary culture' (ibid.: 456).

Disciplines understood in this way may develop a teaching excellence which is sensitive to the epistemological structure and pedagogical processes inherent within the discipline. But they also ask serious questions about prevailing practice and consider alternatives. One way in which this questioning can be deepened and widened to address issues of power is through a process of critique. Barnett (1997) suggests that critique allows disciplinary knowledge to be interrogated to reveal its partiality and implicit values and interests. It involves stepping outside the deep structures of a discipline to get a purchase on key questions through the vantage point of another discipline. This stepping outside offers the opportunity to look reflexively at the discipline and to take part in meta-cognitive analysis. He states: 'Critique is a way of placing the discipline... essentially critique seeks to set the discipline in a wider perspective than that in which the internal debates are conducted. The intellectual field can be the subject of critical evaluation. Critique is metacriticism' (ibid.: 18).

It is important to point out that such meta-criticism is not an end in itself, but a process which strengthens the epistemological base of any claim to understand the world. It enables issues of disciplinary power to be addressed by subjecting the discipline to external evaluation. This entails asking difficult questions that disciplinary inmates may fear to ask, such as 'the extent to which ethical considerations play a part, the degree to which the discipline represents sectional interests, or the influence exerted by particular epistemologies' (Barnett, 1997: 18). Teaching excellence as disciplinary critique would involve understanding the epistemological structure and key pedagogical processes of other disciplines as a means to think and practise reflexively within one's own discipline. This reflexivity enables questions of power to be addressed as the assumptions, values and vested interests of disciplinary deep structures are made public and scrutinized.

Conclusion

Currently there is an emphasis on subject-based understandings of teaching excellence in many countries. Although there was some experimentation with interdisciplinary study in the 1970s, this failed to take root to any significant degree, and those new subjects that emerged during this period (for example, Women's Studies) are currently in decline or under threat. What has emerged in recent years is not simply a return of the established higher education curriculum. In the context of recent higher education policy, there has been a shift towards subjects rather than disciplines. For some, this new emphasis on subjects is thought to be narrowly conceived and symptomatic of a broader shift towards skill-based, training-derived models of university education. For others, the new emphasis reflects an uneasy yet inevitable compromise between traditionalists and those wanting to make higher education more responsive to the economy.

Work on new forms of disciplinarity identify what disciplines as opposed to subjects can imply for excellence in teaching. Reflective disciplines induct students into their deep structures while also encouraging them to reflect on their epistemological assumptions and cultural practices. Critique takes the process further, requiring disciplines to develop a reflexive understanding of their partiality in relation to other disciplines and ensuring that internal interests and power structures are subject to evaluation. In the light of the current socio-political context, it is difficult to see how these broader understandings of the subject *discipline* will gain much purchase on how teaching excellence is understood within policy and practice. Educational reform movements linked to globalization theories stress the relationship between higher education and the economy and are responsible, in part, for an emphasis on the subject, with its incorporation of key skills.

The following chapter is the first of four contributions to Part 3 of this book. Part 3 comprises Chapters 6 to 9 and is called 'Alternative explorations'. It opens up new areas for enquiry about teaching excellence which have received little attention to date. Chapter 6 considers 'ordinary' teacher and student perceptions of teaching excellence. It starts from the premise that ordinary people can help to deconstruct teaching excellence and its underlying assumptions.

Part 3
Alternative explorations

Local knowledge? 'Ordinary' teacher and student perceptions

Introduction

In Part 2 of this book, three 'familiar contexts' for exploring teaching excellence were identified: the individual, the institution and the subject discipline. These contexts have featured significantly in official policy initiatives and helped to shape the discourse of reformers. Chapter 3 focused on individual teachers who win awards for teaching excellence. One of the points noted was that receiving an award may confer an ambivalent status for those working in research-intensive institutions. Within such institutions, an emphasized teaching identity can represent a 'poisoned chalice', attracting negative or ironic comments from colleagues and taking time away from disciplinary research.

In this chapter, I explore *ordinary* teacher and student understandings of teaching excellence. By ordinary I mean those teachers who have not been singled out through awards for excellence and all those students they interact with each and every day, often in unremarkable, unnoticed and customary ways. There is a special quality to being 'ordinary' which features in the poem 'Born Yesterday' by Philip Larkin (Larkin, 1954). Larkin suggests that ordinariness is more likely to lead to happiness and a balanced appreciation of self and the world. Wishing for more can unsettle this balance as people lose the ability to witness the beauty of 'everyday' routine encounters and sentiment. In this chapter I explore teaching excellence from the standpoint of ordinariness; this involves finding out what 'rank-and-file' teachers and their students think about teaching and learning and schemes to promote teaching excellence.

It is important to state from the outset that it is very difficult to get a clear sense of what ordinary teachers and students understand by teaching excellence. Their observations are seldom available to us as most teachers and students are too caught up in the routine experience of pedagogical encounters to write about it. They are also too busy and too removed from positions of power and influence to be directly involved in the cultural production of teaching excellence through the formation of policy or the authoring of books and articles. Although it is clear that a performative discourse on teaching excellence has emerged and intensified in recent years (see Chapter 1), this may not be a discourse of teachers' and students' own making. Higher education reform has led to new policies and practices being introduced to identify and promote teaching excellence, and these communicate ideas about what excellence means and the purposes it should serve. Such reform usually follows consultation exercises with restricted and time-bound opportunities to respond to published proposals. However, it is unlikely that the majority of teachers and students will have participated in these exercises or felt that they played a significant part in the reform process.

In this chapter, teacher and student understandings are compared and contrasted with 'official' interpretations of teaching excellence. A key issue that is addressed is the extent to which ordinary teachers and students take up these official discourses or whether they mediate or resist them, adopting their own preferred understandings. As teachers work and interact with students in real learning situations, they develop a 'professional craft knowledge' (Cooper and McIntyre, 1996: 75–6). This is a knowledge that is born of experience, rooted in practice and one that is highly contextual, recognizing the possibilities and limitations within everyday teaching encounters. Students also learn to distinguish between the claims of course handbooks, the theory of teaching, and its reality. Furthermore, they are not simply passive in the educational process; their interactions with teachers can transform learning situations (Doll, 1989). Together, therefore, teachers and students create a 'local knowledge' (Geertz, 1993) of teaching excellence. The position taken in this book is that any adequate understanding of teaching excellence needs to take into consideration such knowledge.

There have been few reported studies of teacher and/or student perceptions of teaching excellence, although a number of academic articles have been written about award winners' understandings of teaching, their educational concepts and philosophies and their teaching/learning practices (see, for example, Dunkin and Precians, 1992; Dunkin, 1995; Johnston, 1996; Baiocca and DeWalters, 1998; Kreber, 2000; Hativa *et al.*, 2001). In this chapter I draw upon my own and previous research to gain some insight into what ordinary teachers and students understand by teaching excellence, what they think about policies to promote it (such as award schemes), and how they are likely to respond, therefore, to educational development initiatives that aim to enhance teaching and learning.

The value of local knowledge?

Local knowledge about teaching and learning has come under threat in recent years. In the UK, a sustained and successful attack on teachers has been waged since the 1980s by government and politicians (Hartnett and Naish,

1990: 9), which has blamed them for all kinds of social problems from delinquent behaviour to poor national economic performance. 'Discourses of derision' have mainly been targeted at compulsory school teachers, leading to calls for poor practitioners to be weeded out from the profession. Higher education has not completely escaped associated claims that 'education is in crisis' and has suffered from what might be termed 'collateral damage' (Yorke, 2000). Teachers in higher education have not faced the same intensity of scrutiny and criticism as colleagues in compulsory education, but their professionalism has been questioned given that, until recently, there was no expectation or requirement for new entrants to undertake any formalized teacher training. In addition, broader processes of educational reform, involving all sectors of provision, have eroded the professional autonomy of teachers, and decisions about curriculum content and methodology are increasingly being taken out of their hands (Nixon *et al.*, 2001). Any opposition to this process of deprofessionalization or to other associated aspects of higher education reform (for example, student expansion, marketization, the proliferation of computer technologies and so on) tends to be characterized as a failure on the part of individuals to accommodate to the rigours of social and educational change (Clegg *et al.*, 2003a; Morley, 2003).

Students in higher education are also often discursively positioned in negative ways. For example, with the introduction of fees, students are identified as 'consumers' who are thought to make judgements about teaching purely on instrumental grounds. There are concerns, therefore, that students are becoming less intellectual in their orientation to higher education (McNay, 1994) and that their conceptions of teaching are limited and linked to 'surface' concerns with success and employability. Students tend to be viewed as passive recipients of higher education policy, who want and need performative indicators of excellence in order to make practical decisions about what and where to study. We are encouraged therefore to interpret student behaviour as a natural and understandable form of 'competitive individualism' (Ball, 1994: 145) as they do their best to plot a personal path within the education market that precedes them.

Through these discourses of derision and instrumentality, ordinary teachers and students in higher education are silenced and robbed of any authentic voice. Their local knowledge is discredited and we are encouraged to think that they have little of value to say. But there are three important reasons why it is important to clarify what ordinary teachers and students understand by teaching excellence: (i) distinctiveness, (ii) reflexivity and (iii) educational change.

Distinctiveness

Ordinary teachers and students have a valuable local knowledge about teaching and learning which is distinctively experiential, context-sensitive and interactionally constructed. This knowledge is an important potential contribution to our understanding of teaching excellence. For example, people 'in the field' are well placed to recognize the practical constraints that militate against the realization of any ideal conception of excellent teaching, since they are more in touch with environmental, curricula and interpersonal blocks to success.

Reflexivity

The very distinctiveness of this local knowledge can assist a process of meta-deliberation about teaching excellence which is vital for higher education in a democratic society. What can we learn about teaching excellence from the particular standpoint of ordinary teachers and students? How do their insights as 'insiders' compare with the perspectives of policy makers and reformers?

Educational change

For any educational change to be successful, politicians and curriculum planners ignore at their peril the perspectives of the wider population of teachers and students. This is because teaching and learning are social processes and people at grass-roots level inevitably mediate policies and curriculum plans through their action and inaction: consciously or unconsciously accepting, rejecting or refashioning the rational plans of policy makers, educational experts and 'change agents' (Fullan, 1982). It is crucial, therefore, that all those involved in the process of educational change have some insight into the values, experiences and perspectives of ordinary teachers and students within the sector. Any mismatch between local knowledge and policies that seek to promote teaching excellence needs to be addressed.

Ordinary teachers and students may have a different understanding of teaching excellence to that which informs official discourse and policy. Whilst official discourse has internal differences, it is characterized by the commitment to performativity: 'a rationalistic assumption that it is possible – and indeed, desirable, to "measure" performance' (Broadfoot, 2001: 136–7). It has been suggested that some newly qualified teachers may find it difficult to think outside a performative discourse of teaching and learning (Zukas and Malcolm, 2002: 6) and that the 'lifeworlds' of even their more experienced colleagues are becoming increasingly 'colonized' by a distorting 'technical–rational' language of teaching specifications and prescriptions (Abbas and McLean, 2003: 72). Investigating the perceptions of ordinary teachers and students helps to reveal the extent to which official discourses of teaching excellence have been taken up within the sector. They also allow us to consider whether there is a 'reverse discourse' in operation: one that more closely reflects the local knowledge of teachers and students.

Previous research studies

Much of the existing work on teacher and student perceptions of teaching and learning has tended to focus on what is 'good' or 'effective' rather than what is considered to be 'excellent'. For example, Utley (1998) found that students want the sort of teacher 'who can grab our attention, who wants to be there . . . [teachers] who know how to talk to students as human beings [and who are] enthusiastic, approachable, light humoured, personable and above all organized'. Those writing on behalf of students nationally recommend that feedback on teaching should be treated seriously and that students' learning experiences should be negotiated with teachers (Opacic, 1994). Some studies have sought to establish connections between student approaches to learning (for example, 'deep' and 'surface') and the quality of the teaching environment, using researcher definitions of 'good teaching' (Prosser and Trigwell, 1999: 65–6). Ramsden (1979: 420) gives examples of students who have positive perceptions of teaching based on their lecturers' personal enthusiasm and use of real-life examples.

As noted earlier in the chapter, studies of teacher perceptions of teaching and teaching excellence have tended to focus on award-winning or 'expert' individuals. An exception to this is found in the work of Evans (2000), who offers a critique of teaching excellence from a position of 'ordinariness'. He argues that in a mass system of higher education, the primary aim should be to develop high standards of teaching among the majority rather than excellence in the few. Locating the desire for teaching excellence within the tradition of elitist university education, he uses a transport metaphor to make the case for 'good-enough' teaching: 'I am not interested in whether my 747 pilot can loop the loop: I want him or her to take off or land unobtrusively every time on time and deal competently with emergencies' (ibid.: 7).

Fox (1983) identifies different theories that underpin teaching, based on conversations with ordinary teachers. He does not focus on teaching excellence, but argues that more experienced teachers tend to hold 'developed' as opposed to 'simple' theories. Developed theories take into consideration the previous experiences, existing understanding and motives of the learner. They are not concerned with simple transfer of information. Fox argues that our theories of teaching underpin all aspects of the pedagogical process from course planning to choosing methods and forms of assessment.

A study by Morley (2001) of women academics reports their ambivalent reactions to Subject Review and its assessment of teaching excellence. Subject Review is a quality assurance process for teaching and learning in

UK higher education. Institutions try to score a 'perfect 24' (out of 24) as a marker of teaching excellence (anything at 21 or above is technically meant to represent 'excellence', but in practice 24 has become the 'gold standard'). Six aspects of teaching and learning provision are audited and given a mark out of four (for example, 'curriculum development and organization' is one aspect). Interviews carried out by Morley suggest that some women viewed their contribution to Subject Review as an opportunity to gain authority and influence in their organizations, particularly in relation to issues such as equity. Others found the experience 'a highly corrosive form of performance and regulation' (ibid.: 466). In preparing for Subject Review, one informant said how upset she had been when a colleague criticized her teaching for being too emotional and overly concerned with gender issues. Morley suggests that rather than being a neutral category, teaching excellence within Subject Review implies orthodoxy and normalization techniques: people are encouraged to teach in line with 'common goals'.

Having scored a 'perfect 24', academics in the Economics Department of the University of Warwick claimed that Subject Review was meaningless and futile, a superficial, paper-based exercise rather than a process that could recognize teaching excellence or support its development. They also estimated that the exercise had cost their department between £150,000 and £200,000 in staff time (*Guardian* 2001).

Two studies that have focused directly on teacher and student perceptions of teaching excellence have been undertaken by Vielba and Hillier (2000) and Hillier and Vielba (2001). Both of these investigations adopted small-scale, qualitative methodologies. In the first focus-group study, the researchers tried without success to use criterion statements from a national award scheme (the NTFS) to explore teacher and student perceptions of teaching excellence. They found a significant difference between teacher and student perspectives and 'public models of teaching excellence', with the former emphasizing the 'personal qualities of the lecturer and their involvement with their subject. An excellent teacher was seen as someone who not only knew their subject but was also someone who was enthusiastic, creative and imaginative' (Vielba and Hillier, 2000: 10). An excellent teacher was perceived by students and teachers to be 'people and relationship oriented' whereas official discourses, the authors argue, stress 'planning, deployment of resources, assessment or evaluation' (ibid.: 9–10).

The second study used repertory grid methodology (Kelly, 1955) to explore teacher and student perceptions of teaching excellence. It found that the participants used 'soft' characteristics to describe excellence, emphasizing the personal qualities of the teacher, communication skills, and their ability to manage complex human interactions and relationships. The authors concluded that there was a mismatch between teacher/student understandings and official discourses of teaching excellence promulgated by the QAA and the ILTHE in the UK. They suggest that one explanation for this mismatch is that 'softer' expressions of teaching and learning are not reducible to the readily quantifiable and measurable indicators of performance that are required by the quality assurance and enhancement movements (Hillier and Vielba, 2001: 9–11).

Uncovering teacher and student perceptions of teaching excellence

As part of a broader study of the NTFS and understandings of teaching excellence (see Skelton, 2004), four focus groups with teachers and students from two institutions of higher education in the UK were conducted (two with teachers, two with students). One benefit of using focus groups is their ability to allow different perspectives to emerge and be subjected to critical scrutiny through the interactions of participants. The focus groups were undertaken between May and June 2001, during the second year of the NTFS. The teachers and students were from a variety of subject disciplines, attended different types of institution and ranged in age from 25 to 56 years (teachers) and from 20 to 52 years (students). There were three main purposes of the focus groups: (a) to find out what ordinary teachers and students understand by teaching excellence; (b) to elicit their views about the NTFS as a prominent, national-level award scheme; and (c) to explore their preferred images of teaching excellence. Participants were given background information about the study and the NTFS. Following a content analysis of the focus-group discussions, a number of major themes were identified and are outlined below.

Understandings of teaching excellence

- Teaching excellence needs to be distinguished from didactic teaching. There was a strong consensus that teaching facts, teaching from textbooks, 'talking at' students, 'performing' and not explaining ideas ran counter to teaching excellence. The latter required an interactive process (involving dialogue and group work), with students taking ultimate responsibility for their own learning: 'Professor X is a really intelligent guy and you go to his lectures and it is fantastic...but whether he is a good teacher is another thing' (FG3; male student); 'There's nothing worse than somebody who teaches you purely by reading a book. You can't explain things that way...You don't want somebody talking for three hours [and] They're not there just to give you information, you're supposed to be able to interact with them' (FG4; female students).
- Teaching excellence requires a collaborative relationship between teacher and student. This involves the teacher checking out student

responses to educational experiences and getting feedback from them about different methods and alternative ways of approaching teaching: 'I see it [teaching excellence] as a collaborative exercise in which all parties are engaged. I think a lot is gained when the learning process itself is thought about and talked about in a sort of atmosphere of equality and there are attempts to reach some sort of agreement or certainly take people on board' (FG2; male teacher); and, 'I think that is also one of the things that a teacher needs to be proactive in: asking questions. Are there any better ways they could do their teaching? Students are different so different students would prefer different styles of teaching' (FG3; male student).

- Teaching excellence involves teachers making appropriate choices from a repertoire of techniques and methodologies, to suit both the students concerned and the context of learning. Focus-group participants maintained that excellent teachers facilitate learning by varying their approach dependent on the subject discipline, the purpose of sessions and the stage of development of the student group. Teaching excellence was concerned with achieving 'learning excellence': 'One of the themes that seems to come out here is we are talking about variety, we are talking balance. So a few PowerPoint slides is fine but once it is PowerPoint every week what is the point of PowerPoint? So it is matching the right thing to the right activity' (FG1; female teacher); 'I think excellence is about having a repertoire of techniques that you can use in different situations with different audiences. Something might work with one group but it is hopeless for another group' (FG1; male teacher).

- Excellent teachers can be distinguished by their commitment to a long-term continuous process of professional development through critical reflection. Teaching excellence was therefore not perceived to be an end point, something successfully achieved or reached. Rather, it was a process of ongoing development and change: 'I tend to think of excellence in teaching in terms of self-consciousness of a practitioner about methods, styles, etc. [and] a willingness to be critical and therefore engage in a development process and not making quantitative statements about those things' (FG2; male teacher). Several people in the focus groups commented on the difficulty of maintaining such an orientation to practice given the pressures of work loads and the research culture of higher education.

- Excellent teachers can be distinguished by a number of personal qualities and commitments, such as enthusiasm, energy, approach-ability, the interest they show in students as people, their communica-tion skills, and their ability to relate to and empathize with students: 'it [teaching excellence] has got a lot to do with a kind of inherent enthusiasm and energy...if someone has got that you can feel it from them it is obvious and I think it is a special quality which not everybody has got, have they?' (FG1; female teacher).

- Teaching excellence involved demonstrating a concern for 'weaker' students, helping them with their learning difficulties and being available for 'remedial' help. Teaching excellence was not associated with achieving good grades or working successfully with the 'best students': 'I believe that anybody can accompany a first class student and see them produce first class work but the true, in my limited experience, excellence in teaching is the ability to encourage, inspire and show the methodology of learning to people who don't find it so easy' (FG2; female teacher).

The National Teaching Fellowship Scheme

Although most participants were positive in principle about schemes to promote teaching and learning in higher education, they were sceptical about the NTFS. Whilst one person maintained that the NTFS would ensure that teaching-intensive institutions would receive some recognition for what they did best, and several people expressed interest in particular projects that Teaching Fellows were undertaking, most people did not support the scheme. After a content analysis of the focus-group data, the following themes emerged:

- The NTFS was perceived to be 'tokenistic'. It would do little to challenge the privileging of research within the sector and was simply government 'propaganda' to give the false impression that something significant was being done to improve the quality of teaching and learning: 'I can imagine Tony Blair talking about the NFTS in "we support excellence in teaching" and really it is ... tokenistic. If the government really want to support excellence in teaching they need to throw lots of money at it which they haven't done'; and, 'it is a propaganda exercise: it is more of a showcase than an incentive' (FG1; male teachers).
- The NTFS was perceived to be elitist and divisive in recognizing and rewarding a small group of 'superteachers'. It was suggested that a greater number of awards should be given, with a smaller development project fund allocation. This would increase the impact of the NTFS within the sector. 'It is highly competitive, highly elitist and it is a competition between institutions and within institutions. Also, the criteria for judging are quite soon taken out of the context of the teacher and the learners into a wider quasi-political arena where you are supposed to positively influence the whole of the higher education community, which I think is far too ambitious'; and, 'It [the NTFS] implies that you're doing your teaching on your own, you are excellent

and the people around you have nothing to do with it' (FG2; female and male teachers respectively); 'If you doubled the amount of people and halved the amount of money, I don't think you'd lessen the effect' (FG3; male student); 'I think obviously there are dangers and one of them is definitely what about the people who don't get rewarded? The "superteacher" [idea] creates more rivalry and more discontent' (FG1; male teacher).

- Several people in research-intensive institutions felt that it would be 'career suicide' to win one of the fellowships. They felt that the time required to undertake a development project would take time away from their own substantive research interests and would seriously damage their own department's RAE submission: If you take two years out to do research into teaching which wouldn't count for your RAE you are placing yourself and your department under pressure'; and, 'To take up a two year teaching fellowship you have given up on your career. I would love to do it but I would have to say no because otherwise I am just saying goodbye to an academic career' (FG2; male and female teachers respectively).

- A number of concerns were raised about the development projects the Fellows were to undertake. Some felt it was ironic that some of the Fellows had bought themselves out of teaching to undertake their project ('So you've got a good teacher, you reward him for being a good teacher, and then he stops teaching to do [pedagogical] research' (FG4; female student); others were doubtful that excellent teachers were necessarily good at writing project proposals; and finally it was suggested that project money would be better spent on those teachers most in need of support and development (rather than those already deemed 'excellent').

Images of excellence

Given the difficulty of talking about complex concepts, focus-group participants were asked to describe their preferred images of 'teaching excellence'. Three types of image predominated:

- Excellent teachers as 'unsung heroes': one group explored the image of the midwife to denote an act of unselfish giving and the nurturing of life; a second group identified the 'water carrier' as a vital if sometimes taken-for-granted presence, necessary to sustain life in difficult circumstances.
- Excellent teachers as 'travel guides': here the teacher is the person who guides the student through difficult if exciting terrain, with the help of navigational aids, contour maps and experience of similar journeys.

The teacher enables the student to explore unfamiliar territory in relative safety.

- Excellent teachers as givers of light/life/growth: one group explored the image of the 'benign gardener'; another considered the parent guiding the child. References to light, life and growth were frequently made in the groups and appeared at times to have an almost spiritual quality to them.

Discussion

Given the themes and perspectives which have been expressed, it is clear that the teachers and students in the study presented here do not simply follow and reproduce official understandings of teaching excellence. In place of these understandings, which are characterized by a belief in and commitment to performativity, the teachers and students concerned adopted a psychologized discourse emphasizing the personal qualities of the teacher, their human potential and their relationships with students.

The adoption of a psychologized discourse of teaching excellence is perhaps unsurprising given the current climate of higher education. Official discourses, informed by regulatory frameworks, either ignore the human potential of the teacher or seek to minimize its limitation and impact through careful planning, management and measurement of performance. There is little mention in the teacher and student perspectives presented here of course objectives, effective delivery and learning outcomes. Teachers and students in the study appear to be resisting this discourse by restoring the teacher to the heart of the teaching and learning process.

'Soft' characteristics of teaching excellence are an important part of teacher and student understanding, incorporating the individual attributes of the teacher, their communication skills, and their ability to manage complex human interactions and relationships. These are all aspects of teacher and student perceptions of teaching excellence that have been identified in previous studies (Vielba and Hillier, 2000; Hillier and Vielba, 2001). The present study has shown, however, that 'student-centred' methodologies, a commitment to ongoing professional development and a concern for 'weaker' students are also part of what it means to be an excellent teacher for local students and teachers.

Whilst the adoption of soft characteristics of teaching excellence may resist dehumanizing tendencies, it may unintentionally place greater expectations on teachers and allow governments to neglect the wider structures of teaching/learning that affect quality. Higher education teachers who are prepared to give their 'emotional labour' (Morley, 1998) to their institutions may help to remedy problems caused by years of expansion and under-investment, but only at a cost to themselves. Many of the preferred images of excellent teachers in the focus groups portrayed them as heroic, selfless individuals, with an almost mystical quality, bringing life and light to others.

When asked to comment on the NTFS, the teachers and students mounted a powerful critique of the scheme, viewing it as tokenistic, elitist and divisive. This may reflect the timing of the study: people may not have had sufficient opportunity to appreciate the potential contribution the NTFS might make to long-term developments within the sector. On the other hand, the structures of the NTFS, with their emphasis on individual performance, may threaten the keenly felt collective ethos of teaching in higher education.

Conclusion

This chapter has sought to gain an insight into what might be termed the 'local knowledge' that ordinary teachers and students have about teaching excellence. This is a knowledge that is derived from experience, rooted in practice and context-sensitive. From the work presented here, it is clear that teachers and students adopt a psychologized discourse of teaching excellence. This runs counter to official discourses which, despite their internal differences, share a belief in and commitment to performativity.

The local knowledge that teachers and students have about teaching excellence presents us with a number of dilemmas. For example, given that such knowledge is constructed from the 'everyday', seemingly 'practical', experiences of teaching, why is it that their understandings of excellence are about relationships and interpersonal communication? In a similar vein, one would have expected official discourses of teaching excellence to have permeated the consciousness of teachers and students, yet they appear to 'talk a different language', seemingly oblivious to regulatory frameworks. Does this mean that teachers and students find it difficult to change or are they resisting the dehumanizing changes implied by performative discourses?

The value of a psychologized understanding of teaching excellence is its ability to render teaching and learning meaningful and rich in human potential. Such a discourse is limited, however, in two main respects: first, in raising expectations of teachers and suggesting that their 'emotional labour' can counteract years of under-investment; and second, in its focus on teacher–student interactions which ignore the broader social, political and economic context within which these interactions are located.

While positive in principle about schemes to promote teaching and learning in higher education, the majority of focus-group participants were very sceptical about the NTFS. These comments, together with concerns about the potentially alienating impact of teaching award schemes that have been reported in large-scale national surveys in other countries (Ramsden and Martin, 1996: 312), raise serious doubts about the extent to which the

NTFS will be taken up by the sector. The findings of this study suggest that there is an important mismatch in the way teaching excellence is perceived. Such differences in perception need to be addressed by all those involved in educational development if the full potential of schemes to promote teaching and learning, such as the NTFS, is to be realized.

In Chapter 7, I consider how teachers might respond to cultural variations in pedagogy. The chapter maintains that in the light of internationalization, any adequate understanding of teaching excellence has to address such variation and consider appropriate responses. Drawing on insights from the literature, I suggest that it is important to recognize the cultural specificity of teaching excellence and to learn from cultural differences.

Chapter 7

Internationalization and intercultural learning

Introduction

The number of students who are choosing to study in a different country to their own has risen dramatically in recent years. Drawing upon the United Nations Educational, Scientific and Cultural Organization's statistical records (UNESCO, 1997), Bruch and Barty (1998: 18) state that 'there were 1,502,040 foreign students in the top 50 host countries in 1994/5, an increase of some 13 per cent compared to the previous year. In the last 25 years, international student mobility has risen by more than 300 per cent'. Some commentators suggest that this mobility will continue to increase at current levels (Blight, 1995).

The situation in the UK closely resembles the general trend. In 1995/6, there were 196,346 international students in publicly funded higher education institutions (Higher Education Statistics Agency, 1997). Bruch and Barty (ibid.: 19) point out that this represents an increase of 20 and 127 per cent over 1994/5 and 1989/90 figures respectively. In 1995/6, the majority of international students studying in the UK came from the European Union (43 per cent) and Asia (29 per cent). A survey conducted by the Higher Education Information Services Trust (HEIST) in 1994 found that there were three main reasons why non-EU undergraduate students want to study in the UK. These were the opportunity to speak and learn in English, the recognition of UK qualifications around the world and the quality of UK higher education (HEIST and UCAS, 1994).

International students are attractive to higher education institutions for a range of reasons. They can help to enrich the curriculum, broaden its knowledge base and enhance critical thinking through the exchange of perspectives. Their presence can lead to increased cultural sensitivity and international understanding. With the reduction of state funding for higher education, however, come further powerful motivations, namely cash and survival. In the early 1980s, the UK government encouraged higher education institutions to charge higher 'full-cost' fees to international students and regulations were introduced to allow them to do so without contravening the Race Relations Act of 1976. It has been estimated that these fees amount to between five and ten times the equivalent fee that would be paid by a self-financing UK student (Bruch and Barty, 1998: 25). In October 1998, Prime Minister Tony Blair announced the easing of visa requirements for Chinese students wishing to study in the UK. Leon (2000) suggests that this change in policy was motivated predominantly by financial reasons:

> The decision was more than a sweetener to the Chinese government after the western cold-shoulder following the Tiananmen Square massacre of students ten years earlier. He [Blair] was staking the UK's claim to the thriving market in overseas students.

(Ibid.: 30)

International students are therefore lucrative business in the growing global higher education market. UK institutions are well placed to exploit this market, given the previously discussed associations between UK higher education, quality and the recognition of its qualifications. Performative indicators of excellence help to attract international students as an 'objective' marker of quality. But as an English-speaking country, the UK also has an advantage in possessing the leading global language of business and telecommunications. It is not surprising, therefore, that the UK attracts international students who seek to benefit not only from their chosen subject studies, but also from the language of instruction.

With increasing internationalization, however, comes increasing responsibility as well as opportunity. Many higher education institutions now have international offices, codes of practice to ensure appropriate marketing of courses, and language and study support units and services. Despite these developments, there is a sense that some institutions still only pay lip service to the needs of international students. Research into international students' experience of UK HE has revealed that whilst promotional material suggests a warm welcome, their actual experience before arrival, on arrival and during their stay suggests otherwise. For example, admissions procedures, immigration controls and high fees can represent significant obstacles to entry (Bruch and Barty, 1998: 24–7). Institutions may be unsure how to respond educationally to international students since what 'internationalization' means and how it can be fully realized has not been articulated (Patrick, 1997). Some have also claimed that higher education institutions have a limited understanding of cultural difference and how to deal with it (Rizvi and Walsh, 1998).

Although institutions may recognize the need to internationalize the curriculum in response to overseas recruitment, progress to date in this area has been disappointing (Bruch and Barty, 1998: 26). One issue that has received relatively little consideration to date is how individual teachers and institutions accommodate different cultural conceptions of teaching and learning. This is becoming a pressing issue as 'cultural shocks' relating to pedagogy become more commonplace. For example, Wu (2002) has written about her problematic experience of coming to the UK to study as a postgraduate student. She states:

> On arrival in England, postgraduate Chinese students are surprised. We had unconsciously expected discipline. At an ancient English University one had expected the mellow warmth of old gardens, a correct English accent and a civilised relationship with a gowned pedagogue who would subtly keep one up to the most rigorous standards .... In reality ... the lack of discipline continues to be a shock to successive newcomers.

> (Ibid.: 389)

Teachers who strive to be excellent may experience some uncertainty about how to respond to cultural variations in pedagogy. Should they expect students from different countries to forget the way they are used to being taught and value what is on offer? Or should teachers and institutions change their approaches to teaching and learning to accommodate student expectations? This chapter considers how teachers might respond to cultural variations in conceptions of teaching, drawing upon a range of theoretical models. It argues that, given that higher education institutions are becoming more international and culturally diverse, any adequate understanding of teaching excellence has to be informed by this diversity. This involves recognizing the cultural specificity of teaching excellence and learning from the similarities and differences between different cultural conceptions of teaching.

Cultural conceptions of teaching and learning

Understandings of what constitutes 'good', 'bad', 'appropriate' and 'excellent' teaching and learning are culturally specific. This is becoming more evident as conflicts occur more often around issues of pedagogy. Leon (2000), for example, in an article entitled 'Be sensitive to Chinese minds', argues that 'if Britain wants to attract foreign students, lecturers must understand their education and social background better' (ibid.: 30). She states that overseas students are good business for universities yet often feel isolated and lonely. One reason for this, she argues, is that they are used to a higher degree of support from academics and administrators. What is meant by 'support' here is not made explicit, but it may refer to a form of 'pedagogical support' that is associated with teachers exercising authority, leadership and control. Cultural reforms in China post-1978 have resurrected traditional teaching and learning practices. Leon maintains that:

> the classroom layout in China, with its rows of desks and a black-board, is reminiscent of pre-1970 UK. This contrasts with a shift in the West towards group work, continuous assessment, independent learning and open debate. Classroom layout has become circle-shaped with either a single round table or clusters of tables.

(Ibid.)

Wu (2002) compares her experience of studying at an ancient English university with her schooling in Taiwan and concludes:

> it seems there are two poles of pedagogy...At one pole there is the classical pedagogue, familiar to the Chinese. The teacher is remote, austere, highly respected, strict, demanding, parental, unforgiving, meticulous, punitive, quoting Confucius, quoting correct conservative authorities, and with the aim of producing good hard working loyal and obedient citizens. The teacher 'fills the pot' as if each student was an empty vessel, in the hope that once full it would somehow spontaneously start boiling... At the other pole there is the Liberal pedagogue, more familiar to the English. The teacher is empathetic, 'one of the boys' (or girls), informal, eliciting, Socratic, wearing jeans, quoting Rousseau, Foucault. The teacher's aim is to produce orig-inal rebellious and iconoclastic inventive unpredictable enthusiasts. Scorning to fill the pot, instead one aims to 'light the fire'.

(Ibid.: 390)

Wu did not enjoy the liberal experience, commenting on the 'lack of discipline' and minimal formal supervision that was on offer. Her individual experience speaks to a bigger problem: how should teachers respond to cultural variations in pedagogy?

Bodycott and Walker (2000) offer interesting insights into this problem through their writing about 'teaching abroad' in Hong Kong. They point out that much of the existing literature on cultural conceptions of teach-ing focuses on the experiences of Asian students coming to terms with studying in a different pedagogical culture. Instead they focus on their own experience, as 'imported' foreign academics, and their attempts to negotiate Hong Kong students' assumptions and expectations about teaching and learning. They state: 'In so-called Confucian societies... many many local staff are wary of 'foreigners', and are concerned with what they see as an invasion of Western cultural and educational ideologies and values' (ibid.: 81). They recognize a cultural clash between their own commitments to 'student-centred learning' and 'transmissional' models that are favoured in the setting. Their response to this situation changed over time, moving to one that involved intercultural learning and rethinking their educational beliefs:

> When we began teaching 'overseas', our initial, uninformed or even arrogant, assertion was that it was the students' responsibility to adapt to our teaching. However, our recent experiences have caused us to rethink these beliefs. We now argue that the development of inter-cultural understandings and related teaching practices must begin with the *teacher's* attitude. [Emphasis added]

(Ibid.)

Responding to cultural difference

One way of responding to cultural difference is to see it as a threat to existing standards. From such a position, teaching excellence is viewed as a stable entity which will be undermined by the attempt to accommodate student diversity. The traditional understanding of teaching excellence (see Chapter 2) has a view of the typical university student (white, able-bodied, good scores in formal assessments) and is suspicious of 'non-traditional' entrants (Williams, J., 1997). Racializing discourses may play a significant part in maintaining the distinction between excellence and diversity. For example, it has been found that some teachers use stereotypical representations to explain contemporary problems such as low attainment and poor motivation (Clegg *et al.*, 2003). Excellence and diversity may therefore be seen as competing tendencies. Excellence may be viewed as a continuation of recognized standards over time whereas diversity threatens to undermine them. This view of the relationship between excellence and diversity is commonplace. For example, a conference held at the University of Cambridge in the UK in 2001 was called 'Excellence, Enterprise and Equity: *competing* challenges for higher education' (my italics). Many of the papers relating to the 'equity' theme were about widening access and participation. The purpose of the conference was to explore the relationship between the three themes and, in particular, to consider the extent to which the quality of higher education can be maintained in the light of student expansion.

If teaching excellence and cultural diversity are viewed as competing tendencies, what implications does this have for the teacher? Teaching excellence from such a position would involve paying scant attention to the pedagogical assumptions and prior experiences that international students bring with them into the teaching situation. An implicit assumption is made that 'what we do here is best' and that the international student will benefit from the teaching experience that they have sought out and looked for in a different country.

In drawing upon research that has been undertaken in school-based education where there has been considerable debate about how to respond to cultural diversity, three main adaptation models can be detected: assimilation, multiculturalism and anti-racism (see, for example, Arnot, 1985, particularly chapters three and four; Figueroa, 1991, chapters three and four; and Troyna, 1993: 23–6). The traditional view of the relationship between teaching excellence and cultural diversity seems to be consistent with the assimilation model. Assimilation involves people taking on the cultural assumptions and behaviours of the 'host' country. This can be likened to a situation where international students (and 'imported' teachers) are expected to take on and assimilate into the pedagogical culture of the country where they are studying (or teaching). It has been noted that support programmes for students from different countries to induct them into routine work habits and skills may have limited pedagogical value, since they tend to be *ad hoc*, one-off or tacked on to existing higher education courses (Burwood, 1999: 451). But what is more significant for our purposes here is to note that such programmes represent an assimilationist response model which seeks to ensure access to the 'home' pedagogical culture through 'remedial' help.

Multiculturalism, on the other hand, involves attempting to respect a wide variety of cultures and give them some form of expression within the curriculum. In the school sector, multicultural approaches have been associated with superficial and exotic representations of other cultures ('saris, samosas and steel drums'). Translated to the pedagogical culture of higher education institutions, multiculturalism would involve incorporating the contributions to knowledge of different cultural groups and their preferred teaching and learning practices within the curriculum. A multicultural pedagogy of this sort would be seen to enrich the educational experience for all concerned. One of the potential problems with such an approach, however, is its 'tokenistic' quality. Some authors, for example, argue that although pluralist societies and their institutions encourage and accommodate cultural diversity, they also contain it (Bhabha, 1990). According to this view, Western societies 'appreciate cultures in a kind of muse imaginaire; as though one should be able to collect and appreciate them' (ibid.: 208). Clegg *et al.* (2003) state that 'such an imaginary leaves "civilized" values untouched and limits the ways in which cultural difference might act as a challenge to the dominant norms' (ibid.: 164). In short, multiculturalism may not allow an authentic dialogue between cultures to take place since underlying power structures and interests remain invisible.

Cultural variations in pedagogy may be given some expression within the curriculum but they will always be contained so as not to threaten the pedagogical preferences of the dominant group.

An anti-racist conception of the relationship between teaching excellence and cultural diversity would be premised on rather different assumptions. It would seek to identify and counteract the implicitly racist assumptions which underpin pedagogical practices. From this perspective, 'institutional racism' is considered to be endemic in the structures and practices of educational institutions and responsible for serious injustice and disadvantage. Commenting on the situation in the school sector, Gillborn (1998) states that 'racism is common place and routine; in studies of primary and secondary schools alike, teachers' notions of race and ethnicity have important consequences for the lives of all students' (ibid.: 12).

These studies have shown that teachers often work with stereotypes of pupils and their behaviour which can have significant implications in terms of patterns of attainment and future career prospects. For example, African–Caribbean students are seen as having behavioural problems whereas Indian/African Asians and Chinese students are considered to be socially conformist, hard working and high achieving. Clegg et al. (2003) suggest that 'The idea of "racisms" appears particularly useful, therefore, since it captures the ways in which different groups of school and university students are likely to find themselves the subject of different racialised stereotypes' (ibid.: 163). Teachers may hold stereotypical views, therefore, of international students and their pedagogical commitments and preferences. An anti-racist approach to cultural variations in pedagogy would involve identifying the racializing discourses that teachers use in making sense of these variations. It would also seek to establish how these discourses enable the dominant 'white' cultural group within the academy to preserve its power, interests and preferred pedagogical practices.

Responses in the higher education setting

Within the field of higher education, there has been relatively little work to date on how to respond to cultural variations in pedagogy. Notable exceptions include Ofori-Dankwa and Lane (2000); Bodycott and Walker (2000) and Grey (2002). Ofori-Dankwa and Lane identify four different responses to cultural diversity: neutrality, similarity, diversity and diver-similarity. When discussing the first of these responses, neutrality, they state: 'Teachers using the neutrality paradigm pay little attention to cultural similarities or differences' (ibid.: 493). From such a perspective, teaching is viewed as being independent of culture. Excellent teaching can occur anywhere and is characterized by 'universals' of high-quality teaching, for example: the depth of the knowledge base that informs it; the interpersonal qualities of the teacher; and their ability to motivate learners.

Teachers faced with students from a different culture would focus on these universals, believing them to be independent of culture and a sound basis for higher education in any context. They may see each student as an individual, and individual differences (relating, for example, to personality type, learning style, motivation and so on) as being more important and/or significant than cultural differences. The advantage of this perspective is that difficult issues about culture and its relationship with teaching and learning can be avoided, thereby assisting practical decision making.

The second approach to cultural diversity that Ofori-Dankwa and Lane identify is the similarity paradigm. According to this, teachers stress the similarities that exist between teaching and learning practices in different cultures. Global forces affecting higher education are seen to be more significant than 'local' cultural differences. The contribution that higher education teaching makes to economic prosperity, the importance of new technologies and the internationalization of the curriculum are considered to be overriding concerns for all teachers irrespective of their culture. From a similarity perspective, the globalization of higher education inevitably leads to a 'flattening out' of local cultures and specific approaches to teaching and learning. Irrespective of what individual teachers feel about globalization, it is something that is given, which has to be responded to in an appropriate way.

The third approach is called the diversity paradigm. Here the emphasis is on variations between cultural conceptions of teaching. Some of the accounts that have been referred to earlier in this chapter (Wu, 2002; Leon, 2000) reflect such an approach. They emphasize cultural variations in pedagogy and point out the conflicts that can occur when students from one culture study in another. In identifying two poles of pedagogy ('Filling the pot or lighting the fire?), Wu (ibid.: 393) suggests that one way of encouraging Chinese students to be more independent in their learning is to offer them a 'highly disciplined stable pedagogic environment'. Drawing upon the work of Sapochnik (1997), she argues that this seemingly paradoxical relationship (discipline leads to independence) is a way of respecting the Chinese students' understandings of pedagogy while encouraging them to take risks. The advantage of the diversity paradigm is that it encourages the teacher to identify and understand cultural variations in pedagogy. They are better placed to understand the experience of students in an 'alien' culture and to respond to their educational needs.

The final approach is called the diversimilarity paradigm. This emphasizes both similarities and differences in cultural conceptions of teaching and learning. For example, through their close observations of Hong Kong students' responses to their teaching, Bodycott and Walker (2000) became less certain about cultural variations in pedagogy. They reframed their own underlying beliefs about teaching and learning and developed new practices. Initially, they had felt that a cultural clash existed between their own commitments to 'student-centredness' and the 'transmission' model of teaching valued by the students. Gradually, however, this simple distinction became less clear and a more complex understanding emerged. Their use of group work is a good example. They started off thinking that Hong Kong students did not value group work because the quality of interaction was poor and it was difficult to find people who were prepared to report back findings. The students did not appear to like commenting on academic texts in class for fear of 'losing face', although they were willing to talk about personal experiences. On closer inspection, Bodycott and Walker found that if allowed to use their mother tongue in small groups, the students' interaction during group work improved and there was a high level of activity. Subsequently it became easier to find students who were prepared to report back from discussions, as the report was based on a shared understanding rather than an individual opinion. The two authors had wondered initially why students from a seemingly 'collectivist culture' appeared to struggle with group work as an educational method. But once they became more aware of cultural sensitivities and adapted the methodology, both the quality of group work and its appreciation by the students improved dramatically.

Grey (2002) writes about three international students' responses to an undergraduate business degree course in Australia. The students were from Indonesia, Malaysia and Hong Kong. In developing a pedagogical response to these students, Grey worked from the premise that international students are often overlooked and not given an opportunity to talk about their experiences and concerns. She developed a 'pedagogy of possibility', 'where identities, histories, cultures and experiences can be explored and used as a basis for learning' (ibid.: 154). Refusing to identify any clear conceptions of pedagogical difference (for example student-centred versus transmission), she invited the students to write about and illustrate any 'significant issues, questions and concerns' they had in relation to the course. Through the students' work, undertaken at different points, a picture emerges of a group of international students who initially express feelings about being vulnerable and disadvantaged 'as they struggle to be heard at a social, academic and institutional level' (ibid.: 165). By the final set of drawings, however, a process of transformation had occurred, as the students had become more comfortable with the university environment and had 'chosen ways of thinking, speaking, behaving and making meaning that they see as liberating' (ibid.). Grey concludes that the process of dialogue is crucial for teachers and students in coming to terms with cultural difference and its impact upon pedagogy. Dialogue allows students to discuss their previous and current experiences of teaching and learning. It enables teachers to understand these experiences and to respond appropriately. Grey suggests that personal perspectives on pedagogy are never reducible to cultural norms; however, these norms, together with personal identity and specific histories, play a significant part in shaping people's pedagogical assumptions and preferences.

Teaching excellence, diversimilarity and intercultural learning

In a context where student populations in higher education are becoming more and more international and culturally diverse, teachers have to find a way of responding appropriately to this diversity. Neutrality, similarity and assimilation models offer limited help because they play down the significance and import of cultural diversity. Cultural differences are deemed to be irrelevant to the practice of teaching, subservient to global forces or a barrier to successful integration into the 'host culture'. Whilst multicultural responses seek to recognize cultural diversity and give them some form of expression within the curriculum, they can lead to superficial and tokenistic responses to difference. These responses can contain difference and maintain existing power structures. Together with the diversity paradigm, multiculturalism can also emphasize cultural diversity over similarity, leading to a situation where it becomes difficult to find any point of agreement for a teaching programme to unite teachers and students from different cultures. Anti-racism alerts teachers to implicit racialist discourses and other structures that can significantly influence the way in which students from other cultures and their understandings of pedagogy are perceived. It also helps us to understand how dominant 'white' interests and pedagogical preferences are preserved within the academy. With its emphasis on identifying racist assumptions and practices, however, the anti-racist approach can induce feelings of guilt and paralysis in teachers as they struggle to change long-held views, practices and institutional structures. Given these considerations, I want to argue here that the diversimilarity paradigm offers the most potential as a means to respond to cultural variations in pedagogy. This paradigm is sensitive to both cultural similarities and differences, and draws upon these in the design and implementation of teaching programmes.

A teaching excellence that is informed by the diversimilarity paradigm seeks to:

- recognize the cultural specificity of one's own approach to teaching;
- engage in a real dialogue with students from different cultures to understand their current and prior experiences of teaching/learning and their preferred practices;
- recognize that the real, embodied perspectives of particular groups of students may differ from cultural and racialized stereotypes

(for example the passive Chinese student who can't work independently and needs 'spoon feeding');

- undertake intercultural learning in the light of the above dialogue. This involves identifying both similarities and differences between cultures in terms of pedagogical assumptions and practices. It also involves understanding how cultural variations in pedagogy relate to underlying social norms and values (for example 'good hard working loyal and obedient citizens'; 'iconoclastic inventive unpredictable enthusiasts' – see Wu, 2002: 390);

- develop a course or programme of teaching in the light of intercultural learning. This involves reflecting on one's own educational values and practices in the light of alternatives. Responding to cultural difference may involve asking serious questions about existing institutional structures. When working with international students, choosing to retain and work with pedagogical practices that are accepted and valued within one's own culture does not necessarily imply a process of 'colonization'. Students from different cultures may find such practices useful and valuable. They might transform the pedagogy in the process of its adoption;

- make explicit the educational approaches and values that inform the course/programme, making connections between different cultural expressions of teaching and learning, and pointing out the benefits from learning from different approaches.

Some teachers may experience difficulty in learning in such a way given that there may be an association between particular cultural expressions of teaching and 'progress'. For example, the shift from didactic teaching to student-centred learning may be seen as a general move towards social progress. Any cultural expression of teaching and learning that appears to support didactic teaching may therefore be experienced as out of date.

This association between particular cultural expressions of teaching and progress is problematic. For example, a recent article on US-controlled teacher training in Iraq discusses the impact of Western pedagogies and associates them with the development of 'democracy' and 'freedom' (Asquith, 2004):

> Attendance was overflowing, and teachers were eager to learn what progress had been made in education in the past 35 years. But like many western organizations struggling to usher in reform, US educators met with resistance from an old-school culture that prizes rigid adherence to the curriculum, the silent child and the unquestioned authority of the teacher.

> (Ibid.: 9)

In the context of the Iraq War and disputes about its moral and legal basis, it is difficult to establish whether this pedagogical intervention is seeking to support freedom or whether it represents a form of post-colonial control through the 'benign' act of education. The article states that 'Most [participants] complained that their current teaching style relied on memorisation, one-sided viewpoints and curricula written by the Ba'ath party' (ibid.). It ends with a parting comment from an English-language teacher in Iraq who appears to express in essence a diversimilarity perspective which is context-sensitive and willing to learn from cultural differences in pedagogical approach:

> American classrooms are very free. I see in the movies that the students challenge the teachers . . . Maybe we won't do everything like they do. But we want to be exposed to all the new techniques and then we will decide what is useful to us.

> (Ibid.)

Concluding comments: issues and dilemmas in intercultural learning

'Learning from cultural variations in pedagogy' is an important but challenging enterprise. Recognizing the cultural assumptions that underpin one's own approach to teaching can be difficult given that they tend to be taken for granted. Understanding other cultural forms of teaching and relating these to broader values and purposes is fraught with problems as one attempts to do this from within one's own cultural standpoint. The purpose of this section is to make explicit some of the issues and dilemmas related to intercultural pedagogical learning which represent important areas for further enquiry:

1. This chapter has focused on *international* students, who bring cultural differences relating to pedagogy into sharp relief when they study in a different country to their own. Many of the issues discussed in the chapter, however, are also relevant to many 'home' students who, given attempts to expand and broaden access to higher education, are themselves becoming more culturally diverse. Zepke and Leach (2002), for example, have written about their attempt to create an appropriate pedagogy for Maori students on a distance learning adult education course in New Zealand. They ask whether 'western constructs from adult learning have any place at all in Maori contexts' (ibid.: 315). Drawing upon the work of Metge (1984) and Tangaere (1996), the authors established a picture of preferred Maori approaches to learning: 'They like working in groups; prefer a holistic approach

to learning incorporating all four dimensions of the person – wairua (spiritual), hinengaro (intellectual), tinana (physical) and whatumanawa (emotional); like face-to-face contact and discussion, and like their learning to be related to real-life tasks' (Zepke and Leach, 2002: 316). The authors revised their planned methods for the course in the light of Maori opposition. They adopted an 'intermediate' technology which 'gets ideas and theories off paper and into visual and oral forms' (ibid.: 318). The video was narrated by a Maori guide who interprets and explores adult education concepts in the context of her own life and research. Zepke and Leach conclude that their response to cultural diversity is rather like being in a marriage: 'It is precisely the metaphor of marriage that seems apt as we must learn how to value and honour each other's pedagogy and knowledge without being colonised by it' (ibid.: 319).

2. Much of the discussion in the chapter is premised on an assumption that it is possible to identify single, unified and coherent cultural expressions of teaching and learning. How accurate and/or useful is this premise? To what extent does a focus on an overarching cultural expression of pedagogy preclude the study of internal pedagogical differences within cultures or the preferences of *sub-cultures*?

3. Reflecting on and learning from cultural conceptions of teaching and learning may suggest that there is a set of 'meta-criteria' by which competing claims can be resolved. What are these meta-criteria? One answer to this would be to suggest that any particular teacher has to make an informed judgement about how to teach based on a consideration of possibilities and that this judgement can only be enhanced by exposure to different cultural forms. A second possibility would be to suggest that there are universal meta-criteria to which any cross-cultural understanding of teaching excellence is subject (for example, 'truth', 'freedom', 'democracy' and so on – but note the points made earlier).

4. Will the process of 'globalization' lead to a 'flattening out' of cultural expressions of pedagogy? Are the forces of commercialization, privatization and marketization influencing the way we think of teaching excellence across different cultures? Is teaching excellence itself both a product and an instrument of these forces?

5. The chapter has mainly focused on international students who study in a different country to their own. But there are signs that 'methods of delivery' are changing, with leading institutions developing campuses in overseas locations. What significance will this have for intercultural pedagogical learning? Will this increase the tendency towards assimilationist pedagogies or lead to serious attempts to realize diversimilarity?

In Chapter 8 I consider how the press reports teaching excellence in higher education. The press plays an important role in mediating messages about excellence that are embedded in higher education policy. I look in particular at whether the press offers readers any tools with which to engage critically with teaching excellence, drawing on my own research into the NTFS.

Seduced by glitz and glamour?
Press reporting of teaching
excellence

Introduction

This chapter considers how the press helps to shape our understanding of teaching excellence in higher education. It argues that far from simply taking ideas about teaching excellence produced in one context and reporting them faithfully for audiences, the press *media*tes these ideas through a process of selection and emphasis. The press is a major influence on public attitudes (Cunningham, 1992) yet the power of the press to shape our understanding often goes unnoticed. It is only when the press or other media sources challenge the views of dominant groups in society that their 'hidden power' comes to light: something that recent criticism of BBC reporting of the Iraq War demonstrates so vividly.

The chapter draws upon the theoretical ideas of Bernstein (1986a; 1986b) and Fairclough (1989) to examine press coverage of teaching excellence. To add some focus to the investigation, I refer to my own research on the NTFS, which included an analysis of how the scheme was reported. This is supplemented with a small-scale, comparative investigation I conducted into press reporting of the Australian Awards for University Teaching.

Theoretical framework

The sociologist Basil Bernstein (1986a; 1986b) distinguishes between three interdependent contexts of educational discourse, practice and organization: (1) a *primary context* – the intellectual field of education which develops new ideas, practices and discourses; (2) a *secondary context*, which selectively appropriates educational discourse within practice at primary, secondary or tertiary levels; and (3) a *recontextualizing context*, which serves to 'regulate the circulation of texts between the primary and secondary contexts' (Bernstein, 1986a: 35). The recontextualizing context involves the work of various agents including the specialized media of education (such as the educational press and television programmes devoted to educational issues) and those not specialized in educational discourse, for example, local newspapers.

In a discussion of Bernstein's framework, Evans (1990) states:

> At the heart of Bernstein's argument is the claim that when a text produced in the primary context by educationalists of one sort or another is appropriated by recontextualising agents (educational or non-educational), it usually undergoes a transformation prior to its relocation in the secondary context. In the process of appropriation ... the text may be modified by selection, simplification, condensation and elaboration or it may be 'repositioned and refocused'.

> (Ibid.: 157)

The process of appropriation is crucial and critical, according to Evans, because as Bernstein states (1986a: 36), 'the major activities of recontextualizing fields is creating, maintaining, changing and legitimising discourse'.

Writing from within the field of critical language study, Fairclough (1989: 49–55) offers further insights into how this appropriation process works. For example, he refers to the 'hidden power' of media discourse. He argues that an increasing proportion of discourse in contemporary society involves participants who are separated in time and place, and mass-media discourse, involving television, radio and newspapers, accounts for an increasing part of this non-'face-to face' discourse. Due to the separation between producer and audience in media discourse, 'ideal subject positions' are built into whatever it is that is being communicated. These are aimed at a typical reader, listener or watching member of a television audience and the perspective this person is meant to hold. For this reason, therefore, media representations are never neutral or value-free; rather they have a ready-made subject position incorporated within them. These ideal subject positions are created through the practice of selecting and constraining contents (that is, what information is presented) and drawing upon particular sources (that is, whose perspective is adopted in reports).

Fairclough (ibid.: 51) maintains that although there is always the possibility that the media may challenge orthodox or common-sense understandings, they tend to reproduce dominant ideologies: 'In the British media, the balance of sources and perspectives and ideology is overwhelmingly in favour of existing power holders.' If, however, actual viewers, listeners or readers are able to detect the hidden power of the media, they consciously negotiate a relationship with the ideal subject; Fairclough adds: 'people do *negotiate* their relationship to ideal subjects ... this can mean keeping them at arm's length or even engaging in outright struggle against them' (ibid.: 54).

Drawing upon these ideas from the work of Bernstein and Fairclough, I analysed press reporting of teaching excellence in its coverage of the NTFS in 2000. This was the year in which the NTFS was introduced within the sector, which gave rise to much press reaction. The work on the NTFS is supplemented by a small-scale comparative analysis of press reporting of the Australian Awards for University Teaching (AAUT). These awards have been in operation since 1997, so I was interested in the quality of press reporting of a 'mature' scheme. A number of questions are raised, notably:

• In the process of appropriation by the press, to what extent do award schemes and their assumptions about teaching excellence undergo a transformation?
• Are understandings about excellence modified by selection, simplification, condensation and elaboration?
• Are they repositioned and refocused?
• What ideal subject positions are offered to readers?
• Whose perspectives are given exposure?
• Are readers offered tools with which to engage critically with teaching excellence?

Press reporting of teaching excellence

The analysis of the NTFS I undertook was based on a report carried out by POLO Public Relations Marketing Services (Fisher, 2000), who were commissioned by the ILTHE to provide media relations support for the 2000 scheme. In the light of this report, 110 press articles about the 2000 NTFS which appeared between April and August 2000 were identified and examined. Ninety-nine of these articles were published in regional, general-interest newspapers and 11 in two key educational press publications in the UK: six in *The Times Higher Educational Supplement* (*THES*) and five in the *Guardian Education* (*GE*).

A further small-scale investigation of press reporting of the AAUT was undertaken to complement the more detailed analysis of the NTFS. This focused on the coverage in one of the key educational press publications in Australia: the higher education section in the Wednesday edition of *The Australian* newspaper. Using their on-line archive facility, a search for articles written in the last two years produced six relevant publications. A discussion of these articles enabled a comparison to be made of press reporting of new (NTFS) and long-standing award schemes (AAUT) and their underlying assumptions about teaching excellence.

Regional press articles about the NTFS

A high percentage of all the articles about the NTFS during 2000 were published in regional newspapers. Most of these were short, descriptive accounts of the NTFS at three stages of its development: (a) call for nominations; (b) nominations; and (c) winners. The majority of these articles were structured around press releases given by POLO and were therefore highly scripted and controlled. For example, most of the 'call for nominations' pieces publicized the monetary value of the award ('Dedicated lecturers in Hull could be rewarded with a £50,000 prize for their support for learning'), the short time period in which to make a nomination ('The University of Reading has two weeks left to nominate a lecturer to win £50,000'), brief details about the selection process ('The judges are seeking lecturers who are able to inspire students and colleagues and have a track record in influencing the wider community') and the ILTHE's perspective on the scheme ('This is a high-profile scheme unparalleled elsewhere that will not only reward teaching excellence but will also serve to raise the profile of teaching and learning across the sector').

This early regional press coverage of teaching excellence and the NTFS therefore had a practical and procedural emphasis. It focused on key characteristics of the scheme such as its monetary value and reported details about the selection process. What 'teaching excellence' means received little comment in the coverage. The absence of such comment suggests that the meaning of teaching excellence was deemed to be either irrelevant or commonly understood. Due to being structured around the POLO press releases, the articles privileged the perspective of the managers of the NTFS, the ILTHE. We are not offered at this stage the perspectives of other groups of people, for example, student and/or lecturer perspectives on the introduction of the scheme. The ideal subject position offered readers is that teaching excellence is a good thing which can be recognized and rewarded by award schemes. Teaching excellence is associated implicitly with a range of attributes, for example, 'dedication', 'inspiration' and the ability to influence the 'wider community'. In offering a cut-down account of the scheme and its purposes from the ILTHE's perspective, the regional press coverage simplifies and legitimizes 'official discourse' about teaching excellence and the NTFS. The articles provide basic information but little extended discussion about the scheme or its implicit assumptions about teaching excellence. The selection process is presented as unproblematic and professional, with titles of articles proclaiming: 'Cash fund *will* reward the best lecturers' (emphasis added).

Many of the winners' articles included a photograph of the successful teacher. Fairclough (1989) notes: 'Not all photographs are equal: any photograph gives one image of a scene or person from among the many possible images. The choice is very important, because different images convey different meanings' (ibid.: 52). Most of the chosen photographs of the award winners showed them smiling (often at the award ceremony where they received their prize) or looking authoritative when pictured at work (for example, next to a computer, at the lectern, leaning against a bookcase). These images are combined with text which states how they feel on being recognized as excellent: for example, they are 'proud'; it is a 'joy' and 'honour'. The ideal subject position that readers have to negotiate here is one that believes these teachers are happy and authoritative individuals who are truly excellent and deserve to be recognized as such. They are also humble recipients of the honour bestowed upon them. The perspectives which are made available through these articles are those held by the award winners themselves, the ILTHE, managers from the institutions of the successful teachers, the Chair of the Selection Panel and then the Education Secretary, David Blunkett, who comments in one piece: 'Excellence in university and college teaching is of great importance . . . Students deserve the very best. I'm sure these awards will further raise the status of teaching in higher education.' Different perspectives are therefore brought to bear in these articles, yet they are all from proponents of the scheme. The articles included references to how the award winners felt on receiving their prize and brief details about the development work they planned to undertake. They are identified as 'role models' who will disseminate their ideas and practices to other colleagues within the sector. One article which develops this theme was entitled: '*Model* academics win share of £50k' (emphasis added).

Educational press coverage

Eleven articles about the NTFS appeared in the *THES* and *GE* between April and August 2000. Most of these pieces were in-depth reviews of the scheme, often including details about nominees or winners. From an analysis of these articles, three distinct phases of educational press reporting can be detected. During the first phase, following the call for nominations, a 'performance and glamour' discourse on teaching excellence prevailed. Two articles in *GE*: 'Star lecturers to vie for £50,000 teaching award' (MacLeod, 2000a) and 'Oscars are coming' (MacLeod, 2000b) pushed the teaching-as-theatrical-performance analogy hard, the first article beaming: 'The glitz, the tension, the tears, the inflated egos – Oscar fever is about to grip university common rooms up and down the land.'

Together with the title, the second piece was accompanied by an image of an Oscar statuette and made reference to a proposal for video tapes of 'star lecturers' first mooted in the Dearing Report (NCIHE, 1997). Although the article informed the reader that these proposals had been dropped before the introduction of the NTFS, it continued the excellence-as-performance line through references such as, 'The Don's Oscars will reward a variety of lecturing styles', and 'students' views of their lecturer's performance will be taken into account'. Whilst the two articles gave some information about the scheme and sought to reassure the reader that the award money would be spent wisely, their main impact was to 'talk up' teaching excellence and the NTFS by focusing on the performance and glamour of the awards.

They therefore created, maintained and intensified discourse about teaching excellence while refocusing it on 'performance'. This would have undoubtedly frustrated all those involved in the development of the NTFS, given their attempts to devise a scheme that would recognize and reward a teaching excellence based on 'reflective practice' rather than the art of lecturing (see Chapter 3, pp. 56–7).

The ideal subject position offered in these two articles is one that accepts stereotypical and outdated understandings of academics and their work: for example, it is suggested that academics have nothing better to do than congregate in common rooms and get excited by an award scheme ('Oscar fever'), and teaching excellence is reduced to lecturing performance. The articles 'work' by juxtaposing the presumed dreary and entrenched world of academia with the excitement of life in the film industry, with its commitment to innovation and change.

The second phase of educational press reporting began once institutional nominations had been made. During this phase, a different tone can be detected. The 'performance and glamour' discourse became less evident and overshadowed by one that was more serious and questioning, offering readers some limited 'tools' with which to think more deeply about teaching excellence and the NTFS. For example, the article in the *THES*, 'Make winners of class acts' (Currie, 2000a), begins with the traditional stereotype: 'Academia will be donning its glad rags in a few weeks when the results of the first NTFS are announced', but then swiftly moves on to discuss briefly the meaning of teaching excellence, the selection process at institutional level, the criteria for excellence identified by the NAP and the gender characteristics, subject spread and geographical distribution of nominees. It also introduced the views of a number of educational developers who had concerns about the NTFS. Two main issues were mentioned: first, that the scheme rewards individuals not teams and much higher education teaching is undertaken collaboratively; and second, that promoting people on the basis of their teaching ability is a much better lever for raising the status of teaching and learning in higher education than teaching awards. The latter, it was argued, was more likely to encourage a superficial and tokenistic commitment to change, with only a small number of teachers (the 'gloss on the dross', according to one respondent in the article) taking teaching seriously. These reported concerns offered readers some critical tools with which to reflect on the NTFS and its assumptions and to consider alternative conceptions of teaching excellence.

A range of perspectives was therefore included in this article. The ideal subject position that the reader had to negotiate was one that questioned whether award schemes for individuals were the best mechanism for recognizing and rewarding teaching excellence. What we understand by excellence is seen to be relatively unproblematic and within the capability of experts, however, the article stating: 'How to award the best teachers in higher education does not seem to have flummoxed the ILTHE advisory panel, which drew up a list of qualities that constitutes a good teacher.' Other points reassure the reader that all is well with the operation of the current scheme: 'While nearly two-thirds of the nominees are male, the subject spread is surprisingly wide ... scotching early fears that education departments would dominate the proceedings.' The real focus is on alternative mechanisms for recognizing and rewarding teaching excellence, therefore, rather than on what we mean by the term or the operational functioning of the NTFS.

The third phase of reporting followed the identification of the 20 winners of the NTFS in July 2000. In addition to a now muted 'performance and glamour' discourse and continued, if limited, critical engagement with the scheme and its understanding of teaching excellence, something new emerged: an interest in the individual award winner and their particular ideas and practices. This is evident in the *GE* article 'By example' (MacLeod, 2000c), which offered case studies of two of the award winners and in the *THES* article 'And the first prize goes to ... teaching' (Currie, 2000b), which provided details of each of the award winners' development projects. In the first article, the ideas and practices of two seemingly contrasting teachers, one from dance, one from medicine, were considered in some depth and related to their institutional contexts (one worked in a prestigious, research-intensive ancient university, the other in a teaching-intensive university). Despite these differences, the article comments: 'On closer inspection both [teachers] are linked by their willingness to experiment with new technology in their teaching ... [and] Both are passionately committed to teaching students.'

Some glitz and glamour remained in the second article, with reference being made to the 'champagne-drenched celebrations' of the awards ceremony, but this spirited introduction soon gave way to an account that provided space for some of the Teaching Fellows to talk about the NTFS and for all of them to give details of their planned development work (summarized under 'How they will spend their awards'). Allowing teachers to get on with teaching (rather than administration), raising the status of teaching relative to research and supporting 'less able' students were some of the potential benefits that the teachers said the NTFS might achieve. The commitment to innovation and the use of new technology are evident in the descriptions of development projects, with 10 of the 20 Teaching Fellows stating that they were planning to use technological applications to help improve teaching and learning. Two main concerns were also raised in the article. First, the point was made that 'It is ironic that the £50,000 fellowships can be used to buy some time out from hectic teaching schedules', and second: 'If one thing is missing from the remit of the NTFS scheme, the fellowship holders say, it is an emphasis on the role of teamwork in good teaching.'

In these two articles the focus is on the perspectives of the award winners themselves. The reader is given information about their development work and offered short quotes from the successful teachers talking about their ideas and practices. Photographs of the teachers in action are also provided. Two of the three pictures are of a dance teacher in motion. One of them is accompanied by a caption quoting the person saying: 'You can't pull a lecture out of a filing cabinet.' Taken together, the picture and quotation convey the message that teaching excellence is about innovation and change. Attributes that are associated with excellence in these two articles are 'passion', 'intelligence', 'energy, 'inspiration' and 'hard work'. The reader is encouraged to think that these teachers deserve the awards for their ability and industry. The ideal subject position offered is one of excitement about the range of development work the award winners will undertake and the benefit this will have for the sector as a whole. The development work is represented as future oriented, drawing upon the latest pedagogical ideas and technological applications.

Press reporting of the Australian Awards for University Teaching (AAUT)

These awards aim to 'celebrate excellence in university teaching'. Press coverage in *The Australian* can be split into three types of article which appear to follow distinct phases in the selection process: (1) nominations; (2) teachers who are short-listed; and (3) award winners. The first two types of article are short, descriptive accounts of the AAUT which discuss the different types of award, their monetary value and details of the selection process (for example, the date on which the winners will be announced). They are informative and factual and are clearly not concerned with raising broader questions about the scheme or its understanding of teaching excellence. In this sense they are similar to regional press coverage of the NTFS in the UK.

In the first article, 'Wealth of talent lines up – Australian awards for University teaching' (*The Australian*, 2002a), the only perspective on the scheme that is presented is that of the Education Minister, Brendan Nelson, who stated that 'the quality of nominations showed Australia was producing world-class university teaching'. In the second article, 'Short list announced' (*The Australian*, 2002b), a list of finalists was presented together with a short comment on a couple of history teachers who are 'partners in life as well as work'. They are credited with 'revitalizing teaching of first-year Australian history, at a time of declining interest in the subject at other universities'. This type of press coverage simplifies and legitimizes discourse about the AAUT and teaching excellence. The ideal subject position we are offered is one that is interested in procedural matters and supportive of awards and their ability to recognize and reward teaching excellence. The perspectives featured come from proponents of the scheme (Education Minister and finalists). Teaching excellence is associated with 'revitalizing' subjects that are in decline and linked, by the Minister, to Australia's place in the competitive global knowledge economy.

Four further articles in *The Australian* give individual profiles of AAUT winners from the 2002 and 2003 schemes. They are similar in kind to the 'third-phase' reporting of the NTFS in the UK whereby the focus is on the individual award winner and their ideas and practices. In these articles teaching excellence is associated with trying out new approaches and being innovative. For example, the piece entitled the 'Art of Chinese whispers' (Giglio, 2004) describes an approach to language learning used by a Chinese-born award winner: 'Humming, whispering and stomping feet are not the most conventional ways of learning Mandarin Chinese . . . During classes they [students] hum, clap, mime and gesture to learn the language. And that's after a relaxing lie-down on the floor.' In a different article, 'Classes squirm as they learn about parasites' (Illing, 2003), an innovative approach to teaching parasitology is described which involves inspiring students by using tricks to engage them and shock them into submission: 'The students are transfixed as [award winner] slowly opens the bottle of tapeworms. He draws them out with his gloved hand, spouting the virtues of their high-protein content [and] with apparent relish begins stuffing them into his mouth.' Here connections between excellence, innovation, performance, entertainment and student motivation are made. In these and the other two articles: 'Winners are a class act' (Morris, 2002) and 'Award for real-life solutions' (Giglio, 2003), excellent teachers are portrayed as being supportive of teacher training for academics, technological applications and problem-based learning. They are represented as role models for others, as long-serving and dedicated people humble in receipt of the award. For example, one person was reported to have said that although the award was an honour, teaching was her real reward.

The ideal subject position offered in these four articles is of one who is inspired and excited by the innovative practices of the award winners. Their work is presented as future oriented, drawing upon the latest pedagogical ideas and signalling a departure from traditional teaching. The perspectives that are offered in these articles are from proponents of the scheme: award winners themselves, the Chair of the Awards Committee and the Education Minister. Recognizing and rewarding teaching excellence through award schemes is seen as beneficial and non-problematic.

Conclusion

Press coverage of the NTFS and the AAUT on the whole has been very positive. In Bernstein's terms, non-educational press coverage of the NTFS maintained, legitimized and simplified the discourse on teaching excellence initiated by the NTFS and made it available to the wider public. Excellence was associated with the attributes of 'dedication', 'inspiration' and the ability to influence the wider higher education community. The perspectives of different proponents of the scheme were privileged and readers were reassured that the selection process would be undertaken in a professional way. The ideal subject position offered in these articles is that of a person who believes in the legitimacy of award schemes and their ability to recognize and reward teaching excellence. Such a person also accepts that the 'right' people have been selected: people who are positive and authoritative yet humble in the receipt of the award.

In reporting on the NTFS, the specialized educational press shifted from an initial 'performance and glamour' discourse to one that was more serious and critical, offering readers some (limited) tools with which to think more deeply about the NTFS and teaching excellence. Three main limitations of the NTFS were considered and offered to readers (its superficiality as a mechanism for promoting teaching excellence; its emphasis on individuals rather than teams; and the tendency of award winners to buy themselves out of teaching). Award winners' ideas and practices were covered in some detail, teaching excellence being associated with innovation and change, the latest pedagogical developments and technological applications. A small-scale investigation of the AAUT showed that themes identified in the analysis of the NTFS continue to dominate press reporting of 'mature' schemes that have been in operation for some years (the AAUT were introduced in 1997).

In the light of my analysis, there is some support for Fairclough's (1989: 51) claim that although there is always the possibility that the media may challenge orthodox or common-sense understandings, they tend to reproduce the ideas of powerful stakeholders. It is clear that although some critical questions were posed in educational press coverage of the NTFS, this coverage has served to legitimate the scheme and has favoured the perspectives of its proponents. The press has largely reproduced and circulated the understandings of teaching excellence embedded in the NTFS and the AAUT. It has reassured readers that those teachers who have won the awards deserve them for their personal qualities and application. Early educational press reporting refocused teaching excellence away from its reflective practice emphasis in the NTFS towards a 'traditional' concern with lecturing performance. However, although this might be seen initially as a serious challenge to reformist thinking, on closer inspection, the use of humour and stereotypes of academia mainly serve the purpose of 'talking up' interest in the scheme. This type of reporting gradually changed, and later coverage supported the 'official' line within the NTFS which views excellence as future oriented and linked to technological innovation. A similar emphasis on innovation and change is evident in the coverage of the AAUT in *The Australian*.

Fairclough (1989: 52) also points out that the media can 'disguise power' by failing to attribute causality to events or by avoiding 'difficult questions'. In terms of the press coverage of teaching excellence and the two award schemes considered here, there are several such difficult questions that gain little or no mention in any of the articles yet have great significance. For example:

- On what basis do we reconcile competing understandings of teaching excellence?
- What economic and political interests are served by particular representations of teaching excellence?
- To what extent are selection criteria for teaching excellence based on research evidence?
- What negative impact may award schemes have for 'ordinary' teachers?
- What are the perspectives of people who are not supportive of teaching award schemes?
- Does the emphasis on award schemes distract attention away from the basic material conditions of teaching and learning in higher education?

The analysis presented here demonstrates that it is important to be able to read press coverage of teaching excellence critically. The press does not simply report ideas in a neutral way; it *media*tes them through a process of selection and emphasis. This chapter has given some insight into how the process works through the practice of selecting and constraining content (that is, what information is presented) and drawing upon particular sources (that is, whose perspective is adopted in reports). Although some limited tools have been offered readers to allow them to engage critically with the NTFS and understandings of teaching excellence, for the most part press coverage has legitimized and reproduced the perspectives of proponents of this scheme and the AAUT, and fostered compliance. As Fairclough notes, people do negotiate their relationship with the subject positions that are offered in newspaper articles. This chapter has sought to assist this process by clarifying these subject positions and identifying those difficult questions that the press has failed to address. These questions are important to consider as part of any critical understanding of teaching excellence.

In Chapter 9, I examine the relationship between teaching excellence and professional development. I look in particular at how teaching excellence might be supported through professional development courses and consider the following areas: existing and emergent professional development opportunities for teachers in higher education; the assumptions underpinning different types of courses; whether excellent teachers need to be exposed to formal training; and what sort of approach to professional development is likely to foster teaching excellence.

Chapter 9

Professional development and teaching excellence

Introduction

In current circumstances it may seem strange to suggest a relationship between professional development and teaching excellence. It is unusual, for example, for professional development to have teaching excellence as a stated goal or for teaching excellence to pursue professional development in its service. What is more familiar is for professional development in higher education to be linked with competence in teaching and other job-related activities. The emergence of 'academic practice' courses in the UK in recent years is a good example of such a link. These courses aim to make new lecturers competent in three core 'functional areas': teaching, research and administration (for an interesting discussion of what constitutes 'academic practice' and tensions between different activities and roles, see Staniforth and Harland, 1999).

In this chapter I provide a brief outline of how this current situation has arisen. Much of the discussion focuses on the UK context although many of the issues are also pertinent to other countries. I begin by examining the traditional model of professionalism that underpinned the work of academics for much of the twentieth century. This model of professionalism viewed teaching excellence as an inevitable consequence of expert knowledge and the service ethic. In the light of social change, student expansion and the increasing epistemological and ontological insecurity of the university, this traditional professionalism began to be questioned. Teaching, in particular, came under attack, leading to calls for it to be 'professionalized'. The critique of traditional teaching was epistemological, relational and political. With the state seeking to increase its return from higher education, 'imposed' professional development was introduced in the light of this critique, following recommendations made by the Dearing Report (NCIHE, 1997).

After the Dearing Report, courses on teaching and learning for university lecturers proliferated, becoming compulsory for entrants to the profession in many institutions. These courses, with their emphasis on competence and surface learning, are increasingly being standardized through accreditation by the Higher Education Academy (previously by the ILTHE). The limitations of the competence approach are considered and alternative approaches to professional development explored. One of the key issues that emerges out of this exploration is the need to put the notion of *professional* back into professional development for teaching and learning. This is a form of development that takes the distinctive characteristics of professionals (knowledge, responsibility and autonomy) and interprets what they might imply for teaching and learning within the contemporary context. This is not a 'return to tradition' but a more robust and compelling response to the critique of traditional professionalism than that provided by imposed competence. In the final section of the chapter I forge a mutually enhancing relationship between professional development and teaching excellence that helps us move beyond our current fixation with competence-based models.

Traditional models of professionalism and higher education teaching

During the period 1945 to the early 1970s, Nixon *et al.* (1997) state that

> professionals achieved legitimacy through society's acknowledgment of their specialist knowledge and expertise. Based on the assumption of professional autonomy and status, the relationship between professionals and their publics was not at issue: 'doctor knows best' was not just a platitude; it was an underlying code whereby the right to make decisions on behalf of majorities, to exercise judgment on behalf of others, and to pursue the larger aim of providing goods and services in a fashion calculated to obtain public approval, was ceded to particular occupational groups.

(Ibid.: 7)

Occupations which by common consent were recognized as professions included academia, medicine, the law, the church, architecture, engineering and the military (see Hoyle and John, 1995). These had all achieved some measure of autonomy and self-regulation. What the traditional understanding of professionalism required in return was a service ethic and a commitment to the intrinsic goods of professional practice. Contributing to a more just and rational society rather than pursuing self-interest was central to this understanding of professionalism.

During this period there was little sense that professional development specifically for higher education teaching was appropriate or required. Teaching excellence was assumed to flow naturally from subject expertise acquired over time and the service ethic that motivated academics as professionals. Nixon *et al.* (1997) state that 'one of the underlying assumptions of the traditional model of professionalism was of specialist knowledge and expertise as essentially static: a body of received wisdom over which professionals kept guard' (ibid.: 8). During this period, therefore, there was little sense that higher education teaching needed remediation. Once specialist knowledge and technique had been acquired (often through a lengthy period of education), it was regarded as robust and intransient. This knowledge provided a firm foundation for teaching and a career for life (Esland, 1980: 219).

The 'professionalization' of university teaching

Gradually the traditional model of professionalism that influenced the way academics understood and practised teaching began to be challenged in the light of profound social and political changes. By the 1970s, there were consistent calls to modernize and 'professionalize' university teaching in the light of fundamental epistemological and ontological concerns. Universities were thought to be increasingly out of touch with advances in knowledge and technology, and the expanding student body posed serious questions about appropriate methods of instruction. Larger questions were also beginning to be asked about the nature of universities and their contribution to wider society.

Some of the initial impetus to professionalize university teaching gained pace as early as the 1960s. Three key reports (the Hale Report, 1964; the Brynmor Jones Report, 1965; and the Parry Report, 1967) were published in the UK during this period, all examining the condition of teaching and learning in universities. Increasing concern began to be expressed about the quality of university teaching. There was a sense that universities were not keeping pace with the rapidly changing knowledge base, the increasingly heterogeneous student body and new ideas about how to teach derived from training and research publications. A 'deficit' view of university teaching increasingly gained currency and the changing social and economic context within which higher education was located was largely held to be responsible for 'unprecedented teaching problems' (Layton, 1968).

The growing deficit view of university teaching formed an important backdrop to an agreement made in 1974 between the Universities Authorities Panel and the Association of University Teachers. This agreement linked a three-year probationary period with induction courses, mentoring and reductions in teaching load. Induction courses were subsequently established in many universities, although they were often 'short, ad hoc and unstructured' (Gosling, 1996: 204). Educational technology units which had been established to identify technological solutions to teaching problems often contributed to these courses. Some of these units undertook systematic investigations into the improvement of teaching and learning whereas others 'were little more than audio and visual aids units, producing primarily videos and audio tapes, but also often with graphic designers producing overhead transparencies and slides as aids to teaching' (ibid.: 205).

In the 1970s and 1980s research units were also set up to investigate teaching and learning methods in higher education and to feed back their findings through professional development activities. These units rarely had a high profile within institutions but they did contribute to the emergence of a developing knowledge base within universities and the former polytechnics. In the light of this knowledge base, 'traditional' methods of teaching (see Chapter 2, pp. 26–9) and assessment in higher education became less tenable. Student expansion and reduced funding were also drivers for change, leading to a situation where 'The complicit silence on teaching methods began to break down towards the end of the 1980s under the combined pressures of rapidly growing student numbers ... and increasingly severe resource constraints' (Gosling, 1996: 207). A period of pragmatism followed (Gibbs, 1995), with teachers in higher education drawing upon practical advice and research findings that helped them to manage changing conditions of work.

An influential report written in the early 1990s on *Teaching Standards and Excellence in Higher Education* (Elton and Partington, 1993) addressed a range of practical difficulties that universities faced in developing teaching and learning. The report acknowledged that British higher education had a good international reputation but questioned the quality of its teaching, citing three main reasons for this situation:

- In comparison with research, teaching is not adequately rewarded. This has clear implications concerning the values attached by individuals and institutions to these two major academic activities.
- University teachers have not been trained as teachers. Hence they tend to teach in a manner similar to that in which they were taught – a very conservative process. Training is therefore needed not only to improve teachers' current performance, but to enable them to respond to changing circumstances, which will require of them substantial changes in role.
- The circumstances in which university teaching takes place have undergone and will continue to undergo profound changes.

(Ibid.: 1)

It is important to note that the report concluded that addressing the first of these points (the need to reward teaching through the promotion system) represented the most effective way of improving the quality of teaching and learning within the sector: 'a more equitable approach to the awarding of promotions on the basis of both excellence in research and in teaching will send out a powerful signal with potentially far reaching effects towards raising teaching standards quite generally' (ibid.: 2). Given the focus in this chapter, it is significant to note that this report also concluded that there was some doubt about whether teacher training for university lecturers would necessarily lead to significant improvements in current performance:

> we would readily concede that it [teacher training] is more relevant for the improvement of the competence of the average...than for the development of excellence in the best. The far more important function of staff development, i.e. training for change, has not been challenged.

> (Ibid.: 2).

The momentum built up in the 1980s and 1990s culminated in a major review of higher education undertaken in 1997 chaired by Sir Ron Dearing. The review was called the National Committee of Inquiry into Higher Education (NCIHE) and the report (*Higher Education for a Learning Society*) became known thereafter as the Dearing Report (NCIHE, 1997). By the time the Committee met, there was some consensus in the sector about three main concerns relating to the 'professional' quality of teaching: (a) the need for academics to keep up to date with developments in knowledge within their field and for this to feed into their teaching; (b) the low status of teaching relative to research meant that some academics were not treating teaching seriously; and (c) academic freedom meant that some institutions and individuals were impervious to change.

Acting in the light of these concerns, the Dearing Report made recommendations that were to have a significant impact on professional development and the status of teaching. For example, one of the recommendations stated:

> We recommend that institutions of higher education begin immediately to develop or seek access to programmes for teacher training of their staff, if they do not have them, and that all institutions seek national accreditation of such programmes from the Institute for Learning and Teaching in Higher Education.

> (NCIHE, 1997: recommendation 13)

The report recommended the immediate establishment of the ILTHE to perform three main roles:

- The accreditation of programmes of training for higher education teachers
- Research and development in teaching and learning
- The stimulation of innovation.

In the light of these developments, Nicholls (2001) notes that the role of professional development changed and was given new dimensions and directions. She states:

> these include the need for new lecturers to enrol on induction courses and programmes that are assessed in some form ... there has (also) been the introduction of continuing professional development plans that are closely linked to appraisal, promotion and professional standing.

(Ibid.: 3)

Nicholls argues therefore that calls to 'professionalize' university teaching have led to imposed or enforced professional development, a situation that will be considered in the next section.

Imposed professional development, teaching competence and surface learning

With the creation of the ILTHE we have now entered into a period of imposed or enforced professional development. A national system for accrediting professional development courses for university lecturers has been introduced 'of which participation is not in essence through choice' (Nicholls 2001: 19). Imposed professional development assumes that there is something wrong with current practice; it is a 'deficit' model which assumes that external regulation is required to bring teaching up to required standards.

Imposed professional development threatens to undermine professional autonomy. It fosters a culture of compliance and adherence to set 'standards' which are subject to minimal critical scrutiny. Imposed professional development infers that academics are not already professional and underestimates the activities of discipline-based societies and learned bodies through which many academics derive their professional identity. An assumption is made that a great deal of teaching that takes place in higher education is of poor quality. This claim is rarely supported by research evidence.

Imposed professional development has become the norm in higher education as governments around the world have sought to derive more from university teachers. Human capital theories underpin these moves, with teaching viewed as an important element in producing the next generation of skilled workers necessary for vibrant national economies. Nicholls observes astutely that teachers in higher education did not ask for the ILTHE to be introduced, which casts some doubt over the notion that it is a professional body owned by the profession itself. There has been considerable opposition to the ILTHE in the UK which cannot be ignored or deflected by claims that university teachers are simply unable or unwilling to change (Morley, 2003). In addition to concerns about the principle of imposed professional development, many higher education teachers are concerned about the form this development has taken. These concerns relate mainly to the competence model that has been adopted by the ILTHE and the type of learning it fosters.

Of course, there are different understandings of 'competence' (Barnett, 1994). Nicholls (2003) argues that the ILTHE adopted an 'operational' view of competence which is premised on the goal of attaining practical effectiveness in one's teaching rather than a deeper cognitive understanding. The emphasis on learning outcomes in the ILTHE's model of professional development limits possibilities for teacher reflection on their practice. According to Nicholls, reflection should not simply be about assessing the degree to which one has been successful in achieving particular outcomes; teachers also need to know how such outcomes have been achieved and whether they represent educationally valuable goals in the first place. This relies on teachers developing their understanding of concepts, ideas and theories related to the teaching of their discipline. Although the ILTHE may have wanted to support a reflective approach to teaching and learning in higher education, this is a narrow view of reflection, directed towards practical effectiveness.

Criticisms of the ILTHE and its operational competence model have to be set alongside some of the progress it has instigated in terms of our understanding and practice of professional development. For example, in recognizing the importance of subject disciplines in its accreditation requirements, the ILTHE has supported a shift away from notions of generic teacher training, which ignores the disciplines or views them as an impediment to learning. Although the emphasis is more on *subject* rather than the deep structures of *disciplines* (see Chapter 5), this represents an attempt to recognize the contexts in which higher education teachers work and the significance this has for their identity and understanding of pedagogy. Compared with the approach taken by the Staff and Educational Development Association (SEDA), which accredited professional development courses on teaching and learning before the ILTHE, the ILTHE's requirements have also placed less emphasis on the painstaking recording of evidence of teaching competence. Within a context where the ILTHE aimed to develop a mass membership, a 'liberal' interpretation of how courses offered by different institutions would meet accreditation requirements appears to have been adopted, which moved some way to recognizing the diversity in courses that were already in place before the ILTHE and the development of its membership criteria (for further discussion of differences between ILTHE and SEDA approaches, see Healey and Jenkins, 2003: 48–50).

It is important to recognize that a competence model moves some way towards addressing those problems associated with traditional professionalism and its implications for university teaching. For example, an adherence to set standards is preferable to an approach that assumes that teaching will look after itself so long as disciplinary knowledge has been acquired. It also ensures that people are kept in touch with 'best practice'. Imposed professional development for teaching also attempts to make sure that teaching becomes an important part of the service ethic of academics rather than the poor relation in the teaching–research nexus. Some erosion of academic freedom is necessary to ensure that people are open to change and willing to consider the views of all those who have an interest in and perspective on teaching and learning in higher education.

The imposed competence model has some advantages over traditional professionalism and its implications for teaching and learning. But I wish to argue here that it was an inadequate response to the critique of traditional professionalism that gave rise to calls to 'professionalize' university teaching in the first place. The basis of this critique was epistemological (out-of-date knowledge to inform teaching); relational (teaching was becoming a low priority in academics' work) and political (notions of academic freedom meant that some individuals and institutions were impervious to change). Imposed competence provides a temporary fix to the dilemmas posed by this critique. For example, it simplifies our understanding of what con-stitutes knowledge about teaching and learning (thereby avoiding the real epistemological challenge); it forces an engagement with teaching and learning (thereby encouraging instrumentalism and a 'jumping through hoops' mentality – something likely to undermine the status of teaching and learning in the medium to long term); and it fosters adherence to recognized standards of 'good practice' (while stifling innovation and individual creativity). Any immediate gains that arise from this temporary fix may feel shallow in the medium to long term given the importance of the issues at stake. In the next section I want to situate the competence model in relation to alternatives in order to try to identify an approach that offers a more sustained and robust potential for change.

Alternative models of professional development

A critical understanding of professional development for higher education teachers needs to consider different possible models and their distinctive characteristics. This helps to locate current practice, which is dominated by competence-based models, within the range of possibilities available to the sector.

Gosling (1996) identifies five different models of educational develop-ment. Although professional development in relation to teaching and learn-ing is only one aspect of educational development, his framework is useful for our purposes here. The first model proposed by Gosling is premised on reflective practice. In this model, 'an effective professional needs to reflect critically on his/her own performance in a continuous process of review, evaluation, leading to further planning and implementation, which is again subject to review' (ibid.: 211). Professional development is seen as an ongoing process which does not have fixed certainties underpinned by set standards. Rather, practice is dynamic and subject to evaluation.

The second model is called the 'educational researcher' model. Here professional development for teaching and learning involves practitioners applying 'the same level of critical examination to their teaching as they do their own subject area' (ibid.: 212). This ensures that teaching and learning in higher education is 'research-led' and allows teachers to become involved in generating knowledge and an evidence base. This approach is contrasted with the 'professional competence model', which is premised on the notion that it is possible to identify skills and competences that lecturers need in order to carry out their duties successfully. 'Competence' may not simply apply to behaviours, with practitioners being required to demonstrate that particular values and principles underpin their professional work. Gosling suggests that the competence model is a response to observations that professional life is becoming more complex. In order to cope with this complexity and to respond to increasing demands for public accountability, lecturers need specific training to perform their teaching tasks effectively.

The three models that have been referred to so far consider professional development from the perspective of the individual practitioner. The fourth approach in Gosling's framework focuses on the institution and is called the 'human resources' or 'managerial' model. Here the emphasis is on 'mechanisms available to the institution to achieve its mission' (ibid.: 216). In relation to professional development to support teaching and learning within higher education, such an approach would incorporate training for specific roles (lecturing, personal tutoring, small group work and so on), rewards for teaching excellence, criteria for promotion and systems of evaluation and appraisal. In referring to this model, Gosling states: 'The characteristic discourse associated with this model is that of "systems", "structures", "business objectives"; staff are described not as people but as "human resources" . . . [and] Given that the "core" business objectives can be clearly specified, the development needs of individuals become subservient to the needs of the organization' (ibid.: 217).

The final approach is called the 'expert' model. Drawing on Plato's Republic, Gosling suggests an approach to development where the developer is viewed as a member of 'a highly selected elite who, by virtue of their education, training and experience, are uniquely capable of seeing the "truth" which other members of the republic are unable to see' (ibid). The developer's role is 'essentially remediation, putting people right, setting them onto the right track, bringing them up to standard' (ibid.: 218). This model helps to explain those initiatives where 'expert teachers' are identified as role models for other teachers. Expert teachers may be people who have won awards for teaching excellence and/or those who hold senior positions within disciplinary communities who are recognized for their contributions to teaching. Such teachers may become centrally involved in professional development as contributors to courses on teaching and learning or through the dissemination of ideas and practices. One problem with this approach, however, is that many expert teachers have received little or no professional development in teaching and learning themselves and have little under-standing of the latest pedagogical research (Yorke, 2000).

Gosling recognizes that tensions exist between these models since they are underpinned by competing theories and different assumptions about what development entails. In addition to the characteristics of each model, he considers their limitations. For example, drawing upon the work of Gibbs (1995), he suggests that unless careful attention is paid to the conceptual tools that practitioners use for reflection, the 'reflective practitioner' model has only limited value. Referring to the 'educational researcher' model, he states that the commitment to critical enquiry and the questioning of exist-ing practice is unlikely to be favoured by institutional managers attempting to achieve some human resource strategy. Language that is associated with research is missing from the competence model. Gosling observes that 'understanding, critical reason, contextualisation, critique, relativities, social transformation, emancipation – are not simply absent from the competency model, but are alien to it' (Gosling, 1996: 215). This 'lack of fit' between the competence model and the intellectual culture of higher education is problematic.

The 'human resources' model, with its business terms and concepts, has been criticized for being profoundly anti-educational and damaging to the collegial values of higher education (Badley, 1996). The 'expert' model, as previously noted, overestimates its own importance. Questions arise as to the validity of the claim for expert status. *Who* should decide what counts as 'good' or 'excellent' teaching and on what basis? Commenting on the teaching quality movement in the UK, Gosling also suggests that one of the implications of remediation models is that practitioners increasingly begin to develop a surface orientation to teaching and learning. They think 'what do the assessors want?' rather than ask themselves what is the real basis of quality teaching and learning.

Professional development for teaching and learning

All the developmental models discussed in the previous section have their strengths and weaknesses. The competence model is no more or less per-suasive as a basis for development than the other models, although Gosling does suggest that there appears to be a particular 'lack of fit' between this model and the culture of higher education. What is missing from the alternatives offered by Gosling is a model of educational development that is informed by *professionalism*. In this section I want to articulate an understanding of professional development for teaching that puts *professionalism* at its centre. This draws on traditional understandings of professionalism or those characteristics that are held to be distinctive of occupational groups that are recognized as professional by common consent – knowledge, responsibility and autonomy – but interprets what these characteristics imply for teaching within the contemporary context. I aim, therefore, to offer a more compelling response to calls to professionalize teaching and learning in higher education than has been provided to date by the move to imposed, competence-based forms of professional development. This involves offering a more robust response to the epistemological, relational and political critique of traditional professionalism referred to earlier.

Professional development for teaching in higher education needs to provide an adequate knowledge base. But in our current conditions of high modernity or postmodernity, knowledge is increasingly being regarded as transitory and unstable. Most knowledge fields could be described as suffering from 'supercomplexity' (Barnett, 2000), split by rival claims or 'voices'. There is an awareness of the partiality of different knowledge claims, the circumstances that lead to different perspectives and the vested interests that can militate against claims to 'truth'. Teaching and learning are not separate from this supercomplexity. They are also contested, value-laden concepts. For this reason, it is difficult to evaluate different approaches to teaching and learning and their 'success', since they may have different standards of judgement. This is the epistemological challenge that educational professionals need to face. Professional development for teaching has to recognize this as a precursor to deeper cognitive understanding and more effective practice. One current question relating to knowledge about teaching and learning in higher education is from where such a knowledge might be derived. Professional development needs to provide a context in which higher education teachers can explore the potential relative contributions of subject and pedagogic knowledge. To what extent does the conceptual structure of disciplines inform the way they are taught? How important is it for higher education teachers to understand pedagogic research that has been undertaken outside their specific discipline? These are important questions that need to be addressed in any programme of professional development for teaching.

Professional development must foster responsibility for teaching and a commitment to restore teaching to the heart of university life. This is more likely to be achieved in the medium to long term if teaching and learning are presented as intellectually inspiring and challenging pursuits. Bringing teaching and research into a more productive relationship through a focus on learning and scholarship is also more likely to arouse interest than an approach that intensifies their separation. A focus on higher education policies that discourage staff from giving more time and energy to their teaching (for example, research assessment exercises carried out in Australia, Hong Kong and the UK) would also help to foster understanding and identify possibilities for strategic action.

The political critique of traditional professionalism focused on notions of academic freedom and the inability of some individuals and institutions to respond appropriately to social change. Nixon *et al.* (2001) argue that a 'new professionalism' would not imply a return to conditions where academics were cloistered off from the rest of society protected by notions of 'academic freedom'. Rather, new professionalism would imply a 'capacity to listen to, learn from and move forward with the communities they serve' (ibid.: 81). They suggest that if academic freedom is reinterpreted as a 'freedom for others', it can continue to be an important concept. Academic freedom understood in this way points up the importance of universities to society in that they represent 'an important, structural part of the culture of independence' (ibid.). If academic freedom is abandoned, Nixon *et al.* argue, then all that we have left is the market or state intervention. Professional development from such a perspective would need to defend the right of academics to have some degree of autonomy over their teaching. The justification for this would not be to preserve traditional notions of academic freedom, but to ensure that university teachers were able to draw upon their expertise and had a role in deciding what and why something was taught in universities and how this teaching might best take place. From this perspective, therefore, higher education teachers are not passive recipients of expert knowledge and policy; rather, they have an important contribution to make to the dialogue about teaching and learning within the sector.

Professional development and teaching excellence

Teaching *excellence* and *professional* development have much to offer each other. They can be mutually enhancing and enable us to think about excellence and development in different ways. For example, a professional development that has teaching *excellence* as its goal encourages us to think beyond our current fixation with competence models. A teaching excellence that is informed by *professional* development, on the other hand, points up the importance of knowledge, responsibility and autonomy. In order for teachers to be viewed as excellent they need to respond adequately to the critique of traditional professionalism and its implications for teaching and learning in higher education. The important questions are: what constitutes an appropriate knowledge base for teaching in higher education? How can teaching be placed centre stage? And what are the educational values that underpin our practices?

A professional development for teaching excellence which devotes sufficient time to these questions is clearly at odds with many current quality control mechanisms and planned systems of professional accreditation. For example, Nixon *et al.* (2001) state:

> Within the UK, the Dearing-inspired ILT(HE) in Higher Education is currently establishing a system of professional accreditation that is wrong-headed both in its restricted emphasis on threshold competencies and in its assumption that there is a single 'right' way to conceptualize teaching.

(Ibid.: 74)

They argue that a new notion of professionalism is 'necessarily and primarily a matter of addressing issues of principle and value in one's own teaching and learning practices ... [and that] Without this emphasis on the moral purposefulness of practice there would be no claim to professionalism' (ibid.: 81). Rather than address fundamental epistemological, relational and political questions, imposed professional development either avoids these questions (notions of 'good practice') or stifles any debate about them through the introduction of short-term solutions and control measures (compulsory courses on teaching and learning; standardized practices). Imposed professional development positions higher education teachers as a new proletariat (Halsey, 1992): people who increasingly lack ideological control over their work but are expected to adhere to values and practices that are decided by others.

An emphasis on adherence underpins current developments in the UK, where Universities UK recently undertook a national consultation entitled 'Towards a framework of professional teaching standards'. The document states: 'We understand "professionalism" as an individual's adherence to a set of standards, code of conduct or collection of qualities that characterize accepted practice'. This document therefore positions higher education teachers as passive recipients of standards established by others. It also assumes that they are surface learners who prefer to implement 'accepted' practice rather than investigate it or consider the educational worth of different possibilities. As mentioned earlier, there is no one 'right' way to teach or learn, and our existing evidence base does not allow such certainty. To suggest this is to engage in ideological folly. In short, the consultation document fails to recognize that teaching is a contested concept.

A *professional* development for teaching *excellence* would seek to foster an approach that transcends a simple adherence to set standards. The aims of such development would be:

- to enable university teachers to develop an informed understanding and practice of teaching and learning in higher education;

- to enable people to consider alternative approaches to teaching and learning, their underlying assumptions and respective strengths and weaknesses;
- to encourage people to develop their practice of teaching in the light of these approaches and research evidence, while recognizing that this evidence is contested and value-laden;
- to promote the idea that teaching and learning are intellectually interesting areas of study that have intrinsic value;
- to provide opportunities for university teachers to conduct systematic investigations into teaching and learning in higher education and to thereby contribute to the knowledge base;
- to explore ways in which teaching and research can be brought together in a productive relationship. An emphasis on 'learning' and 'pedagogical research' can avoid the increasing polarization of research and teaching;
- to support people in developing an informed understanding and practice of pedagogical research. This will help them to 'read' such research more critically and to improve the quality of their own investigations;
- to promote the idea that higher education teaching is not simply a technical concern; to offer opportunities for people to explore what their educational values are, how these may inform teaching and learning practices and what helps or hinders their realization;
- to encourage people to engage with (the sometimes contradictory) policies that help shape teaching and learning practices in higher education; to support people in taking a serious, reasoned and critical stance towards regulatory mechanisms and their impact on teaching and learning.

The next chapter is the first of three contributions to Part 4 of this book called 'Future horizons'. It draws upon interviews with teachers from the Carnegie Scholars Program in the USA to suggest a way of bringing together teaching excellence and scholarship.

Part 4

Future horizons

Chapter 10

Lost in the translation?

Introduction

In April 2004, I was invited to a meeting in San Diego, California, by the American Association of Higher Education (AAHE). The meeting took place during the AAHE's 'Learning to Change' Conference. The purpose of the meeting was to bring together award-winning teachers/scholars from the UK, Canada and the USA, all of whom had been recognized for excellence in teaching and learning. It aimed to foster collaborations between excellent teachers and to consider the possibility of future networks and educational projects. I was invited to the meeting in the light of my research into teaching excellence on the NTFS in the UK. The international standing of the meeting, its forward-looking orientation and the freshness of the collaborative spirit all suggested a significant moment or turning point: a sense of 'where do we go next with teaching excellence? And what are its future possibilities?'

On the flight over to San Diego I watched the film *Lost in Translation*. The significance of this film for my visit became more and more apparent during my stay, as I grappled with some of the subtle cultural differences that exist between the UK and the USA and their respective higher education systems. As I got to know more about the Carnegie Scholars Program (USA) and Canadian 3M awards and compared them with the NTFS in the UK, it also became clear that there were both similarities and differences between these three schemes and some 'grey areas' in between. The differences were not immediately noticeable given the network-building emphasis of the meeting, but their significance became more apparent during my stay.

The purpose of this chapter is to try to learn from these differences and to explore their implications for teaching excellence and its future possibilities. I draw upon interviews with Carnegie Scholars undertaken during the visit to suggests ways in which a more integrated understanding of teaching excellence – which builds upon contemporary developments across national boundaries – might be achieved.

One meeting, three schemes

Following an initial round of introductions at the San Diego meeting, participants worked in small groups and plenary sessions to determine how they might work together in the future. I felt somewhat ambivalent about my role in that I had been invited as an educational researcher rather than a teacher/scholar who had won an award for teaching excellence. A range of potential collaborative projects was explored before a few were identified with significant common interest. My suggestion of a cross-national evaluation of teaching award schemes received some initial support but did not make it to the final stages. A number of people sought me out, however, at different times during the meeting, commenting that such an evaluation would be worthwhile and offering their support.

The three schemes that were represented at the meeting seemed an interesting group for a cross-national evaluation. The Canadian 3M Teaching Fellowships Program, for example, is a long-standing scheme which was introduced in 1986 to recognize teaching excellence as well as educational leadership. 3M is mainly a traditional award scheme (see Chapter 3, pp. 42–3) which rewards recognized achievement and contributions to the support and development of teaching and learning. It includes a citation and an invitation to participate in an all-expenses-paid three-day retreat at Chateau Montebello in Quebec. This retreat provides the winners with an opportunity to share past teaching experiences and discuss new ideas. The Carnegie Scholars Program, on the other hand, is more like an educational development grant (see Chapter 3, pp. 42–3). It offers an opportunity for teacher scholars to undertake systematic educational enquiry and uses a residency scheme to provide support for the refinement of research plans. The NTFS in the UK combines elements of both of these programmes in offering recognition for past achievement and financial support for future educational development work. It requires winners to undertake individual projects and to participate in collective activities.

Whilst the UK and Canadian schemes explicitly seek to recognize and reward 'teaching excellence', the Carnegie Scholars Program aims to support the 'Scholarship of Teaching and Learning' (SoTL). I was intrigued by this different language and its potential significance. I was also interested in why Carnegie Scholars rather than award winners from the US Professors of the Year Program had been invited to the meeting, since the latter was more explicitly designated as an award for teaching excellence. During the visit I was fortunate to have an opportunity to interview some of the Carnegie Scholars about these issues and their programme. Their presence at the meeting proved invaluable for my thinking about teaching excellence. Their experiences and comments suggested ways in which a more integrated understanding of teaching excellence, which draws on scholarship, might be realized in practice.

The Carnegie Scholars Program (CSP)

CSP was introduced in 1998 as part of the broader Carnegie Academy for the Scholarship of Teaching and Learning. The web site for CSP states:

> The Carnegie Scholars Program is *not* an award for teaching excellence; nor is it a teaching-improvement workshop. Its purpose is to create a community of scholars, diverse in all the ways that matter in teaching and learning, whose work will advance the profession of teaching and deepen student learning. The central work of the Carnegie Scholars is to create and disseminate examples of the scholarship of teaching and learning that contribute to thought and practice in the field. Toward this end, each Scholar designs and undertakes a scholarly project aimed at deepening understanding of and practice related to an important issue in the teaching and learning of his or her field.
>
> (Emphasis added; http://www.carnegiefoundation.org/CASTL/ highered/scholars_program.htm)

When I first read this statement I was surprised by the way in which the CSP appeared to distance itself from awards for teaching excellence. Both the Canadian and UK schemes seemed to share, through the notions of 'retreat' and 'fellowship', the importance of creating a community. There also seemed a parallel commitment to scholarship. The NTFS Fellows, for example, undertake and disseminate findings from their individual projects, and 3M applications or dossiers can include research into teaching/learning problems and 'special projects' related to university teaching. Why was it, therefore, that two of the schemes represented at the meeting seemed happy to identify themselves as an award for teaching excellence while the third wanted to be thought of in a different way?

The interviews with Carnegie Scholars offered an opportunity to talk about this issue and to follow up themes that had emerged in my evaluation of the NTFS. In the evaluation (see Chapter 3), two significant issues that emerged were (a) the absence of a collective identity among the Teacher Fellows and (b) the need for greater support to be given to the Fellows in the design and implementation of their individual development projects. The structure of the CSP suggested that more emphasis was placed on these two aspects. For example, the Scholars participate in two two-week residencies in consecutive summers and also spend shorter periods together during the academic year. I was interested, therefore, in finding out more about the residency experience and what support was offered for individual projects.

Talking to Carnegie Scholars

I interviewed an opportunistic sample of six Carnegie Scholars during a colloquium on the SoTL at the AAHE Conference. They had won awards in different years (1998–2002) and were from a range of subject disciplines. Each interview lasted approximately 45 minutes and was structured around the following areas: the aims of the CSP; the meaning of scholarship; the residency experience; the nature of the individual's development project; the impact of CSP; and the experience of winning an award.

From these interviews, the following themes emerged.

A unified and coherent movement

There was a strong sense in the interviews that the Carnegie Scholars were part of a unified movement with a history, vision, developing body of work and commitment to systematic educational enquiry. The CSP is part of the work of the Carnegie Foundation for the Advancement of Teaching in the USA which was founded in 1905. Ernest Boyer, appointed president of the Foundation in 1979, wrote the influential work *Scholarship Revisited* in 1990 (Boyer, 1990). His work identified the scholarship of teaching as a legitimate pursuit for academics which carried equal value to the scholarship of discovery (research). Several people I spoke to talked about CSP as a social and educational 'movement' and there was a high level of agreement among interviewees about the fundamental aims and purposes of CSP, the value of educational enquiry and its key characteristics.

Scholarship is different to excellence

All the people I spoke to distinguished SoTL from teaching excellence. They pointed out that teaching excellence was being recognized and rewarded by the US Professors of the Year Program and related more to performance than a process of enquiry. One scholar commented:

> There are lots of excellent teachers who have absolutely no interest in investigating their practice and changing it. Some of the best teachers I ever had teach the same class the same way every time and really aren't interested in how they're influencing their students, they're interested in performing and they're so good at it that it doesn't matter ... I think all of our Carnegie Scholars are excellent teachers but I'm not convinced that all of them would win teaching excellence awards ... But all of them are enquiring teachers and so it doesn't matter if you're good, it matters if you want to be better.

The view was expressed that teaching excellence awards were more for people at the latter stages of their career who were known for the quality of their teaching. SoTL had little to do with age or rank: someone may have had a significant educational enquiry they wished to explore with the support of others, irrespective of their experience and years of working in the sector. As one Scholar noted, 'It's not about what you've done, it's about what we're going to do together.' Given these comments, I asked how people felt about being invited to a meeting which brought together excellent teachers. Some people felt that the different programmes were all playing their part in raising the profile of teaching and learning in higher education. Others felt that there was some potential tension between SoTL and awards for excellence, although it was pointed out that some US Professors of the Year had also become Carnegie Scholars.

Teachers as 'knowledge producers'

In the CSP, teachers are viewed as 'knowledge producers' who, with appropriate guidance, are able to carry out pedagogical research. They draw upon their own disciplines to inform their enquiries, one person stating: 'The methodologies of a field biologist are identical to a good pedagogue.' Carnegie Scholars are exposed to a range of disciplinary methodologies with potential for the exploration of educational phenomena during the residency period (see below). During this period they are asked to talk to their peers about how they understand the process of research and data collection. This is interspersed with contributions from Program Staff about SoTL and previous studies. Through the refinement of their research enquiries in the critical company of others, the Carnegie Scholars are expected to contribute and take forward the knowledge base about teaching and learning within their disciplines. 'Going public' is an important part of this, whereby scholars disseminate their work through journals and at disciplinary associations and educational conferences.

Residency, community building and interdisciplinarity

The residency period clearly plays an important role in forming a shared identity among Carnegie Scholars. People were extremely positive about the experience of working together intensively over (two) two-week periods. For example, one person said:

> You come here and they treat you like princes and princesses, they treat you like you have something to offer, you have something to contribute to the world and they are going to help you contribute ... they honour and respect you ... the role of respect and validation and honouring in a program like this is very meaningful for people's guts ... every person I spoke to in my cohort felt exactly the same way that it has been a profoundly validating experience.

One of the key features of the residency is community building, where people are encouraged to work together across disciplinary boundaries. A commitment to working in this way is emphasized in the call for applications. Early on in the residency there is an interdisciplinary sharing of project designs. Scholars are placed in interdisciplinary project groups (of between six and eight people) to discuss their provisional project plans and receive feedback from others. This was viewed very positively, one person said:

> The group I was in had two lawyers in it, three economists and a philosopher... and I'm a psychologist... the whole ethos is... supportive of the enquiry process... my first time doing it I loved it, it was incredible to receive feedback from a bunch of lawyers, it's like wow they have something interesting to say about this problem.

Compared with the NTFS in the UK, people appeared to be more positive about working together across disciplines. Senior Carnegie Scholars played a part in facilitating the development of project designs, which may have contributed to the success of the process. The interdisciplinary working was interspersed with stimulus and support discussions led by Program staff.

Impact on professional lives, career changes and tenure

When asked about the impact of a Carnegie scholarship on their professional lives, most people stressed how significant and positive the experience had been. For some, the experience of SoTL had changed their careers dramatically as they became less focused on research within their discipline and more involved with SoTL. Others found that SoTL led to them moving out of the classroom and becoming more involved in management or educational development. The move to management was not always a personal choice, but institutions would suggest this, given their tendency to associate SoTL with a broad interest in learning and its institutional support, an interest in students and their welfare, and the ability to talk to teachers from across different faculties. The loss of enquiring teachers from the classroom was viewed as unfortunate by some of the Scholars, although it was pointed out that representation at senior levels within organizations was likely to help SoTL have a greater impact in the medium to long term. Most of the Scholars said that being involved in SoTL made it more difficult for them to receive tenure in their institutions. This was particularly true for people in research-intensive institutions. One person achieved tenure only after a protracted process where they were left in no doubt about what colleagues thought of their research into teaching and learning. Attitudes changed only gradually after significant funding and a national profile for this research work had been achieved. Suddenly the person became, in their own words, 'King of the dunces... (but) with a lot of friends.'

Learning from difference

There are many similarities in the comments on professional impact from Carnegie Scholars and National Teaching Fellows. Teaching awards can change career trajectories and bestow an ambivalent status, particularly in research-intensive institutions.

In exploring the differences between the two schemes and their preferred language, a significant question that emerged for me was: 'Why should teaching excellence not involve educational enquiry or scholarship, but be thought of as an end state, a completed journey, rather than a process of continuing enquiry?' It seemed strange to think of someone deemed excellent as having little or no interest in investigating their teaching or thinking about how students learn. Focusing on one's own performance also implied a teaching excellence that was somewhat claustrophobic.

At the same time, it is not difficult to imagine how SoTL might be enhanced by a teacher's experience, accumulated wisdom and knowledge of the disciplinary field. There seemed to be no reason, therefore, why the different understandings of teaching excellence displayed at the meeting could not be integrated and schemes improved by reference to key differences. For example, the Canadian 3M scheme rewards recognized achievement and offers a three-day retreat to share past experiences and future ideas. One aspect that might be considered in the light of the discussion here (and assuming additional support is available) is whether the retreat experience could be developed in a way that supports systematic educational enquiry. Turning attention to the CSP, its separation from the US Professors of the Year awards may unintentionally reinforce a notion that teaching excellence and educational enquiry are uneasy bedfellows. There is considerable potential, therefore, for forging new alliances between excellence and scholarship. We need a teaching excellence that is dynamic and enquiring, and a scholarship that is tethered to experience.

In its very conceptualization the NTFS has the potential to combine recognized achievement with educational enquiry. But in practice this ambition has been difficult to realize. In seeking to foster a teaching excellence that integrates achievement, experience and enquiry, it could learn much from the CSP. If Teaching Fellows are to contribute to pedagogical knowledge within their disciplines and to engage in collective activities, the residency programme in CSP has much to offer. The community building and support offered for educational enquiry are of key importance here. There is also an issue of history and vision. Although the NTFS has been running for four years, it is not located within a clear movement or educational tradition like the CSP, which is underpinned by the Carnegie Foundation. The ILTHE initially managed the NTFS, and was still forming an identity and vision when replaced by the Higher Education Academy. The work of the ILTHE is now included within the remit of the HEA but there may be a period of adaptation or change as the new organization evolves. This history has clearly influenced the degree to which the NTFS has been underpinned by a clear sense of value and direction.

Future possibilities: teaching excellence and scholarship

Three versions of 'teaching excellence' were implicitly present at the San Diego meeting. One emphasized recognized achievement, one systematic enquiry and the third attempted to forge a relationship between these two aspects. It is possible to imagine a future scenario where two large movements – one called 'excellence' and once called 'scholarship' – follow their own separate paths within the higher education community. This would have the benefit of avoiding some of the difficult tensions that emerged for the NTFS in the UK.

The implications of separating excellence from scholarship, however, are potentially far-reaching. A teaching excellence that is concerned with recognized performance but has little interest in investigating its impact on student learning appears to be short-sighted. On the other hand, an excellence premised on systematic enquiry with little grounding in experience or a knowledge of the field lacks substance. Both of these understandings of teaching excellence have their strengths and weaknesses, but taken together, they offer a much more powerful and compelling impetus for the development of teaching and learning within the sector.

If teaching excellence were to involve scholarship, what would this entail? In the CSP, there is a view that SoTL has the same qualities as any good piece of research: there is the same intellectual commitment, and the quality of research is assessed with reference to standards of judgement that are equivalent to those used in discovery research (for example, a concern to conceptualize the enquiry, to adopt appropriate methodology, to be systematic in data collection and rigorous in interpreting potential findings). This approach to SoTL gives legitimacy to the knowledge generated by teacher/scholars. One of the limitations of the NTFS in the UK concerns the quality of knowledge that is generated through its project investigations (see Chapter 3, p. 53). The Teaching Fellows receive little in the way of academic support for these projects and little opportunity to learn from an interdisciplinary sharing of project designs.

Insights from the CSP help us to understand how excellent teachers might undertake systematic enquiry and make legitimate contributions to the developing knowledge base about teaching and learning. However experienced teachers may be within their own disciplines, they can benefit from a sense of what educational enquiry involves and examples of previous studies. My interviews with Carnegie Scholars suggested that it is important to encourage people to initiate educational enquiries with methods that are familiar to them. Some people will have developed, through their disciplinary-based research, methods of enquiry that may have potential for SoTL. Having considered familiar approaches in the context of specific enquiries, and once they have developed the confidence to contemplate alternatives, it is likely that people will develop their methodological repertoire (see Hutchings, 2000). Interdisciplinary sharing of possible methodologies supports this process, allowing people to pool ideas and think about different ways in which to approach a problem or issue. Those offering academic support can also support the process of educational enquiry by giving details of previous SoTL work and methods employed. This helps to prevent what one Carnegie Scholar termed the 'Discovering America' syndrome: that situation where enthusiastic teachers feel they have discovered something new about teaching and learning only to find later that it has already been researched by many others!

A teaching excellence which integrates recognized achievement with ongoing scholarship is not only powerful but threatening. If excellent teachers become knowledge producers, they break out of the classroom and the limiting discourse of 'performance'. The systemic enquiries they undertake, located within SoTL, cannot be cast aside amidst accusations that they lack legitimacy or because they are not grounded in experience and accumulated wisdom. Furthermore, as experienced professionals who often hold senior positions within institutions, excellent teachers who undertake systematic enquiries are well placed to disseminate their work with authority.

A teaching excellence that involves scholarship threatens established territory. For example, Faculties of Education (FOE) may feel that they are best placed to develop knowledge about teaching and learning. It was interesting to note that comments made by the Carnegie Scholars were often similar to those made by NTFS Fellows about FOE. It was suggested that FOE are not necessarily interested in questions about teaching and learning, that they tended to focus on school-based education and that their work was often not seen to be of high status by members of different faculties given that education was regarded as an applied field rather than a distinct discipline.

Central government and state agencies responsible for higher education may also be threatened by knowledge-producing teachers. Following attacks on the teaching profession in many countries and the development of an associated discourse of 'education in crisis', governments have sought to impose greater central control over teaching and learning through national curricula and other regulatory frameworks. These limit the degree of freedom teachers have to determine what and how they teach, with the result that they have become increasingly seen, in government circles, as 'deliverers' of knowledge rather than knowledge 'producers.' It is interesting to note that in one of the NTFS interviews (see Chapter 3), one Fellow commented that there must have been some initial anxiety, within HEFCE, about how the first group of Teaching Fellows would interpret their role. Would they see themselves as a group sympathetic to government policy or one that advocated a different set of values? Would they be content with developing practical tools in support of government policy (for example, technological applications to support increasing numbers of students entering higher education) or would they produce knowledge of a different kind?

Excellent teachers as knowledge producers

A teaching excellence that seeks to integrate recognized achievement with ongoing scholarship has to consider the scope of that scholarship. In the design of systematic enquiries, excellent teacher/scholars could conceivably ask questions related to the purposes, content and methods of higher education: these might be termed in short the 'why', 'what' and 'how' of scholarship. Enquiries may also be located at different levels of analysis, for example, at the level of the system, institution, department or one's own practice.

Drawing on work undertaken within the NTFS and CSP, it is possible to get a sense of the scope of scholarship within these two programmes. Within the NTFS, the individual development projects undertaken by Teacher Fellows resemble a form of practical action research. They focus on the teacher's own practice and are concerned principally with changes to delivery methods, often drawing upon new technologies. In the CSP, again the focus is the teacher's own practice, but the questions asked appear to be broader in scope and include conceptual work and attempts to make sense of learning situations.

Most of the NTFS projects were located within existing educational policy. This meant that HEFCE did not have to suffer the embarrassment of an award winner challenging policy or using their project to consider policy alternatives. During my interviews with Carnegie Scholars, some people mentioned that systematic enquiries into their own practice had revealed the need for action at other levels to ensure the success of a teaching innovation (for example, support from senior management). Both of these examples suggest forms of scholarship that are relatively new and emergent. One Carnegie Scholar thought that as the SoTL movement became more mature, the standard of work produced would be of a higher quality. With greater confidence derived from experience, they argued, teacher/scholars would begin to contextualize their work more fully in terms of theoretical concepts, context, methods and strategy. This suggests the possibility of a broader-based notion of teachers as knowledge producers. A teaching excellence that incorporates scholarship should not only involve teachers investigating delivery methods; it should also encourage them to ask questions about the purposes of teaching and learning in higher education and the different contexts within which these practices are located.

Of course a range of difficulties arise when teachers seek to contribute to the knowledge base about teaching and learning in higher education. Some of these difficulties became apparent in my own research of the NTFS in the UK, while others were identified by Carnegie Scholars and Senior Program Staff. A teaching excellence that incorporates serious scholarship has to address a number of issues, including:

- How to make connections with previous work that is relevant to the scholarship. This can be difficult in the field of higher education teaching and learning given that the field is fragmented and constituted by a range of often competing voices (these include work undertaken by educational developers, adult educators, educational researchers in FOE, practitioners within disciplines who contribute to SoTL and senior colleagues within the SoTL movement).
- Cumulation: how to ensure that scholarship actively takes forward existing knowledge. This is related to the above but different in the sense that it addresses issues of progression and development.
- Theory building: how to develop meta-level theory about teaching and learning in higher education from scholarship that is often practice-based and context-specific.
- Getting work recognized by the wider community: not just 'preaching to the converted' but persuading colleagues from outside the SoTL movement. Bringing together the existing 'excellence' and 'scholarship' communities would represent a start in this direction.
- Influencing educational policy: how to ensure that teacher scholarship is treated seriously by policy makers. This can be difficult if scholarship engages critically with policy or adopts methodologies which do not lead to generalizable findings. It is interesting to note that one suggested area of collaboration at the San Diego meeting focused on exploring the role of excellent teachers in educational policy and change. All the schemes at the meeting are beginning to give greater thought to this issue. For example, one of the aims of the new Council of 3M Teaching Fellows (a subset of award winners from the Canadian Scheme) is to contribute to policy in becoming 'a national voice on teaching and learning issues'.

Conclusion

In this chapter I have attempted to anticipate what the future holds for teaching excellence. I have made reference to an international meeting in

San Diego which brought together award-winning teachers and other individuals interested in teaching excellence to foster collaborations and joint projects. The teachers came from the USA, the UK and Canada, and all had been recognized for excellence in teaching and learning. As I got to know more about the three different programmes which gave awards to these teachers, it became clear that there were both similarities and differences between them and some confusing areas in between. One of the confusing areas that interested me in particular was the use of the term 'scholarship' in CSP which was preferred to teaching excellence. As I explored this and other questions through interviews with the Carnegie Scholars, I was able to gain a deeper understanding of the CSP and how systematic educational enquiry is supported through a residency system. The interviews also suggested that although excellence and scholarship might be viewed as two separate entities, they had much to offer each other. I concluded that a teaching excellence that incorporated scholarship was one of increased strength and resilience, since the commitment to serious enquiry would allow teaching excellence to remain dynamic and reflexive. I then looked at what would be required to support such an understanding of teaching excellence within the CSP, the NTFS and the 3M Scheme, suggesting ways in which the schemes might develop in the future. The chapter therefore demonstrates that important lessons can be learned from comparing understandings of teaching excellence across national boundaries – something that I hope to be able to pursue in greater depth in subsequent research.

The focus of the next chapter is research into teaching excellence. It offers some initial discussion on the current state of pedagogical research in higher education, an outline of work on excellence carried out to date and suggestions for future practice. Four key themes emerge during the chapter. These are: who should undertake research into teaching excellence? How will it be conducted? What ought to be the focus of this research? And what role might evidence play?

Chapter 11

Research into teaching excellence in higher education

Introduction

The last chapter made reference to the Carnegie Scholars Program in the USA which maintains that, with appropriate guidance and support, practising teachers are capable of undertaking pedagogical research and contributing to our knowledge base about teaching and learning in higher education. In this chapter, I want to explore pedagogical research in more depth, focusing in particular on research into teaching excellence. Four themes which feature in the course of the discussion are:

- *Who* will undertake this research?
- *How* will it be conducted?
- What should be the *focus* of research into teaching excellence in higher education?'
- What role might *evidence* play?

In order to set the scene, I offer some important background information on the current state of pedagogical research in higher education and recent calls for an 'evidence-based' approach to teaching and learning. I then identify different ways in which people have researched teaching excellence to date before outlining 'alternative visions' for future practice.

Pedagogical research in higher education

In Chapter 9, it was noted that since the 1970s there has been a growing recognition that university teaching is struggling to keep pace with advances in disciplinary knowledge, the needs of an expanding and diverse student body and new ideas about how to teach derived from training and research publications. There is now a broad consensus that more pedagogical research needs to be undertaken to support teaching and learning in higher education (Yorke, 2000; Steirer and Antoniou, 2004). There is also agreement that practitioners need to be encouraged to engage with pedagogical research and to draw upon such research in the development of their teaching (DfES, 2003: 54).

In recent years, higher education policy in many countries has sought to promote the development and dissemination of pedagogical research. In the UK, its strategic significance to the development of a mass higher education system was recognized in the Dearing Report (NCIHE, 1997). One of the remits of the ILTHE, which was established on the recommendation of Dearing, was to support 'Research and development in learning and teaching' (ibid.: para. 8.64ff). The Higher Education Academy (HEA), which has now replaced the ILTHE, also lists as one of its strategic aims: 'Lead[ing] the development of research and evaluation to improve the quality of the student experience through evidence-based practice' – (http://www.heacademy.ac.uk/184_187.htm). The HEA has taken over responsibility (from the ILTHE) for the accreditation of professional development courses for university lecturers. Such courses offer one important way in which higher education teachers can gain access to pedagogical research and its potential implications for practice.

Given the growing significance attached to pedagogical research in higher education, there have been a number of attempts to summarize its current state and future possibilities. Two notable contributions to the debate are Yorke (2000) and Steirer and Antoniou (2004). The picture that emerges from this work is somewhat troubled. The authors maintain that pedagogical research has been undervalued to date and there is a recognition, given the greater value and status accorded to particular approaches in research assessment exercises, that most lecturers choose 'to undertake research in their academic discipline rather than in the pedagogy related to that discipline' (Yorke, 2000: 106). Pedagogical research in higher education is also largely invisible, with few published texts available to support practitioner enquiry. It is perhaps no surprise, therefore, that there is little consensus over what pedagogical research entails and, perhaps more worryingly, a lack of any real debate about these things (Steirer and Antoniou, 2004: 277).

Within this context, a pedagogical research field has developed that is highly fragmented and constituted by different 'voices'. Diverse groups of people are undertaking pedagogical research from a range of starting positions. For example, educational developers (generalists and within disciplines), educational researchers specializing in teaching and learning in higher education, and practising lecturers are all contributing to this emergent field. They disseminate their work to different audiences and there are few meaningful fora for these groups to come together to discuss their work. One reading of the current fragmented nature of the field is positive: it could lead to a vibrant research culture that values experimentation and a plurality of approaches. On the other hand, such fragmentation could also become problematic since a sense of shared understandings and purposes may be difficult to establish. Any sense of pedagogic research in higher education providing a rational foundation for practice seems unlikely in such a situation since it is difficult for disparate studies to build on from one another and '(ac)cumulate' (see Yorke, 2000: 110).

Several attempts have been made to review research into various aspects of teaching and learning in higher education and to draw conclusions from the presented work (for example: Brown and Atkins, 1988; Ramsden, 1992; Biggs, 1999; and Prosser and Trigwell, 1999). But in the absence of a large, established group of professional researchers, a significant proportion of pedagogical research is carried out by practitioners within the disciplines and is characteristically small-scale and context-specific (Steirer and Antoniou, 2004: 283). Some of this research is undertaken as part of professional development programmes (for example, masters-level dissertation work) and tends to adopt a loose 'action research' orientation and structure (Yorke, 2000: 110). The emphasis in much of this work is on the development of the individual's own teaching, often involving the introduction and evaluation of a new method or set of materials. The strengths and weaknesses of this type of research have been noted in Chapter 3, when considering the project work of the NTFS in England and Northern Ireland. Its strengths, for example, include its practical relevance and potential for practitioner collaboration. Its weaknesses are that it can be under-theorized and insufficiently related to previous work in the field, leading to problems of 'reinventing the wheel' (Bell, 1982). The difference between 'methods' and 'methodology' is also rarely acknowledged. Methods are often deployed without due regard for the 'frameworks and concepts in which methods are situated ... which provide the rationale and justification (intellectual, epistemological and ethical) for the methods that are selected and the ways in which they are used' (Steirer and Antoniou, 2004: 278).

A considerable body of pedagogical research has already been conducted in other sectors of education, for example, in schools and adult education settings. This work clearly has potential relevance for practitioners with a disciplinary and research background other than education but, as Steirer and Antoniou point out, practitioner/researchers may find it difficult to engage in and learn from this work due to its lack of 'face validity' (ibid.: 283). This is not surprising since higher education has distinctive surface characteristics, and students differ from school pupils in a number of important ways, for example their adult status, voluntary attendance and 'wider-life' commitments. For these reasons, Steirer and Antoniou (ibid.: 279–80) suggest that pedagogical research in higher education may warrant distinctive methodologies. Recognizing that practitioner/researchers tend to draw, at least initially, on disciplinary understandings of pedagogy and methodology in conducting research into teaching and learning, they advocate the use of *hybrid methodologies* as one way in which this distinctiveness might be expressed. Hybrid methodologies 'represent syntheses of educational research traditions and traditions from their own disciplines' (ibid.: 284). As noted in the last chapter, such hybrids seem to be emerging in the context of the Carnegie Scholars Program, and one recommendation I made in the light of my own work on the NTFS was that award winners would benefit from academic support from experienced educational researchers. This would help them to: 'locate their work within existing research traditions, and to develop disciplinary perspectives on teaching and learning in higher education' (Skelton, 2004: 464).

The development of hybrid methodologies is one of the most exciting challenges facing pedagogical research in higher education. But such development may need to be tethered to more humble yet important projects, such as producing summaries and synopses of existing pedagogical research across a wide range of themes (Yorke, 2000: 112). It is important to note, however, that in addition to the issues that are currently exercising the minds of those who actively research into pedagogical research come other 'imported' concerns from outside higher education and from beyond education itself. In recent years, the calls for 'evidence-based' practice (EBP) across the professions have grown louder and louder, becoming the favoured parlance of politicians and policy makers. It is to EBP we now turn, since this has significant implications for the future development of pedagogical research in higher education which may, in turn, also have an impact on investigation into teaching excellence specifically.

Towards 'evidence-based' teaching in higher education?

There is a growing assumption that pedagogical research can provide the evidence base for teaching and learning in higher education. For example, the theme of an HEA conference in the UK during July 2004 was 'An evidence based approach in higher education – how far can we take it?' In the publicity for this conference, the following question was posed: 'how can we move from states of awareness and action based on our perceptions and beliefs of the way the world works to states of awareness and action that are informed by evidence of how it *actually* works?' (emphasis added). The idea of EBP is gaining prominence in higher education, but where has such an approach come from and what are its merits?

EBP has its origins in the biomedical sciences and has recently been 'imported' into the educational field (Pirrie, 2001: 124). In the light of a sustained attack on educational research (Hargreaves, 1996, 1997; Hillage *et al.*, 1998; Tooley and Darby, 1998) and the ensuing 'moral panic' that followed, EBP has been taken up with almost 'missionary zeal' by many practitioners and researchers in the UK (Harden *et al.*, 1999). In the USA, a similar situation prevails, with educational research being deemed to be in crisis and unable to provide objective and reliable findings that policy makers can trust (NRC, 2002). A critical perspective on this situation, however, maintains that EBP is being used, by the government, as a justification for legislating scientific method in educational research (Lather, 2004).

It has been observed that many of the foremost champions of EBP are those that precipitated the view that educational research was in crisis in the first place (Pirrie, ibid.: 126). The view that education and health care are different activities which require different research approaches has been countered by Davies (1999), who maintains that the processes and outcomes of both are highly complex, often indeterminate and context-specific, making their measurement problematic (ibid.: 112). EBP is now well established in health care (Sackett *et al.*, 1996) and beginning to influence policy and practice in education. School-focused educational research has borne the brunt of the criticisms although it has been noted that peda-gogical research in higher education has suffered by association, becoming 'vulnerable to what military strategists euphemistically term "collateral damage"' (Yorke, 2001: 107).

EBP is being put forward as an antidote to all that is currently perceived to be wrong with educational research, for example its lack of scientific rigour and relevance to the practitioner community. Pirrie (2001) questions EBP, however, stating that its use in education is 'fundamentally misguided'. She points out that there is little evidence to support its intro-duction and take-up within the medical and educational fields, citing the review of EBP by Harden *et al.* (1999). In the context of this and other work, she suggests that if educational practice and research should become more evidence-based, then educational policy should too (Pirrie, 2001: 126). Following on from this, she points out that there is no such thing as 'context-free' evidence, and the belief that evidence 'speaks for itself' hides the social and political context in which research operates. She concludes:

> It would ultimately be to the detriment of educational research if the spirit of critical enquiry were to be crushed in a ragged stampede towards 'evidence-based' practice...It would be a matter of regret if 'educational research' were to be narrowly construed as producing toolkits for teachers.

> (Ibid.: 133)

Similar sentiments have been expressed in the USA, where educational researchers (predominantly but not exclusively from the qualitative tradition) have questioned the evidence-based movement, its championing of randomized field trials as a 'gold-standard' methodology and its narrow view of what constitutes scientific research in education (Tierney, 2001; Cochran-Smith, 2002; Eisenhart and Towne, 2003). There is a concern that EBP is being used to 'discipline' educational research (in the Foucauldian sense), so that it delivers support for government policies and increasing management control (Lather, 2004: 763).

Despite these reservations, EBP is currently being linked with the identification of professional standards for higher education teaching. Following on from this, an important question that needs to be asked is: *who* will create this evidence base? In the last chapter, a 'grass-roots' and 'bottom-up' approach to developing knowledge and understanding about teaching and learning was presented through discussion of the CSP in the USA. In the CSP, higher education teachers are seen as knowledge producers who, with guidance and support, are capable of contributing to the knowledge base about teaching and learning. Here in the UK and in other countries embracing EBP, it appears unlikely that higher education teachers will be trusted to generate the evidence base for professional teaching standards. An implicit distinction is beginning to be made between pedagogical research (PedR) and pedagogical development (PedD). PedR is large-scale 'scientific' pedagogical research that can supply the necessary evidence for teaching and learning practice in higher education. PedD, on the other hand, refers to small-scale investigations that teachers make into their own practice with a view to improving that practice. Sometimes this work is called 'action research' and teachers may disseminate findings to colleagues within their own department or institution, or even to other colleagues within the sector. Much of the work undertaken by practitioners within disciplines resembles this form of PedD. It is also sometimes referred to as research of the 'soft applied' variety (Biglan, 1973), often qualitative in nature and highly context-specific. These characteristics are precisely those that have been vilified in recent attacks on educational research. Alleged weaknesses of such work include its non-cumulative character and the lack of large centres to coordinate activity (Hargreaves, 1998).

In my interviews with HEFCE and ILTHE senior personnel during the NTFS research, it was evident that they made a distinction between PedR and PedD. Even though national Teaching Fellows thought that they were undertaking 'research projects' as part of the award for £50,000, this was not a view shared by HEFCE and ILTHE personnel, who preferred the term 'development activities'. When asked in interview about who would undertake research into teaching and learning in higher education, reference was made to established researchers rather than practitioners within disciplines.

In the following section, I move the discussion to focus specifically on research into teaching excellence. I look at the different kinds of research that have been conducted to date into teaching excellence. I then consider how EBP positions these different approaches and what implications the emerging split between PedR and PedD is likely to have for our understanding of 'what counts' as teaching excellence research.

Researching teaching excellence

The previous sections have clarified the pedagogical research context within which the specific study of teaching excellence is situated. Research into teaching excellence to date shares many of the characteristics of pedagogical research in higher education *per se*, for example its limited quantity, fragmented nature and relative 'invisibility'. In my research for this book I often found it difficult to find work on teaching excellence and, when I did, it was located in very obscure and unexpected places! Looking at the research that has been conducted to date, it is possible to identify three main approaches:

1. *Operational*: research and evaluation studies of initiatives to promote teaching excellence, such as teaching award schemes, and institutional teaching and learning strategies. They are often carried out by 'in-house' researchers or recognized experts in the field who report to a specific brief. For example, the research might consider how effectively an initiative is operating in order to demonstrate value for money to potential stakeholder groups and/or how successful it is in realizing operational objectives. This type of research is often conducted for state agencies and carries significant strategic import. It is conducted independently but is often located within a given policy context or set of operational assumptions. I have included in this category 'defini-tional' and conceptual work about teaching excellence that is focused primarily on supporting developmental initiatives – for example, work that attempts to define teaching excellence and identify its component parts for teaching award schemes (examples of operational research: Elton and Partington, 1993; Brown, 2000; HEFCE, 2001a, 2001b, 2002).

2. *Inductive*: research into the educational philosophies, teaching concepts, practices and personal characteristics of excellent teachers. The research seeks to reveal the 'essence' of teaching excellence that is assumed to reside within the teachers concerned. It seeks to clarify teaching excel-lence so that it can be promoted more generally within the sector, with excellent teachers often held up as 'role models' for others to follow. The research is undertaken by 'expert' educational researchers. What excellence entails is generated inductively from the study of award-winning practitioners. The systems of selection that recognized the teachers as excellent in the first place are largely absent from these accounts; administrative procedures are implicitly or explicitly held to be 'value-neutral' (examples: Dunkin and Precians, 1992; Dunkin, 1995; Johnston, 1996; Baiocca and DeWalters, 1998; Kreber, 2000; Hativa *et al.*, 2001).

3. *Insider*: research into the experiences of excellent teachers and their development work undertaken by the teachers themselves. Much of this

research focuses on the implementation of practical solutions to teaching problems and adopts a loose 'action research' structure. It also includes work, however, that highlights the subjective dimension of winning an award – for example, the meaning of awards for individual teachers and the purposes their development work serves. The subjectivity of insider accounts is both their strength and limitation: we get 'up close' to the teachers and their practices but are offered little about the 'bigger picture' or macro context of teaching and learning in higher education in which teaching awards and their subjective interpretation by teachers are located (examples: work published by national Teaching Fellows and other award winners).

These different types of research offer particular insights and perspectives on teaching excellence. They carry different assumptions about *what* is important to study, *how* to study it and *who* can generate knowledge about teaching excellence. In the next section, I focus on EBP and its potential implications for research into teaching excellence. I examine how EBP positions operational, inductive and insider research, and what significance the emerging split between PedR and PedD is likely to have for teaching excellence research.

'Evidence-based' teaching excellence?

At this time it is difficult to predict with any confidence what impact EBP will have on research into teaching excellence in higher education. Currently EBP is being presented as the foundation for professional standards of teaching and learning rather than for 'higher levels' of practice. Teaching excellence could remain relatively sheltered from the EBP movement or it may be subject to increasing influence. EBP could be charged with the responsibility of finding an evidential base for teaching excellence. Once located, this would make it relatively easy, from a management perspective, to recognize and reward excellent teachers, since there would be more confidence in selection criteria.

In the preceding discussion about EBP, it was noted that higher education policy itself is not necessarily evidence-based (Pirrie, 2001: 126). A good example of this is the proliferation of award schemes for teaching excellence when research has shown them to be one of the least effective ways of promoting teaching (see Chapter 3, pp. 43–6). One of the unexpected consequences of an EBP approach to teaching excellence may therefore be that it encourages a more critical engagement with higher education policy.

As mentioned earlier in the chapter, there is growing support for EBP within the higher education sector. EBP works from the assumption that large-scale, scientifically robust research can generate findings that are objective, reliable and generalizable to the wider population. Experts are expected to carry out such research and disseminate their work to the practitioner community. EBP distinguishes between a PedR that is expert-driven and capable of prediction, explanation and verification, and a PedD that is practitioner-led, descriptive and focused on practice. Proponents of EBP believe that the former can generate a legitimate knowledge base about teaching and teaching excellence, whereas the latter is viewed as having a softer and more 'developmental' quality: it has a context-specific relevance of value to the practitioner/researcher and their immediate colleagues.

From an EBP standpoint, operational and inductive research into teaching excellence has a legitimacy given that it is conducted by expert researchers. It is recognized as PedR, although some inductive work may be viewed as having limited application due to its small sample size. Insider research into teaching excellence, on the other hand, is likely to be considered PedD due to its subjective nature and context specificity. Although there is potential here for the development of 'hybrid methodologies' and fruitful collaborations between practitioners and experts, insider accounts are unlikely to be considered sufficiently robust and objective to generate an evidence-based teaching excellence.

A high proportion of existing pedagogical research is carried out by practitioner/researchers and one exciting contemporary development is the tentative emergence of hybrid methodologies. It would seem to be short-sighted, therefore, if research into teaching and teaching excellence were restricted to 'top–down' studies that require expert researchers. An exclusive reliance on methodologies that can produce findings generalizable to large populations also seems restrictive. This may limit what research questions can be posed, who can pose them and how they are framed. One criticism that has been made of EBP is that it completely ignores the recognized limitations of conducting experimental research in educational settings and the shortcomings of using causal models, given the significance of interaction effects in such settings (Lather, 2004: 763). These limitations point to 'how social science might serve us better than the parade of behaviourism, cognitivism, structuralism and neopositivism that have all failed successfully to study human activity in a way modelled after the assumedly cumulative, predictive and stable natural sciences' (ibid.: 760). Such comments evoke broader debates about the quality of research and the legitimacy of different approaches that have existed for many years in the educational research community. 'Paradigm wars' have been the norm, as conflicts have emerged between positivistic, interpretative, critical and postmodern approaches (Hammersley, 1992). Perhaps one important indication of the maturity of a research community is its ability to tolerate diverse approaches and its capacity to learn from difference (Sparkes, 1992). Working across paradigms and the creation of 'blurred genres' (Geertz, 1983) that do not fit neatly into established traditions have become more commonplace in educational research and with these a greater sophistication and reflexivity among researchers has emerged.

Alternative visions for research into teaching excellence

It is the contention of this chapter that a wide range of approaches to the study of teaching excellence can benefit the sector. Operational, inductive and insider research all have their place, but it is important to recognize their limitations. Hybrid methodologies represent a way in which disciplinary traditions and culture can inform pedagogical research and generate knowledge about teaching excellence that is relevant to particular communities. The coming together of disciplinary and existing educational research traditions offers creative possibilities but also significant challenges. Educational research, beset by paradigm wars, conceptualizes the relationship between theory and data in different ways and operates according to very different standards of judgement (NERF, 2000). Whilst EBP quite properly encourages us to consider the importance of evidence and to move beyond 'common sense' thinking (Ramsden, 2004), when located in relation to existing educational research traditions it represents just one vision for the future among the many that exist.

EBP is premised on large-scale, scientific research that can produce generalizable findings. It has its origins in the biomedical sciences and has much in common with the positivistic paradigm in educational research. Research into teaching and teaching excellence in higher education should not be confined to such a paradigm, since this will limit the research questions that can be addressed. The ideological position of the researcher, and their epistemological and ontological leanings, may also influence their choice of paradigm and the way they frame their research.

Drawing on the four ideal-type understandings of teaching excellence in Chapter 2, it is possible to generate very different research agendas in relation to teaching excellence. A brief outline of some of the issues and themes likely to be pertinent to researchers working from these different ideal-type positions on excellence is given below:

- *Traditional*: the maintenance of teaching excellence in the light of student expansion and increasing diversity; the relationship between teaching excellence and student attainment; teaching excellence as 'research-led' teaching; teaching excellence and the process of knowledge acquisition; the relationship between teaching excellence and subject disciplines (for example, their epistemological structure and cultural practices).
- *Performative*: teaching excellence and its contribution to national economic performance; problem-based teaching and student learning; teaching that is informed by the 'employability' and 'enterprise'

agendas; innovative uses of technology to make teaching more accessible to students; the evaluation of systems designed to assure, enhance and promote teaching excellence.

- *Psychologized*: differentiating teaching to meet the individual needs of students; 'learning-style' research; finding interesting and innovative ways to motivate students; resolving mismatches in student and teacher perceptions of teaching and learning situations; identifying the personal characteristics of excellent teachers and how these contribute to effective teaching and learning experiences; interactional studies, focusing on patterns of communication and group dynamics.
- *Critical*: teaching excellence and student emancipation; how the discourse of teaching excellence distracts attention away from the declining material conditions of higher education; what counts as knowledge in universities and who decides; increasing state control over universities and academic freedom; the development of inclusive learning environments; challenging the normative assumptions built into disciplinary cultures, curricula and pedagogical practices; democratic teaching relationships and formations (for example 'ideal speech situations', see Chapter 2, p. 34).

Conclusion

This chapter has described the broader pedagogical research context within which the specific study of teaching excellence is situated. Existing research into teaching excellence shares many of the general features of pedagogical research in higher education, notably its limited quantity, fragmented nature and relative 'invisibility'. Three main approaches to the study of teaching excellence can be detected in the literature: operational, inductive and insider research.

Two contemporary developments appear to be pulling pedagogical research in different directions. The first is the tentative emergence of hybrid methodologies. These are developed when practitioner researchers, with appropriate guidance and support, forge a productive relationship between their disciplinary and established educational research methodologies. The second development is EBP. EBP originated in the biomedical sciences and has been imported into the educational field. In the light of a sustained attack on educational research, it has gained increasing support and is currently being linked to the development of professional standards for teaching and learning in the UK.

It is difficult at present to predict what impact EBP and hybrid methodologies will have on future research into teaching excellence in higher education. Currently EBP is being put forward as the foundation for professional standards rather than for 'higher levels' of practice. The position taken in this chapter is that it would be short-sighted if research into teaching and teaching excellence became restricted by the EBP movement and a narrow empiricism or instrumentality (Yorke, 2000). Given the limited research into teaching excellence to date, we should be encouraging engagement rather than putting up barriers.

One indication of a mature research community is its ability to respect diverse approaches, to be reflexive, and to learn from difference. With this in mind, four alternative research agendas for future work into teaching excellence have been outlined, drawing on the ideal-type understandings presented in Chapter 2. Funding needs to be available that will support teaching excellence research of different kinds, not simply large-scale studies premised on positivistic assumptions. Further opportunities for researchers to share their ideas and approaches need to be created. If teaching excellence in higher education is important, then research into teaching excellence should be of a high quality. This is something we should insist on as a basis for any rational foundation for practice.

Chapter 12

Conclusion

> The underlying assumption of ... this year's scheme is that we all know
> what good teaching is; therefore it is not really a very big issue. I don't
> feel that for a minute. I think there has been very little debate within
> higher education about what good teaching is and that there is no
> reason at all to assume that the people on the panel are particularly
> good at defining it. My hope at the beginning of the scheme was that
> this would be an opportunity for academics involved in teaching to
> actually come together and work out between themselves what they
> understood to be good teaching.
>
> (National Advisory Panel member, NTFS, 2000)

The importance of debate

Over the last decade a wide range of policy initiatives have been introduced
to raise the status of teaching and learning in higher education. Labelled as
the 'poor relation' of the research/teaching divide, teaching has benefited
from these new initiatives and associated funding streams to spark innovation and embed good practice. Policies and discourses that have focused on
teaching excellence have used it as a performative lever to drive up general
standards. Teachers who have won awards for excellence have been in the
vanguard of this drive: through example and interaction with others, they
have been entrusted with promoting teaching and learning across the sector
as a whole.

In the midst of all the initiatives it is often very difficult to establish what
anyone means by 'teaching excellence' and the underlying purpose(s) it is
meant to serve. In the rush to 'do' something about teaching, to innovate
and to enhance its status among the higher education community, an
important opportunity for serious debate about its quality (referred to in
the comments above by an NTFS Advisory Panel member) has been passed
by. The time is right for such deliberation given the changes that have
occurred recently both inside and outside the academy. The rapid shift from

elite to mass systems, increasing student diversity, the emergence of new technologies and the increasing epistemological and ontological uncertainty of higher education institutions all suggest the need for a proper engagement with teaching and what we understand by excellence in teaching. The title of the series to which this book contributes is 'Key Issues in Higher Education'. One conclusion that emerges from this book is that we have yet to have a satisfactory debate about the key issue of teaching excellence. There has been little real debate about whether the pursuit of teaching excellence is a 'good thing' and little debate of any substance about what it means and the type of higher education it is trying to foster.

Perhaps the first of these 'debating points' is already off the agenda. Given policy commitments in this area, it is unlikely that teaching excellence will be interrogated at this deep level, and if this happens, such debate is likely to be confined to the margins. The second debating point carries more potential. It is possible to view our current situation as 50 per cent complete. Teaching excellence *has* been put squarely on the higher education agenda, but we now need to ask: 'what *sort* of teaching excellence do we want and what is it trying to achieve?'

The intellectual culture of higher education requires such a debate if teaching excellence is to become a meaningful concept (a question that was posed in Chapter 1). Academics expect to interrogate concepts, to understand their origins and to consider competing interpretations. If mechanisms designed to promote teaching excellence are to have any lasting effect in higher education, then there needs to be some recognition, on the part of the academic community, that such mechanisms have been thought through and adequately conceptualized. Sufficient planning time needs to be given to managers of award schemes for teaching excellence to enable them to consider research evidence and provide opportunities for robust deliberation between stakeholder groups.

If there are no real opportunities to debate teaching excellence, this will have significant repercussions. At the very least it will give rise to policies aimed at promoting excellence that are muddled, incomplete or contradictory. The NTFS is a good example of this (see Chapter 3). It set out with noble ambitions but suffered from the tension between wanting to recognize existing achievement and supporting future development. Given this tension, it only achieved moderate success with the latter, due to confusion over the development aspect of the scheme (its relative importance compared to rewarding existing achievement); whether a 'research' project was required (which discouraged some institutions from entering: see Chapter 4); and the limited direction and support given to the Fellows' collective activities (see Chapter 3, pp. 53–4). These difficulties reflect deeper uncertainties about the meaning of teaching excellence that could have been resolved at the outset (see Chapter 10 for a discussion of how recognized excellence and developmental enquiry might be brought together in a productive relationship). Further problems emerged when NTFS panel members sought to conceptualize teaching excellence and clarify criteria for the scheme. Offered little in the way of background material on meta-level debates about education that underpin understandings of teaching excellence, they also had to devise criteria in a context characterized by 'speed and efficiency'. This gave them little time to deliberate on matters of substance, so it was unsurprising that assessment difficulties emerged later, with one panel member attributing this to 'the lack of discussion about the meaning of the criteria'.

Other significant muddles currently surround teaching excellence that are at least partly attributable to the lack of real debate about its meaning and purpose. For example, many countries are pursuing a process of educational reform in which teaching excellence is being used performatively to increase system efficiency and to harness higher education teaching for the good of the economy. This performative use of teaching excellence is an implicit policy goal rather than something that is explicit and subject to serious critical scrutiny. At the same time governments are attempting to respect the histories, missions and autonomy of higher education institutions through policies devoted to diversification. Although the overall aim is still performative in seeking to stimulate system performance through diversity and competition, this policy gives rise to different understandings of teaching excellence, and some of these are not premised on economic productivity.

The new CETL programme in the UK (see Chapter 4, p. 67–8) is a good example of policy support for diversification, with large numbers of institutional centres of teaching excellence being created. It is possible to see this programme as a postmodern 'celebration of difference', with multiple expressions of teaching excellence coming into being. One cannot fail to be impressed by the wide range of innovative work being proposed. In reading through the applications, however, it is difficult not to come to the conclusion that teaching excellence can mean almost anything. In this situation, the potential for tensions between implicit government agendas to do with the relationship between higher education and the economy, policies on institutional diversity, notions of academic freedom and whether there is a need for some shared vision about higher education teaching and its purpose become apparent. Further debate about these tensions and how they might be resolved is crucial in order for teaching excellence to be a meaningful force in the future.

There are also contradictions between policies designed to promote teaching excellence and those that concentrate on excellence in research. For example, award schemes may try to foster teaching excellence but research assessment exercises pull in the opposite direction and encourage people to see teaching as a burden. It is no surprise, therefore, that some people find that receiving an award for teaching, particularly in 'research-intensive' institutions, becomes a 'poisoned chalice' (see Chapter 3, p. 55).

Clearly there is a need for higher education policies to demonstrate 'joined-up thinking' if they are to be effective. But the policy contradictions relating to teaching and research reflect deeper uncertainties about the teaching/research relationship in higher education. This uncertainty, as noted in Chapter 4 (pp. 64–7), is evident in policies and discourses related to teaching excellence. The ambivalent status of 'research-led' teaching demonstrates that there is still some confusion as to what significance disciplinary research has for teaching excellence. And the contribution that pedagogical research might make to it is even more unclear! There is a real need, therefore, for a sustained debate about these issues if teaching excellence is to be given the chance it deserves.

In Chapter 11 it was noted that higher education policy and specific policies related to teaching and teaching excellence do not appear to be evidence-based. Serious debate about teaching excellence and the quality of research that generates evidence about it makes this situation more difficult to sustain. Award schemes for individual teachers have been introduced, for example, more as an act of political will than because they are rationally defensible on the basis of research evidence. Their development also demonstrates a selective appreciation of the research evidence that would provide a sound basis for such schemes. For example, in the development of the NTFS, the ILTHE drew on extensive research it had undertaken into award schemes in the UK and other countries and operational research on how to recognize and reward teaching excellence (for example, Elton and Partington, 1993). More attention might have been given to 'meta-level' debates about education that underpin understandings of teaching excellence (for example, Williams, R., 1961; Williams, J., 1997; Malcolm and Zukas, 1999). This omission meant that there was little self-conscious, rational debate about different understandings of teaching excellence within the NAP.

In the absence of debate, it is likely that the current mismatch between 'official' and 'ordinary' teacher and student perceptions about teaching excellence (see Chapter 6) will continue. Evidence presented in this book supports previous research studies. Ordinary teachers and students adopt a discourse on excellence that celebrates the 'soft' skills and personal qualities of the teacher, their communication skills and their ability to manage complex human interactions and relationships. This is very different to the emphasis on planned systems, resources, standardized processes and pre-determined outcomes that feature in official discourses of excellence. These seek to make teaching 'teacher-proof'. If this mismatch is to be resolved for the good of teaching excellence, then there has to be a robust dialogue between policy makers and ordinary teachers and students (who represent the 'end users' of policy).

A powerful alliance: the ascendancy of performative and psychologized understandings of teaching excellence

Through the discussions in the preceding chapters it has become clear that performative and psychologized understandings of teaching excellence appear to be in the ascendancy in higher education, favoured by politicians, policy makers and institutional managers. As outlined in Chapter 2, performative understandings of teaching excellence emphasize three main aspects: first, the contribution that teaching makes to national economic performance; second, its ability to attract students on to courses which compete in the global higher education marketplace; and third, its use as a lever to regulate, measure and maximize individual, institutional and system performance. Proponents of the performative discourse identify it as an inevitable response to globalization pressures which are driving educational reform across the world.

What is often less explicit in policies and discourse underpinned by performative understandings of teaching excellence is their political and moral agenda. This agenda includes increasing state control over higher education and reducing the freedom that teachers have to exert professional judgement over what and how they teach (Morley, 1997; Nixon *et al.*, 2001). Teaching excellence in the performative university is therefore becoming increasingly characterized by the following of rules and prescriptions for practice. Although many governments claim to value education and the contributions of teachers, in conceptual terms they often view teaching and learning in instrumental terms, adopting a pragmatic 'what works, works' philosophy which denigrates the role of educational theory. In the UK, the New Labour government treats education problems as though there is no debate about what constitutes 'best practice' (McCaig, 2000). A simplistic emphasis on how such practice can be 'delivered' and 'transferred' irrespective of context is also prominent in guidance material and good-practice guides published by the Higher Education Funding Council (see, for example, HEFCE, 2001a).

Psychologized understandings of teaching excellence have originated from a different source. They dominate the literature on teaching and learning in higher education and exert a significant influence on practice. One example of the 'mainstreaming' of psychological discourse is the 'deep' and 'surface' learning dichotomy that is now widely known and accepted, particularly among practitioners who have experienced a professional development course on teaching and learning. Psychologized understandings focus primarily on the micro-level transaction between individual teacher and student. They construct the educational process in a way that makes it possible to predict and control what will be learnt and how. Psychology's scientific paradigm seeks to identify general laws of human behaviour. Objective studies of teaching and learning are undertaken to enable students' behaviour to be understood and responded to effectively by teachers.

Although performative and psychologized understandings of excellence differ in important respects, they share a commitment to the development of universal approaches to teaching and learning that can be predicted and controlled. From a psychologized perspective, this is necessary to ensure that teacher–student encounters are productive and sensitive to individual needs. From a performative perspective, the prediction and control of teaching is associated with improving system efficiency. Together, these two different perspectives form a powerful alliance which significantly influences the way teaching excellence is understood in contemporary higher education. They are supportive of the move to evidence-based teaching practice in higher education (see Chapter 11) which seeks to derive professional standards for teaching from 'scientifically robust' research.

Their power is also evident in the way they have been able to appropriate ideas and practices associated with traditional and critical understandings of teaching excellence. For example, in Chapter 5, it was observed that there is currently a shift from traditional 'disciplines' to performative 'subjects'. Subjects can be broken down into a set of competences or skills and then tested. The role of the teacher is simply to focus on the efficient delivery of the course and the achievement of the specified outcomes. For some, this new emphasis on subjects is thought to be narrowly conceived and symptomatic of a broader shift towards skill-based, training-derived models of university education. For others, the new emphasis reflects an uneasy yet inevitable compromise between traditionalists and those wanting to make higher education more responsive to the economy.

'Student-centred' teaching is increasingly being appropriated by performative discourse. Originally associated with a process of empowerment where the student takes responsibility for their own learning and moves towards self-actualization (Rogers, 1994), it is gradually being transformed by notions of instrumental progressivism. This form of progressivism is outer-directed, focused on employability and 'tethered to the goals of performativity rather than reflexivity' (Symes and McIntyre, 2000: 2).

As noted in the case study of the NTFS in Chapter 3, 'reflective practice' has also been appropriated and stripped of its more radical and 'critical' possibilities. A reflective approach to teaching and support of learning in the NTFS is associated not with *critical* reflection (a process which locates practice within existing power relations and engages with these relations; see Brookfield, 1995), but with a psychologized form of reflection which is practical and apolitical. Psychologized reflection draws primarily on theories derived from psychological theory (for example, theories related to 'personality', 'learning style' and 'motivation'). The focus of the reflection is practical, emphasizing solutions to teaching problems (for example, changes to delivery methods and the creation of new materials to suit new 'types' of 'non-traditional' learners). Reflection in the NTFS takes higher education policy as a 'given' rather than something to be questioned. The practices, perspectives and development projects of most of the award winners are located within current higher education policy arrangements and commitments.

What's to be done?

There are various ways in which we might respond to the ascendancy of performative and psychologized understandings of teaching excellence. One response is to accept and comply with them, which is relatively easy if one shares their assumptions. An alternative response is to try to limit their impact. For example, one could outwardly comply with performative understandings yet retain private reservations about them. In Chapter 6, it was noted that this was the approach that academics from the Economics Department of the University of Warwick in the UK took when their teaching came under scrutiny by the Quality Assurance Agency. They scored a 'perfect 24' (out of 24), but then declared the exercise to be meaningless and futile: a superficial, paper-based process rather than one that could recognize teaching excellence or support its development. The academics concerned estimated that the process had cost their department between £150,000 and £200,000 in staff time and resources (*Guardian*, 2001).

A third possibility is to keep a distance by responding in an ironic way. This reflects the position taken by one individual in the focus groups referred to in Chapter 6, who viewed the NTFS rather like the Eurovision song contest (a competition for singers from European countries who many people believe look to the competition to boost their career opportunities). This person felt that one should not treat award schemes for teaching excellence too seriously, but the celebration events where the winners were identified were a good excuse for a party!

The only problem with 'playing the game' and 'ironic' strategies is that they convey the impression that performative understandings of teaching excellence can be kept at a safe distance with relative ease. This under-estimates the potency of performativity, which works through constant calls for information and the way this 'disciplines' how people think. As noted in Chapter 2, all teachers are now encouraged to become excellent through a process of continuous improvement and self-regulation. This requires people to engage in self-promotion and to publicize particular aspects of their performance. An 'existence of calculation' becomes the norm, which some individuals can find alienating. In these circumstances people can feel confused about what educational values they hold, as attempts are made to separate beliefs and practices important to the self from those required by external agencies (see Ball, 2003: 217–21).

I want to suggest a rather different type of response that involves locating performative and psychologized understandings of teaching excellence within the broader range of possibilities identified in Chapter 2. It is important to remember that teaching excellence is a contested concept and that we need to consider the strengths and weaknesses of different understandings in order to develop an informed point of view. As noted in Chapter 1, it is important that people take responsibility for their views on teaching excellence and recognize that their own understanding is provisional and subject to change. It is important that we remind other people that teaching excellence is not a given, and encourage discussion about its meaning and practice. This is important whatever context we operate in, whether talking to colleagues, students, institutional managers or policy makers.

There should be a healthy debate about teaching excellence and a willingness to enter into dialogue with people who do not share our personal perspective. It is worth noting that the critical stance can only be achieved in dialogue with others who offer different ways of seeing the world. An uncritical 'taken-for-granted' teaching excellence is no good for anybody: it is not acceptable for students, who rightly expect that teaching is treated seriously, and it sits uneasily with the intellectual culture of higher education. As pointed out in Chapter 10, we need to forge a productive relationship between teaching excellence and ongoing scholarship. We need a teaching excellence that has sustainability: one that is dynamic, enquiring and reflexive.

In the different chapters of this book, I have attempted to identify a number of specific actions that might be taken to move us forward and make the most of teaching excellence. For example, in Chapter 3, I said that awards for teaching excellence need to be built on firm foundations. If they are to continue (and a robust case still needs to be made to justify this), then we have every right to expect that they consider relevant background literature, including 'meta-level' deliberations about education. Criteria for teaching excellence can then be devised in the light of this evidence base. Awards for excellence would be enhanced by a clear educational change strategy; this is particularly important for schemes that are seeking to 'add value' through development work. Academic support improves the quality of knowledge and insight generated through such development work and helps foster 'hybrid methodologies' (see Chapter 11). Thought needs to be given to those teachers who experience difficulties in receiving an award within research-intensive institutions. Their difficulties in forging an identity in these circumstances reminds us of the problematic teaching/research relationship in higher education that continues to endure. If award schemes are to prosper and be taken seriously by the sector, then these are important issues to address.

In Chapter 4, I welcomed moves to recognize the contribution that 'teaching-intensive' institutions make to teaching excellence. Discourse that challenges the view that research excellence automatically leads to teaching excellence is to be supported, but if it encourages an overly pragmatic view of teaching, this is also limiting. Some institutions are developing a reputation for 'teaching-led' research, and here excellence might mean a commitment to pedagogic research and research into institutional teaching and learning policy. The continuation of separate funding streams for research and teaching, however, along with the differential status afforded to 'research-intensive' institutions, ultimately maintains a two-tiered, stratified system of higher education. Within such a system, institutions that are associated primarily with teaching are likely to continue to be seen as the 'poor relation'.

Concerns were raised in Chapter 5 that teaching excellence could become associated with a narrow definition of 'subjects' rather than a broader conception of academic 'disciplines'. The appeal of subjects, from a performative perspective, is that they can be constructed into a programme of knowledge acquisition and assessed in a quantitative manner. Subjects incorporate key skills and demonstrate relevance to 'real-life' situations, which is consistent with the performative emphasis on employability. Work on new forms of disciplinarity identifies an alternative agenda and potential for teaching excellence. It stresses the importance of inducting students into the 'deep structures' of their chosen discipline while encouraging them to reflect on its underlying assumptions. I suggested that a process of critique helps disciplines to develop a reflexive understanding of their relationship to other disciplines and ensures that vested interests and power structures are subject to evaluation.

In Chapter 6, as noted earlier, I discovered a mismatch between official and ordinary teacher and student discourse on teaching excellence. Official discourse, informed by regulatory frameworks, either ignores the human potential of teachers or seeks to minimize their limitations through the development of effective systems. In emphasizing personal qualities and interpersonal skills, teachers and students appeared to be resisting official discourse by restoring the teacher to the heart of the teaching and learning enterprise. The chapter concluded that this mismatch needs to be addressed if policy initiatives to promote teaching excellence are to be realized.

The internationalization of higher education was the focus of Chapter 7. One view of internationalization is that it offers institutions an opportunity to increase market position in the developing global knowledge economy. According to this view, teaching excellence can become an objective indicator of quality and a means to attract international students. A different perspective is that internationalization enables teaching excellence to learn from cultural difference. I suggested that higher education teachers might respond to cultural variations in pedagogy by undertaking a process of 'intercultural learning'. This involves, in the first instance, the recognition that one's own approach to teaching is culturally specific. Intercultural learning is preferable to a response mode that either ignores cultural variations in teaching or seeks to assimilate international students into one's own pedagogical culture.

Chapter 8 looked at press reporting of teaching excellence with a focus on award schemes. It found that although the press provides some limited tools with which to think critically about teaching excellence, its coverage is essentially conservative and legitimizes the views of proponents of such schemes. We should expect the educational press in particular to provide a range of perspectives on teaching excellence to ensure balanced coverage. The chapter concludes by reminding readers of the need to adopt a critical perspective on press reporting of teaching excellence.

The relationship between professional development and teaching excellence was the subject of Chapter 9. One view of this relationship is that professional development and teaching excellence have little in common. According to this view, excellent teachers are born not made, and professional development is concerned with ensuring minimum pedagogical standards. I proposed a different view of this relationship, stating that professional development and teaching excellence potentially have much to offer each other. I maintained that a professional development that has teaching *excellence* as its goal encourages us to think beyond competence models. An excellence that is informed by *professional* development, on the other hand, points to the importance of teacher knowledge, responsibility and autonomous judgement.

In Chapter 10, an attempt was made to forge an alliance between teaching excellence and scholarship. I argued that a teaching excellence that is based on recognized performance but displays little concern for investigating its impact on student learning appears to be short-sighted. On the other hand, an understanding of scholarship as systematic enquiry with little grounding in experience lacks substance. The chapter concluded that we need to bring together the excellence and scholarship movements. They both have their strengths and weaknesses, but taken together, they offer a much more powerful and compelling impetus for the development of teaching and learning in higher education.

The identification of a form of teaching excellence underpinned by systematic enquiry led on to a discussion in Chapter 11 of its relationship with research. Two recent developments appear to be pulling pedagogical research in higher education in different directions. The first is the tentative emergence of hybrid methodologies and the second the development of evidence-based practice. The chapter advocated the development of a pedagogical research community that can tolerate diversity.

It supported the broadening out of teaching excellence research and the giving of legitimacy to work undertaken according to different standards of judgement.

A critical approach to the study of teaching excellence

This book has adopted a critical approach to the study of teaching excellence in higher education. As 'critical' can be interpreted in many different ways, I described my interpretation in some detail in Chapter 1 (pp. 10–14). The approach I adopted has informed the various parts of this book. For example, in establishing a framework with four ideal-type understandings of teaching excellence in Part 1, I placed the ways we currently think about teaching excellence (performative and psychologized understandings in the ascendancy) within a broader range of possibilities. This is a first important step in developing an informed, personal perspective on teaching excellence, and refusing 'received wisdom'.

In Part 2 of the book, I 're-engaged' with three 'familiar faces' of teaching excellence that have been presented to us through policy initiatives and operational research. It is important to do this given that these familiar faces have become almost taken for granted. The critical stance taken towards award schemes, institutional teaching excellence and the place of subject disciplines involved avoiding 'convergence', premature judgement and 'closure'. Even though these levels or dimensions for looking at teaching excellence may continue to dominate official discourse and policy initiatives, it is important to retain a critical relationship with them.

New and alternative explorations relating to teaching excellence were the subject of Part 3 of this book. This involved 'deconstructing' teaching excellence from the position of 'ordinariness'; subjecting it to comparative analysis by considering different cultural conceptions of teaching and learning; examining how the press mediates our understanding of teaching excellence and offers limited critical tools for engagement; and exploring ways in which notions of 'professionalism' and 'excellence' can come together to offer an approach to professional development that is willing to challenge and recreate existing practice.

Part 4 focused on future possibilities for teaching excellence. It drew on comparisons between award schemes for teachers in three different countries to propose a more integrated understanding of teaching excellence. The critical approach taken involved recognizing that current understandings, realities and practices could be different and indeed *better*, so it attempted to build on the strengths of respective programmes to suggest new directions for growth. Following a review of existing research into teaching excellence, it became apparent that research constructs the very phenomena it sets out to study. In outlining a range of possible agendas for research into teaching excellence in the future, I wanted to convey the message that a mature research community tolerates diversity and learns from difference. We need to research in ways that support a teaching excellence that is dynamic and complex. Critical approaches can make an important contribution to the development and maintenance of a healthy and vibrant pedagogical research community.

Bibliography

Abbas, A. and McLean, M. (2003) 'Communicative competence and the improvement of university teaching: insights from the field', *British Journal of Sociology of Education*, 24: 69–81.

Anderson, G. (1989) 'Invisibility, legitimation, and school administration: the study of non-events', paper presented at the annual meeting of the American Educational Research Association, San Francisco, March.

Anderson, R. D. (1992) *Universities and Elites in Britain since 1800*. London: The Macmillan Press.

Antoniou, M. and Stierer, B. (2002) 'Are there distinctive methodologies for pedagogic research in higher education?', paper presented at the Higher Education Special Interest Group, British Educational Research Association Seminar, Leeds, June.

Arena (2001) 'Why are there so many award ceremonies?' BBC2, 11.20pm, 13 May.

Arnold, M. (1983) *Culture and Anarchy*. New York: Chelsea House.

Arnot, M. (ed.) (1985) *Race and Gender: equal opportunities policies in education*. Oxford: Pergamon Press/Open University.

Asquith, C. (2004) 'The shock of the new', *The Guardian Education*, 24 February.

The Australian (2002a) 'Wealth of talent lines up – Australian Awards for University Teaching', 6 November.

The Australian (2002b) 'Short list announced', 20 November.

Badley, G. (1996) 'Educational development in the managerial university', *Journal of Education Through Partnership*, 1: 53–69.

Baiocca, S. A. and DeWalters, J. N. (1998) *Successful College Teaching: problem-solving strategies of distinguished professors*. Needham Heights, MA: Allyn and Bacon.

Ball, S. J. (1994) *Education Reform: a critical and post-structural approach*. Buckingham: Open University Press.

Ball, S. J. (2003) 'The teacher's soul and the terrors of performativity', *Journal of Education Policy*, 18: 215–28.

Barnett, R. (1990) *The Idea of Higher Education*. Buckingham: Society for Research into Higher Education (SRHE)/Open University Press.

Barnett, R. (1992) *Improving Higher Education: Total Quality Care*. Buckingham: SRHE/Open University Press.

Barnett, R. (1994) *The Limits of Competence: Knowledge, Higher Education and Society*. Buckingham: Open University Press.

Barnett, R. (1997) *Higher Education: a critical business*. Buckingham: Open University Press.

Barnett, R. (2000) *Realizing the University: in an age of supercomplexity*. Buckingham: Open University Press.

Barton, L. (1994) 'Teaching and research: dilemmas and possibilities', in P. Carrotte and M. Hammond (eds) *Learning in Difficult Times: issues for teaching in higher education*. Sheffield: UCoSDA and The University of Sheffield.

Becher, T. (1989) *Academic Tribes and Territories*. Buckingham: Open University Press.

Bell, G. (1982) *What is to be Called Action Research in Schools?* (Mimeo). Middlesborough: Teesside Polytechnic.

Bernstein, B. (1971) 'On the classification and framing of educational knowledge', in M. F. D. Young (ed.) *Knowledge and Control: new directions for the sociology of education*. London: Collier Macmillan.

Bernstein, B. (1986a) *On Pedagogic Discourse*. London: University of London, Institute of Education, mimeo version.

Bernstein, B. (1986b) 'On pedagogic discourse', in S. Richardson (ed.) *Handbook of Theory and Research for the Sociology of Education*. New York: Greenwood Press.

Bhabha, H. (1990) 'The third space', in J. Rutherford (ed.) *Identity: community, culture, difference*. London: Lawrence and Wishart.

Biggs, J. (1999) *Teaching for Quality Learning at University*. Buckingham: SRHE/Open University Press.

Biglan, A. (1973) 'The characteristics of subject matter in different scientific areas', *Journal of Applied Psychology*, 57: 195–203.

Bird, E. (2001) 'Disciplining the interdisciplinary: radicalism and the academic curriculum', *British Journal of Sociology of Education*, 22: 463–78.

Blight, D. (1995) *International Education: Australia's potential demand and supply*. Canberra: IDP Education Australia.

Bodycott, P. and Walker, A. (2000) 'Teaching abroad: lessons learned about intercultural understanding for teachers in higher education', *Teaching in Higher Education*, 5: 79–94.

Bolton, G. (2000) *Reflective Practice*. London: Paul Chapman.

Boud, D. and Solomon, N. (2001) *Work-based Learning: a new higher education*. Buckingham: SRHE/Open University Press.

Boyer, E. (1990) *Scholarship Revisited*. Princeton, NJ: Carnegie Foundation for the Advancement of Teaching.

Boyer, E. (1994) 'Scholarship reconsidered: priorities for a new century', in *The Universities in the Twenty-First Century* (a lecture series). London: The National Commission on Education.

Broadfoot, P. (2001) 'Empowerment or performativity? Assessment policy in the late twentieth century', in R. Phillips and J. Furlong (eds) *Education, Reform and the State: twenty-five years of politics, policy and practice*. London: RoutledgeFalmer.

Brookfield, S. (1995) 'Changing the culture of scholarship to the culture of teaching: an American perspective', in T. Schuller (ed.) *The Changing University?* Buckingham: SRHE/Open University Press.

Brown, G. and Atkins, M. J. (1988) *Effective Teaching in Higher Education*. London: Routledge.

Brown, S. (2000) 'The implications of the National Teaching Fellowship Scheme for staff and educational developers', *Educational Developments*, Staff and Educational Development Association, August.

Bruch, T. and Barty, A. (1998) 'Internationalizing British higher education: students and institutions', in P. Scott (ed.) *The Globalization of Higher Education.* Buckingham: SRHE/Open University Press.

Brynmor Jones Report (1965) *Report of the Committee on Audio Visual Aids in Higher Education.* London: HMSO.

Burton, L. and Haynes, C. (1997) 'Innovation in teaching and assessing mathematics at university level', *Teaching in Higher Education*, 2: 273–93.

Burwood, S. (1999) 'Liberation philosophy', *Teaching in Higher Education*, 4: 447–60.

Carr, W. and Kemmis, S. (1986) *Becoming Critical: education, knowledge and action research.* Lewes: Falmer Press.

Clarke, J. and Newman, J. (1997) *The Managerial State: power, politics and ideology in the remaking of social welfare.* London: Sage.

Clegg, A., Hudson, A. and Steel, J. (2003a) 'The emperor's new clothes: globalisation and e-learning in higher education', *British Journal of Sociology of Education*, 24: 39–53.

Clegg, S., Parr, S. and Wan, S. (2003b) 'Racialising discourses in higher education', *Teaching in Higher Education*, 8: 155–68.

Cobban, A. B. (1988) *The Medieval English Universities. Oxford and Cambridge to c.1500.* Berkeley, CA: University of California Press.

Cobban, A. B. (1999) *English University Life in the Middle Ages.* London: UCL Press.

Cochran-Smith, M. (2002) 'What a difference a definition makes: highly qualified teachers, scientific researchers, and teacher education', *Journal of Teacher Education*, 53: 187–9.

Collinson, V. (1999) 'Redefining teacher excellence', *Theory Into Practice*, 38: 4–11.

Cooper, P. and McIntyre, D. (1996) *Effective Teaching and Learning: teachers' and students' perspectives.* Buckingham: Open University Press.

Cowan, J. (1998) *On Becoming An Innovative University Teacher.* Buckingham: Open University Press.

Cowie, H. and Rudduck, J. (1988) *Co-operative Group Work: an overview.* London: BP Educational Service.

Crème, P. (1999) 'A reflection on the education of the "critical person"', *Teaching in Higher Education*, 4: 461–71.

Cronin, C., Foster, M. and Lister, E. (1999) 'SET for the future: working towards inclusive science, engineering and technology curricula in higher education', *Studies in Higher Education*, 24: 165–82.

Cunningham, P. (1992) 'Teachers' professional image and the press 1950–1990', *History of Education*, 21: 37–56.

Currie, J. (2000a) 'Make winners of class acts', *The Times Higher Education Supplement*, 9 June.

Currie, J. (2000b) 'And the first prize goes to... teaching', *The Times Higher Education Supplement*, 7 July.

Curzon-Hobson, A. (2003) 'Higher learning and the critical stance', *Studies in Higher Education*: 28: 201–12.

Davies, P. (1999) 'What is evidence-based education?' *British Journal of Educational Studies*, 47: 108–12.

Dean, M. (1995) 'Governing the unemployed self in an active society', *Economy and Society*, 24: 559–83.

Department for Education and Skills (DfES) (2003) *The Future of Higher Education*. London: HMSO.

Department for Education and Employment (DfEE), Higher Education: Quality and Employability Division (1998) *Higher Education Development Projects 1998–2000*. Sheffield: DfEE.

Doll, W. E. (1989) 'Foundations for a post-modern curriculum', *Journal of Curriculum Studies*, 21: 243–53.

Dunkin, M. J. (1995) 'Concepts of teaching and teaching excellence in higher education', *Higher Education Research and Development*, 14: 21–33.

Dunkin, M. J. and Precians, R. P. (1992) 'Award-winning university teachers' concepts of teaching', *Higher Education*, 24: 483–502.

Eggins, H. and Macdonald, R. (2003) *The Scholarship of Academic Development*. Buckingham: SRHE/Open University Press.

Eisenhart, M. and Towne, L. (2003) 'Contestation and change in national policy on "scientifically based" education research', *Educational Researcher*, 32: 31–8.

Ellis, R. (ed.) (1993) *Quality Assurance for University Teaching*. Buckingham: SRHE/Open University Press.

Elton, L. (1998) 'Dimensions of excellence in university teaching', *International Journal of Academic Development*, 3: 3–11.

Elton, L. and Partington, P. (1993) *Teaching Standards and Excellence in Higher Education*, 2nd edn. Sheffield: Committee of Vice-Chancellors and Principals of the Universities of the United Kingdom.

Esland, G. (1980) 'Professions and professionalism', in G. Esland and G. Salaman (eds) *The Politics of Work and Occupations*. Milton Keynes: Open University Press.

Evans, C. (2000) 'Against excellence', *Educational Developments*. Birmingham: Staff and Educational Development Association.

Evans, J. (1990) 'Defining a subject: the rise and rise of the new PE?' *British Journal of Sociology of Education*, 11: 155–69.

Fairclough, N. (1989) *Language and Power*. London: Longman.

Fazackerley, A. (2003) 'Teaching-focused "not worthy" of university title', *The Times Higher Education Supplement*, 6 June.

Figueroa, P. (1991) *Education and the Social Construction of 'Race'*. London: Routledge.

Filmer, P. (1997) 'Disinterestedness and the modern university', in A. Smith and F. Webster (eds) *The Postmodern University? Contested Visions of Higher Education in Society*. Buckingham: SRHE/Open University Press.

Fisher, A. (2000) *National Teaching Fellowship Scheme: media report and press cuttings*. Harrogate: POLO Public Relations Marketing Services, August.

Fox, D. (1983) 'Personal theories of teaching', *Studies in Higher Education*, 8: 151–63.

Fritzberg, G. J. (2000) 'Escaping the Shadow of "Excellence"', *Multicultural Education*, 8: 37–40.

Fullan, M. (1982) *The Meaning of Educational Change*. Toronto: Ontario Institute for Studies in Education Press.

Gamson, Z. F. (1998) 'The stratification of the academy', in R. Martin (ed.) *Chalk Lines: the politics of work in the managed university*. London: Duke University Press.

Gates, H. L. (1992) 'Canon confidential: a Sam Slade caper', in *Loose Canons: notes on the culture wars*. Oxford: Oxford University Press.

Geertz, C. (1983) *Local Knowledge*. New York: Basic Books.

Geertz, C. (1993) *Local Knowledge: further essays in interpretive anthropology*. London: Fontana Press.

Gibbons, M., Limoges, C., Nowotny, H., Schwartzman, S., Scott, P. and Trow, M. (1994) *The New Production of Knowledge: the dynamics of science and research in contemporary societies*. London: Sage.

Gibbs, G. (1995) 'Changing conceptions of teaching and learning through action research', in A. Brew (ed.) *Directions in Staff Development*. Buckingham: SRHE/Open University Press.

Gibbs, G. (2000) 'Institutional and disciplinary diversity', paper presented at a seminar on 'The Relationship Between Research and Teaching in Higher Education', organized by Southampton Institute and the Higher Education Funding Council for England, Southampton, January.

Giddens, A. (1994) *Beyond Left and Right: The future of radical politics*. Cambridge: Polity Press.

Giglio, M. (2003) 'Award for real-life solutions', *The Australian*, 3 December.

Giglio, M. (2004) 'Art of Chinese whispers', *The Australian*, 14 January.

Gillborn, D. (1998) 'Race and ethnicity in compulsory schooling', in T. Modood and T. Acland (eds) *Race and Higher Education*. London: Policy Studies Institute.

Giroux, H. A. (1988) 'Border pedagogy in the age of postmodernism', *Journal of Education*, 170: 162–81.

Gosling, D. (1996) 'Educational development and institutional change in higher education', in K. Gokulsing and C. DaCosta (eds), *Usable Knowledges as the Goal of University Education*. London: Edwin Mellen Press.

Grey, M. (2002) 'Drawing with difference: challenges faced by international students in an undergraduate business degree', *Teaching in Higher Education*, 7: 153–66.

Guardian (2000) 'Lecturers' chance to shine', *The Guardian Education*, 13 June.

Guardian (2001) 'Trial by ordeal', 30 January.

Habermas, J. (1974) *Theory and Practice* (trans. J. Viersal). London: Heinemann.

Habermas, J. (1978) *Knowledge and Human Interests*. London: Heinemann (2nd edn).

Hale Report (1964) *Report of the Committee on University Teaching Methods*. London: HMSO.

Halsey, A. H. (1992) *The Decline of Donnish Dominion*. Oxford: Oxford University Press.

Hammersley, M. (1992) 'The paradigm wars: report from the front', *British Journal of Sociology of Education*, 13: 131–43.

Hannan, A. and Silver, H. (2000) *Innovating in Higher Education: teaching, learning and institutional cultures*. Buckingham: SRHE/Open University Press.

Harden, R. M., Grant, J., Buckley, G. and Hart, I. M. (1999) 'BEME guide no 1: best evidence medical educational', *Medical Teacher*, 21: 553–62.

Hargreaves, D. H. (1996) 'Teaching as a Research-based Profession: possibilities and prospects', Teaching Training Agency Annual Lecture, London: Teacher Training Agency.

Hargreaves, D. H. (1997) 'In defence of research for evidence-based teaching: a rejoinder to Martyn Hammersley', *British Educational Research Journal*, 23: 405–19.

Hargreaves, D. H. (1998) 'A new partnership of stakeholders and a national strategy for research in education', in J. Ruddock and D. McIntyre (eds) *Challenges for Educational Research*. London: Paul Chapman.

Harrison, M. J. (1994) 'Quality issues in higher education: a post-modern phenomenon?' in G. Doherty (ed.) *Developing Quality Systems in Education*. London: Routledge.

Hartnett, A. and Naish, M. (1990) 'The sleep of reason breeds monsters: the birth of a statutory curriculum in England and Wales', *Journal of Curriculum Studies*, 22: 1–16.

Hativa, N., Barak, R. and Simhi, E. (2001) 'Exemplary university teachers: knowledge and beliefs regarding effective teaching dimensions and strategies', *The Journal of Higher Education*, 72: 699–729.

Healey, M. (2000) 'Developing the scholarship of teaching in higher education: a discipline-based approach', *Higher Education Research & Development*, 19: 169–89.

Healey, M. and Jenkins, A. (2003) 'Discipline-based educational development', in H. Eggins and R. Macdonald (eds) *The Scholarship of Academic Development*. Buckingham: SRHE/Open University Press.

Higgins, R., Skelton, A. and Hartley, P. (2002) 'The conscientious consumer: reconsidering the role of assessment feedback in student learning', *Studies in Higher Education*, 27: 53–64.

Higher Education Funding Council for England (1998) *Learning and Teaching: strategy and funding proposals*. Bristol: HEFCE, ref: 98/40.

Higher Education Funding Council for England (2001a) *Strategies for Learning and Teaching in Higher Education: a guide to good practice*. Bristol: HEFCE, ref: 01/37.

Higher Education Funding Council for England (2001b) *Analysis of strategies for learning and teaching*. Research report by Professor Graham Gibbs. Bristol: HEFCE, ref: 01/37a.

Higher Education Funding Council for England (2002) *Teaching Quality Enhancement Fund: funding arrangements 2002–03 to 2004–05*. Bristol: HEFCE, ref: 02/24.

Higher Education Funding Council for England (2004) *Centres for Excellence in Teaching and Learning: invitation to bid for funds*. Bristol: HEFCE, ref: 04/05.

Higher Education Information Services Trust (HEIST) and UCAS (1994) *Higher Education: the international student experience*. Leeds: HEIST.

Higher Education Statistics Agency (1997) *Students in Higher Education Institutions*. Cheltenham: HESA.

Hillage, J., Pearson, R., Anderson, A. and Tamkin, P. (1998) *Excellence in Research in Schools. Research Report RR74*. Department of Education and Employment, Sudbury: DfEE Publications.

Hillier, Y. and Vielba, C. (2001) 'Perceptions of excellence: personal constructs of excellence in teaching and learning', paper presented at Institute of Learning and Teaching Annual Conference, York, July.

Hirst, P. (1974) *Knowledge and the Curriculum*. London: Routledge, Kegan Paul.

Hoyle, E. (1980) 'Professionalization and deprofessionalization in education', in E. Hoyle and J. Megarry (eds) *The Professional Development of Teachers: world yearbook of education, 1980: Professional Development of Teachers*. London, Kogan Page.

Hoyle, E. and John, P. (1995) *Professional Knowledge and Professional Practice*. London: Cassell.

Hutchings, P. (ed.) (2000) *Opening Lines: approaches to the scholarship of teaching and learning*. Menlo Park, CA: The Carnegie Foundation for the Advancement of Teaching.

Illing, D. (2003) 'Classes squirm as they learn about parasites – Australian awards for university teaching', *The Australian*, 22 January.

Institute for Learning and Teaching (2000) *Launch of the National Teaching Fellowship Scheme: scheme structure*. http://www.ilt.ac.uk/news/ntfs_structure.html

Jacobsen, R. H. (1989) 'The impact of faculty incentive grants on teaching effectiveness', paper presented at the Annual Meeting of the American Educational Research Association, San Francisco, March.

Johnston, S. (1996) 'What can we learn about teaching from our best university teachers?', *Teaching in Higher Education*, 1: 213–25.

Kelly, G. (1955) *The Psychology of Personal Constructs*, Vols 1 and 2. New York: Norton.

Kemmis, S. (1987) 'Critical reflection', in M. F. Wideen and I. Andrews (eds) *Staff Development for School Improvement*. London: Falmer Press.

Kreber, C. (2000) 'How university teaching award winners conceptualise academic work: some further thoughts on the meaning of scholarship', *Teaching in Higher Education*, 5: 61–78.

Lacey, C. (1977) *The Socialisation of Teachers*. London: Methuen.

Larkin, P. (1954) 'Born Yesterday', in A. Thwaite (ed.) *Philip Larkin: collected poems*. London: The Marvell Press and Faber & Faber Ltd, 1988.

Lather, P. (1986) 'Research as praxis', *Harvard Educational Review*, 56: 257–77.

Lather, P. (2004) 'Scientific research in education: a critical perspective', *British Educational Research Journal*, 30: 759–72.

Layton, D. (1968) *University Teaching in Transition*. London: Oliver & Boyd.

Leon, P. (2000) 'Be sensitive to Chinese minds', *The Times Higher Education Supplement*, 23 June.

Leon, P. (2002a) 'Received with reservations', *The Times Higher Educational Supplement*, 14 June.

Leon, P. (2002b) 'Chameleon finds quality colours', *The Times Higher Educational Supplement*, 25 January.

Luke, C. and Gore, J. (1992) *Feminisms and Critical Pedagogy*. London: Routledge.

MacLeod, D. (2000a) 'Star lecturers to vie for £50,000 teaching award', *The Guardian Education*, 6 April.

MacLeod, D. (2000b) 'Oscars are coming', *The Guardian Education*, 11 April.

MacLeod, D. (2000c) 'By example', *The Guardian Education*, 27 June.

Malcolm, J. and Zukas, M. (1999) 'Models of the educator in higher education: perspectives and problems', paper presented at the Society for Teaching and Learning in Higher Education Conference, University of Calgary, June.

Malcolm, J. and Zukas, M. (2001) 'Bridging pedagogic gaps: conceptual discontinuities in higher education', *Teaching in Higher Education*, 6: 33–42.

McCaig, C. (2000) 'New Labour and education, education, education', in S. Ludlum and M. J. Smith (eds) *New Labour in Government*. London: Macmillan.

McDonald, G. (1990) 'Excellence, promotion policies, and educational standards', in S. Middleton, J. Codd and J. Jones (eds) *New Zealand Education Policy Today: critical perspectives*. Wellington: Allen and Unwin.

McLean, M. and Blackwell, R. (1997) 'Opportunity knocks? Professionalism and excellence in university teaching', *Teachers and Teaching: theory and practice*. 3: 85–99.

McNair, S. (1998) 'Managing development work in higher education: reflections on the Higher Education Quality and Employability Division experience', discussion paper presented at HEQED Consultation Event on 'Educational Change Within Higher Education', University of Nottingham, December.

McNaught, C. and Anwyl, J. (1993) 'Awards for "teaching excellence" at Australian Universities', *Higher Education Review*, 25: 31–44.

McNay, I. (1994) 'The future student experience', in S. Haselgrove (ed.) *The Student Experience*. Buckingham: SRHE/Open University Press.

McNay, I. (2000) (ed.) *Higher Education and its Communities*. Buckingham: SRHE/Open University Press.

McNay, I. (2003) 'The e-factors and organization cultures in British universities', in G. Williams (ed.) *The Enterprising University: reform, excellence and equity*. Buckingham: SRHE/Open University Press.

Metge, J. (1984) *Learning and Teaching: he tikanga Maori*. Wellington: Maori and Island Division, Department of Education.

Moore, R. and Young, M. (2001) 'Knowledge and the curriculum in the sociology of education: towards a reconceptualisation', *British Journal of Sociology of Education*, 22: 445–61.

Morley, L. (1997) 'Change and equity in higher education', *British Journal of Sociology of Education*, 18: 231–42.

Morley, L. (1998) 'All you need is love: feminist pedagogy for empowerment and emotional labour in the academy', *International Journal of Inclusive Education*, 2: 15–27.

Morley, L. (2001) 'Subjected to review: engendering quality and power in higher education', *Journal of Education Policy*, 16: 465–78.

Morley, L. (2003) *Quality and Power in Higher Education*. Maidenhead: SRHE/Open University Press.

Morris, S. (2002) 'Winners are a class act', *The Australian*, 4 December.

National Educational Research Forum (2000) *Research and Development for Education*. Consultation Paper, December.

National Committee of Inquiry into Higher Education (NCIHE) (1997) *Higher Education for a Learning Society*, Report of the National Committee of Inquiry into Higher Education (The Dearing Report). London: HMSO.

National Research Council (2002) *Scientific Research in Education*, Committee on Scientific Principles for Education Research (R. J. Shavelson and L. Towne, eds). Washington, DC: National Academy Press.

Newman, J. (1976) *The Idea of a University*. Oxford: Oxford University Press.

Nicholls, G. (2001) *Professional Development in Higher Education: new dimensions and directions*. London: Kogan Page.

Nixon, J., Beattie, M., Challis, M. and Walker, M. (1998) 'What does it mean to be an academic? A colloquium', *Teaching in Higher Education*, 3: 277–98.

Nixon, J., Marks, A., Rowland, S. and Walker, M. (2001) 'Towards a new academic professionalism: a manifesto of hope', *British Journal of Sociology of Education*, 22: 227–44.

Nixon, J., Martin, J., McKeown, P. and Ranson, S. (1997) 'Towards a learning profession: changing codes of occupational practice within the new management of education', *British Journal of Sociology of Education*, 18: 5–28.

Northedge, A. (2003a) 'Rethinking teaching in the context of diversity', *Teaching in Higher Education*, 8: 17–32.

Northedge, A. (2003b) 'Enabling participation in academic discourse', *Teaching in Higher Education*, 8: 169–80.

Ofori-Dankwa, J. and Lane, R. W. (2000) 'Four approaches to cultural diversity: implications for teaching at institutions of higher education', *Teaching in Higher Education*, 5: 493–9.

Opacic, S. (1994) 'The student learning experience in the mid-1990s', in S. Haselgrove (ed.) *The Student Experience*. Buckingham: SRHE/Open University Press.

Parker, J. (1999) 'Thinking critically about literature', *Teaching in Higher Education*, 4: 473–83.

Parker, J. (2002) 'A new disciplinarity: communities of knowledge, learning and Practice', *Teaching in Higher Education*, 7: 373–86.

Parry Report (1967) *Report of the Committee on University Teaching*. London: HMSO.

Patrick, K. (1997) 'Internationalizing curriculum', paper presented at Higher Education Research Development Annual Meeting, Adelaide, July.

Patton, M. Q. (1990) *Qualitative Evaluation and Research Methods*. London: Sage.

Pirrie, A. (2001) 'Evidence-based practice in education: the best medicine?' *British Journal of Educational Studies*, 49: 124–36.

Pollitt, C. (1993) *Managerialism and the Public Services: cuts or cultural change in the 1990s*. Oxford: Blackwell.

Prosser, M. and Trigwell, K. (1999) *Understanding Learning and Teaching: the experience in higher education*. Buckingham: SRHE/Open University Press.

Ramsden, P. (1979) 'Student learning and perceptions of the academic environment', *Higher Education*, 8: 411–28.

Ramsden, P. (1992) *Learning to Teach in Higher Education*. London: Routledge.

Ramsden, P. and Martin, E. (1996) 'Recognition of good university teaching: policies from an Australian study', *Studies in Higher Education*, 21: 299–315.

Ramsden, P. (2004) 'The evidence is there, so let's make use of it', *The Times Higher Educational Supplement*, 1 October.

Readings, B. (1996) *The University in Ruins*. Cambridge, MA: Harvard University Press.

Ritzer, G. (2001) 'Let's make it magical', *The Times Higher Educational Supplement*, 6 July.

Rizvi, F. and Walsh, L. (1998) 'Difference, globalisation and the internationalisation of curriculum', *Australian Universities Review*, 41: 7–11.

Robbins Report (1963) *Higher Education: report of the committee appointed by the prime minister under the chairmanship of Lord Robbins, 1961–63.* London: Report and 5 appendices.

Rogers, C. R. (1994) *Freedom to Learn,* 3rd edn. Oxford: Maxwell Macmillan.

Rowland, S. (1996) 'Relationships between teaching and research', *Teaching in Higher Education,* 1: 7–20.

Rowland, S. (2000) *The Enquiring University Teacher.* Buckingham: SRHE/Open University Press.

Sackett, D. L., Rosenberg, W. M. C. and Haynes, R. B. (1996) 'Evidence-based medicine: what it is and what it isn't', *British Medical Journal,* 312: 71–2.

Salter, B. and Tapper, T. (1994) *The State And Higher Education.* Ilford: The Woburn Press.

Sapochnik, C. (1997) 'In and out of fragmentation, improving student learning through course design', in C. Rust and G. Gibbs (eds) *The Oxford Centre for Staff and Learning Development.* Oxford: Oxford Brookes University.

Schon, D. (1983) *The Reflective Practitioner.* New York: Basic Books.

Schon, D. (1987) *Educating the Reflective Practitioner.* San Francisco, CA: Jossey-Bass.

Scoggins, J. and Winter, R. (1999) 'The patchwork text: a coursework format for education as critical understanding', *Teaching in Higher Education,* 4: 485–99.

Skelton, A. (1990) 'Development sites: a gradualist approach to strategic redefinition', *British Journal of Sociology of Education,* 11: 387–95.

Skelton, A. (2002) 'Towards inclusive learning environments in higher education? Reflections on a professional development course for university lecturers', *Teaching in Higher Education,* 7: 193–214.

Skelton, A. (2004) 'Understanding "teaching excellence" in higher education: a critical evaluation of the National Teaching Fellowship Scheme', *Studies in Higher Education,* 29: 451–68.

Skinner, B. F. (1973) *Beyond Freedom and Dignity.* London: Penguin.

Smith, A. and Webster, F. (eds) (1997) *The Postmodern University? Contested Visions of Higher Education in Society.* Buckingham: SRHE/Open University Press.

Sparkes, A. C. (ed.) (1992) *Research in Physical Education and Sport: exploring alternative visions.* London: Falmer Press.

Staniforth, D. and Harland, T. (1999) 'The work of an academic: Jack of all trades, or master of one?', *International Journal for Academic Development,* 4: 142–9.

Stierer, B. and Antoniou, M. (2004) 'Are there distinctive methodologies for pedagogic research in higher education?', *Teaching in Higher Education,* 9: 275–85.

Stenhouse, L. (1975) *An Introduction to Curriculum Research and Development.* London: Heinemann.

Symes, C. and McIntyre, J. (2000) *Working Knowledge: the new vocationalism and higher education.* Buckingham: SRHE/Open University Press.

Tangaere, A. (1996) 'Maori human development learning theory', in B. Webber (ed.) *He Paepae Korero: research perspectives in Maori education.* Wellington: New Zealand Council for Educational Research.

Tapper, T. and Salter, B. (1992) *Oxford, Cambridge and the Changing Idea of the University.* Buckingham: SRHE/Open University Press.

Thomas, E. (1993) 'The first distinguished teaching award in the United Kingdom', in R. Ellis (ed.) *Quality Assurance for University Teaching*. Buckingham: SRHE/Open University Press.

Tierney, R. J. (2001) 'An ethical chasm: jurisdiction, jurisprudence, and the literacy profession', *Journal of Adolescent and Adult Literacy*, 45: 260–76.

Tollefson, N. and Tracy, B. (1983) 'Comparison of self-reported teaching behaviours of award winning and non-award winning university faculty', *Perpetual and Motor Skills*, 56: 39–44.

Tooley, J. and Darby, D. (1998) *Educational Research: an OFSTED critique*. London: OFSTED.

Trowler, P. R. (2002) *Higher Education Policy and Institutional Change: intentions and outcomes in turbulent environments*. Buckingham: SRHE/Open University Press.

Troyna, B. (1993) *Racism and Education: research perspectives*. Buckingham: Open University Press.

UNESCO (1997) *UNESCO Statistical Yearbook*. Paris: UNESCO.

Universities UK (2001) *Research and Development for Education: response from Universities UK*. London: Universities UK.

Universities UK (2004) 'Towards a framework of professional teaching standards'. Consultation Paper. London: Universities UK.

Utley, A. (1998) 'Who gets the thumbs up?' *The Times Higher Education Supplement*, 13 March.

Vielba, C. A. and Hillier, Y. (2000) 'Defining excellence in teaching and learning in postgraduate professional programmes', paper presented at British Academy of Management Conference, Edinburgh, September.

Vygotsky, L. S. (1978) *Mind in Society: the development of higher mental processes*. Cambridge, MA: Harvard University Press.

Walker, M. (ed.) (2001) *Reconstructing Professionalism in University Teaching: teachers and learners in action*. Buckingham: SRHE/Open University Press.

Wallace, M. (1987) 'A historical review of action research: some implications for the education of teachers in their managerial role', *Journal of Education for Teaching*, 13: 97–115.

Warren, R. and Plumb, E. (1999) 'Survey of distinguished teacher award schemes in higher education', *Journal of Further and Higher Education*, 23: 245–55.

Wenger, E. (1998) *Communities of Practice: learning, meaning, and identity*. Cambridge: Cambridge University Press.

Williams, G. (2003) (ed.) *The Enterprising University: reform, excellence and equity*. Buckingham: SRHE/Open University Press.

Williams, J. (ed.) (1997) *Negotiating Access to Higher Education*. Buckingham: SRHE/Open University Press.

Williams, R. (1961) *The Long Revolution*. Harmondsworth: Penguin.

Wu, S. (2002) 'Filling the pot or lighting the fire? Cultural variations in conceptions of pedagogy', *Teaching in Higher Education*, 7: 387–95.

Yorke, M. (2000) 'A cloistered virtue? Pedagogical research and policy in UK higher education', *Higher Education Quarterly*, 54: 106–26.

Zepke, N. and Leach, L. (2002) 'Appropriate pedagogy and technology in a cross-cultural distance education context', *Teaching in Higher Education*, 7: 309–21.

Zuber-Skerritt, O. (1992) *Action Research in Higher Education*. London: Kogan Page.

Zukas, M. and Malcolm, J. (1999) 'Models of the educator in higher education', paper presented at the British Educational Research Association Conference, University of Sussex, September.

Zukas, M. and Malcolm, J. (2002) 'Playing the game: regulation and scrutiny in academic identities', seminar paper presented at University of Sheffield, October.

Index